Don't miss this book! Powerful, provocative, persuasive, practical—it's a masterful exploration of modern miracles and related topics that will encourage you in your spiritual life. With the sharp intellect and inquisitive mind of a seasoned philosopher, J. P. Moreland investigates key issues surrounding God's supernatural activity in today's world. Read it, ponder it, discuss it, apply it—and then tell others about it!

LEE STROBEL, bestselling author of *The Case for Christ* and *The Case for Miracles*

It's a privilege to endorse this life-changing book so needed in the church at this time. After Christian philosopher J. P. Moreland provides clear ways to think about unanswered prayer and offers a grid for recognizing special divine action and helping us see how our lives are surrounded by miracles, he takes us on a fascinating tour of God's works today. I wish I could have read this faith-encouraging book on miracles before writing mine!

CRAIG S. KEENER, F. M. and Ada Thompson professor of biblical studies, Asbury Theological Seminary

As a new Christian at the age of thirty-five, I struggled to see God's involvement in the world around me. I had grown so accustomed to attributing everything to the forces of nature or the efforts of humans that I missed the obvious interaction of God. I so wish I had J. P. Moreland's new book back then. *A Simple Guide to Experience Miracles* will help you recognize God's handiwork in your own life, reenergize your prayer life, and renew your sense of awe and wonder. Don't waste another day overlooking the miraculous, supernatural activity of God. Let J. P. show you what you may have been missing.

J. WARNER WA~~~ ~~~ ~~~~~~~ ~~~
cold-case detecti~
Interest an

T0053513

This remarkable book is filled with numerous fascinating, faith-building reports of miracles that God continues to work even today. Those stories make this book a persuasive refutation of the claim that miracles have ceased. J. P. Moreland also argues for the veracity of these reports, using the analytic skills of a professional philosopher. And he writes with practical pastoral wisdom as he explains why we should still be expecting miracles today and how we can pray more effectively. Highly recommended!

WAYNE GRUDEM, distinguished research professor of theology and biblical studies, Phoenix Seminary

Whether you are still skeptical and doubt the reality of the miraculous or are a passionate proponent of the supernatural, this book is for you. With remarkable depth and clarity, J. P. Moreland brings to bear on this subject his gifting as a philosopher, apologist, theologian, and student of the Scriptures. He explores with profound insight and biblical grounding such issues as the nature of the miraculous, whether we should pray for miracles, and how we might know if a miracle has happened. The specific stories of the miraculous cited in the book as well as J. P.'s personal experience will serve you well as you explore this fascinating topic. I can't recommend this excellent book too highly.

SAM STORMS, PhD, Enjoying God Ministries

J. P. Moreland brings together both the sharp, rational evidence of an acclaimed philosophy professor and heart-inspiring credible stories to convince the skeptic and inspire the believer—God's miraculous intervention is not only real, but practically accessible, as you will see.

JOHN BURKE, *New York Times* bestselling author of *Imagine Heaven* and founding pastor of Gateway Church

J. P. Moreland's unique book sparkles with spiritual vibrancy, fresh insight, and seasoned wisdom. Not only will readers find their hearts strangely warmed, but they will also be greatly encouraged to trust more fully in God's power, to become more fervent and expectant in prayer, and to view life in this world with a renewed kingdom vision. This book is a gem!

PAUL COPAN, Pledger Family Chair of
Philosophy and Ethics at Palm Beach Atlantic
University and author of *Loving Wisdom*

It often takes a scholar with gravitas and a firm reputation to risk moving readers toward an emerging position that is viewed skeptically by many peers. Miracles today? Where's the data? J. P. Moreland is just such a researcher who thinks that the time has come to both take that challenge and place it within a framework that makes good sense. Very highly recommended.

GARY R. HABERMAS, distinguished
research professor, Liberty University

God is on the move today all over the world, and it's important to have careful documentation of divine miracles that are faith building. J. P. Moreland is a highly respected scholar, and he has been very careful to vet and verify five different kinds of contemporary miracles happening all around us. He also provides engaging, inspiring cases of each, along with solid reflections about how to think about the miraculous. I highly recommend this unique and exciting book.

JOSH D. MCDOWELL, author

A Simple Guide to Experience Miracles helped open up new depths of intercessory prayer and discernment in my life when I needed it most. If you are a Christian who has longed to experience more of God's supernatural and gospel-authenticating presence, this book is an answer to your prayers. If you are a skeptic or a seeker, you will find a sober-minded, reasoned approach to considering the reality of a wonder-working God. Dr. Moreland approaches his readers with the warmth of an old friend, taking them on a tour of vetted miracle accounts. Highly practical and a brilliant encouragement!

MRS. RAE DARABONT, graduate
student and philanthropist

J. P Moreland is a brilliant thinker with a tender heart and winsome spirit, an expert who chooses to remain a novice in order to discover more of the King and his kingdom. His humility and hunger for the things of God inspire me. *A Simple Guide to Experience Miracles* is exceptional. It marries what is necessary today but so often easily separated: mastery and mystery, conviction and curiosity, rigorous scholarship and passionate spirituality, logic and fire. I highly recommend this book to everyone eager to encounter the incomparable God who moves in inexplicable ways.

ALAN SCOT, senior pastor, Vineyard
Anaheim, Anaheim, California

A SIMPLE GUIDE TO

EXPERIENCE MIRACLES

INSTRUCTION and INSPIRATION FOR
LIVING SUPERNATURALLY IN CHRIST

J. P. MORELAND

ZONDERVAN
REFLECTIVE

ZONDERVAN REFLECTIVE

A Simple Guide to Experience Miracles
Copyright © 2021 by J. P. Moreland

Requests for information should be addressed to:
Zondervan, *3900 Sparks Dr. SE, Grand Rapids, Michigan 49546*

Zondervan titles may be purchased in bulk for educational, business, fundraising, or sales promotional use. For information, please email SpecialMarkets@Zondervan.com.

ISBN 978-0-310-12419-1 (softcover)

ISBN 978-0-310-12421-4 (audio)

ISBN 978-0-310-12420-7 (ebook)

Cover design: Tammy Johnson
Cover photo: Denis Belitsky / Shutterstock
Interior design: Kait Lamphere

Printed in the United States of America

21 22 23 24 25 26 27 28 29 30 /LSCH/ 14 13 12 11 10 9 8 7 6 5 4 3 2 1

They shall speak of the glory of thy kingdom, and talk of thy power; to make known to the sons of men his mighty acts, and the glorious majesty of his kingdom.
PSALM 145:11–12 KJV

To my Vineyard-Anaheim brothers and sisters, past and present—
you embody what this book is all about.
1 CORINTHIANS 4:20

CONTENTS

INTRODUCTION

In the middle of nowhere, two Christians were driving in the mountains of Iran in a car that was full of Bibles. Without warning, the steering wheel jammed and they were forced to the side of the road. Suddenly an old man was knocking at the car's window, asking them where the books were. Confused, they asked what books he was referring to, and he responded, "The books about Jesus."

Continuing, the old man said an angel had recently appeared to him in a vision and shared about Jesus, and the man later discovered that everyone in his village had just had the very same vision! They had all believed in Jesus. Now the old man had a village full of infant Christians who had no idea what to do next. The old man shared that in another dream, Jesus told him to walk down the mountain and stand beside the road, and someone would bring him books about Jesus. He obeyed and selected the spot where he would stand, and just as expected, a supply of Bibles written in their language was provided for his village.[1]

What do you make of this story? Is it a fabrication? The story is told in a book by Joel Rosenberg, a *New York Times* bestselling author, an expert on Middle East affairs, and a man who did extensive research, much of it while spending time in Muslim countries, about the rising numbers of people who have made decisions to follow Jesus in these places. Is what happened to these two Christians in Iran a coincidence? Obviously not. In this book you will learn how to use a principle to discern between a

1

miracle and a lucky coincidence, but this one is pretty obvious. It was a miracle. Period!

Would you like to see more of this sort of thing happen in your life? In the life of your church? If your answer is yes, this book is for you.

My goal in this book is to invigorate your love for God. In the stories and thoughts I share, I want to build up your confidence that we can truly know the reality of the biblical God and his power today. I also want to increase your expectation and hope that God can and often does miraculously intervene to bring help and comfort, and to show that it makes rational sense to step out and engage kingdom power. I believe that by doing so you will strengthen your courage to witness to and act on behalf of the gospel of Jesus. To put it simply, the varied aspects of the book's purpose center on building strong, confident, and spiritually and emotionally mature disciples who are increasingly manifesting a supernatural lifestyle to a watching world.

I realize you have a multitude of options when it comes to the books you read. My aim here is to offer fresh insights into and a basic understanding of the supernatural work of God by providing credible, confirmed, inspiring, and motivating cases of five kinds of miraculous events that ordinary believers have experienced today. We'll look at specific and verifiable answers to prayer, miraculous healings, miraculous ways in which God still speaks to and guides his children, angelic/demonic manifestations, and near-death experiences (NDEs).

Again, my greatest hope is that this book will foster your love for God. When I speak of love for God, I often refer to it as "attachment love." This phrase may be unfamiliar to you, but I think you will quickly see why I refer to it this way. *Attachment* is a deep and enduring emotional bond that connects people. Think of the attachment an infant develops with its mother, children with their parents, or a husband and wife in a healthy marriage.

Think of attachment love as love that involves an intimate, close, experiential connection between those who love each other. There is a growing emphasis today on healthy attachment as a key element in the development of emotionally and psychologically stable, mature people. Psychiatrist Daniel Siegel notes that healthy relational attachments include the sense of being held in another's heart and mind, of "feeling felt" and close to another.[2]

The idea of attachment has gained a renewed emphasis in biblical studies, often with a focus on the fundamental catastrophe that resulted from the fall of humankind and our separation from God. We were created to function best in loving relational dependence on God, and attaching to him in love is one of the central aims of biblical Christianity. Author Dallas Willard has gone so far as to suggest that a central component of the gospel is a "new and active attachment with God that forms and transforms our identities."[3] To help us grasp what is distinctive about the biblical notion of attachment, I believe it is best to call it "attachment love." When we apply "attachment" to our relationship with God, we learn that one of the most important things in life is the cultivation of *a mutual relationship that is established on a deep, intimate, emotional love for and connectedness to God and the ability to receive this love from him in a felt way.*

"This all sounds great," you may be saying, "but what does it have to do with this book?" There are several ways to cultivate an attachment love with God, but as Dallas Willard insightfully observed, spiritually and emotionally mature persons "have developed the knowledge and habits that keep them constantly turned toward and expectant of God and God's action in their life. This is the primary source of direction and empowerment for all that concerns them and their world."[4]

And so while there are many ways you can read the stories I share in this book, perhaps the most helpful is to allow them to assist you in being more attentive to and expectant of God's actions and interventions. Allow them to create a hunger and expectation in your heart, one that will empower you to see more of God's actions in your own life. So, among other things, read them with your *heart*. Imagine what the people in these stories felt about God, and let those thoughts increase your attachment love for God and create an expectation of his active care for you.

To help you see where we are going in the chapters that follow, here is an overview of what we'll be covering. I begin by showing the need. Why does it matter that we become more attuned to the supernatural, and what role does this awareness play in a flourishing Christian life? Chapter 1 describes the important role that miracles played in the first four centuries of Christianity and goes on to explain how the church lost contact with this vital aspect of ordinary discipleship. We will then look at eight ways to strengthen our trust in and experience of the supernatural, and how to build an expectation for a life of supernatural engagement. Along the way I'll share some of my qualifications for serving as your tour guide on this journey.

The first chapter raises several fundamental questions:

- What is a miracle?
- How can I distinguish a miracle from a serendipitous coincidence?
- How do I respond to the culture's biggest objection against miracles?

Chapter 2 builds on chapter 1 by addressing these questions. It begins by providing a working definition of a miracle. We will consider the false contemporary view of what it means to know something and flesh out how this understanding defrauds people of the confidence and comfort that come from knowing that God is real, Christianity is true, there is a heaven and a hell, and miracles really do continue to happen. To solve this problem,

I'll offer an accurate, simple account of the nature of knowledge. I will explain why our embrace of this account is so important and then offer insights that can set believers free to be confident in what they know, with a special focus on the miraculous. I'll also share a time-tested, well-supported principle that helps us know whether an event is a miracle or a mere coincidence.

But this raises a new problem. What if this whole business of miracles and the supernatural is just superstitious and irrational? To answer this question, I will address what is by far the biggest objection raised against belief in miracles. The foundation laid in chapters 1 and 2 will create a hunger to know what kinds of miraculous events should be part of a biblical lifestyle.

Before we can fully benefit from the amazing accounts of miraculous answers to prayer, I must address some potential confusion about prayer. That's the point of chapter 3, which begins by answering the question, "Why does God have us bring our petitionary prayers to him?" The answer will help us be active rather than passive in our prayer life. The remainder of chapter 3 addresses two further questions about prayer:

- Why should I pray if God already knows what I'm going to ask for and what is going to happen in the future?
- Wouldn't a perfectly good God already set his heart and will toward doing for us what is truly good and keeping us from what is truly bad, regardless of whether we pray?

In other words, if God already knows everything and is truly good, how can prayer make any difference?

Chapter 3 closes with a look at some practical questions we all struggle with from time to time: When should I stop praying? Why should I pray more than once? We will consider two kinds of petitionary prayer, and I'll share several credible accounts of miraculous answers to prayer.

I find the topic of chapter 4 to be one of the most fun and exciting sections of the book. I hope that it will help each of us be confident that God really does listen and often does grant what we ask for. In addition, I hope it will assure us that miraculous answers to prayer don't just come to the spiritual superstars; these answers also come to us "ordinary" Jesus followers who are in need. All of the accounts in this chapter were experienced by either my family or friends, and the stories I share from friends were written by them solely for inclusion in this book.

Moving from the general to the particular, chapter 5 zeros in on miraculous healing. Similar to the previous two chapters, this chapter lays out a framework for understanding the nature and practice of healing prayer, and chapter 6 provides stunning, credible, hope-filled accounts of miraculous healings that resulted from prayer.

Chapter 5 begins by showing our need to be more active in praying to experience more results from healing prayer. We'll look at the importance of healing in church history and some of the confusion that has caused healing to wane. The first section closes with documentation of a revival of worldwide healings since 1970. Building on that, I offer five biblical lines of evidence that give us increased confidence when we pray for healing. I also discuss several skeptical questions about the reality of healings and respond to these faith-stifling objections. Given that it is reasonable and biblical to launch out expectantly in the practice of healing prayer, the chapter closes by addressing three areas where we need to grow in understanding before we begin praying for healing:

- We'll learn how to pray for the sick most effectively.
- We'll examine fourteen reasons why many people do not experience healing.
- We'll gain practical suggestions for growing in faith and expectation in our use of healing prayer.

Chapter 6 embarks on an adventurous tour through a series of wonderful, credible accounts of miraculous healings. For each case I share in this chapter, I provide careful documentation and evidence, and I personally have strong confidence in their authenticity. As you read, my hope is that these stories will convince you that you can embrace the reality of miraculous healings and that you will feel a stirring conviction that your church should make room for healing prayer. Part of what we learn about healing prayer in chapters 4 and 5 involves learning to listen to what God is saying about a situation, which raises the issue of how we learn to hear and discern God's voice. We'll put the focus on that topic in chapter 7, which may be the most powerful chapter in the book for many people.

Can we hear the supernatural voice of God speaking to us today? Chapter 7 starts with four preliminary considerations we need to grasp before we examine the specific ways God speaks to us extrabiblically. We'll consider the claim made by many Christians that God does *not* speak today outside of the Bible (and creation). Then we'll look at the biblical justification for believing that God speaks to us extrabiblically, along with life-changing examples of six ways he does this.

To this point, the book has been building one chapter on the next. The first two chapters lay a foundation for dealing with miracles and the supernatural. The next five build on this foundation and in a logically ordered progression provide instruction and inspiration in the three main areas in which God miraculously intervenes. In chapters 8 and 9, we move on to areas of the supernatural that do not primarily focus on divine intervention— namely, angelic and demonic manifestations and near-death experiences. In this way, we fill out a thoroughly supernatural Christian worldview and encourage learning to live in light of these supernatural realities.

My goal in chapter 8 is that you will become more biblically aware of the spirit world, to know with confidence that it exists, and to live in its reality. In the first half of the chapter, we focus on angels by clarifying their nature and ministry, highlighting how and why we should incorporate their companionship and help in our daily lives. Along the way, we look at the debate over whether adults have guardian angels, and I conclude with some highly credible and comforting accounts of angelic manifestations to help people know they are never alone.

In the chapter's second half, we follow the same trajectory with regard to demons, describing their nature and activities and addressing whether Christians can be demon-possessed. My aim here is to help believers understand both their authority in Christ and the degree to which demons can harm them. Along the way, we will learn four ways of knowing that demons are real and discover how to relate demonization to psychological and psychiatric problems. I then provide several credible accounts of demonization that will help us better analyze and address personal problems as we keep the demonic in mind.

Chapter 9 takes up the issue of near-death experiences (NDEs), arguing that it is appropriate to use these experiences to strengthen our belief in heaven and hell and to increase a *healthy* preoccupation with heaven, one that cultivates daily comfort, purpose, and joy. Two practical problems can prevent the doctrine of heaven from bringing believers daily comfort, purpose, and hope: (1) we *want* heaven to be real and we *believe* it's real, but we don't know with confidence that it *is* real; and (2) given the hazy presentation of the intermediate state (the time between death and the final resurrection), many Christians lack a concrete, imageable picture of what it will be like to be in heaven and what it is like at the moment of death. Thankfully, the powerful evidence from NDEs contributes greatly to solving both of these problems.

Before these stories can be fully appreciated and internalized, some objections to near-death experiences need to be addressed.

Chapter 9 begins with a presentation of six lines of solid evidence for the veracity and knowability of NDEs, followed by a response to naturalistic and biblical objections to NDEs. Once we clear the air of objections, the rest of the chapter is full of encouraging cases that can help rid Christians of any fear of death.

The purpose of the final chapter is to provide the reader with a personal vision for incorporating into their own lives what they've learned. My hope is that what I share will inspire a greater embrace of the supernatural in many churches as well. We begin by "putting it all together" as we summarize what we've learned and place it into a broad framework. Then I highlight different practical steps we can take to benefit from, live more powerfully in, and practice more competently what we've read.

The bibliography at the back of the book provides additional resources for those who want to continue learning about the topics covered in this book. Under each category, I've listed several sources, with each entry marked as either basic (B), intermediate (I), or advanced (A) in difficulty.

In their wonderful work *What Is the Mission of the Church?* Kevin DeYoung and Greg Gilbert persuasively argue that the fundamental—not the sole, but the fundamental—purpose of God's people from Genesis to Revelation is proclaiming, testifying, and bearing witness.[5] And what are we to bear witness to? To the reality and meaning of the death and resurrection of Jesus the Messiah. They add that this proclamation includes announcing the blessings of the kingdom of God that flow out of and point back to this gospel. Moreover, at the core of those blessings reside the mighty miracles of God performed on behalf of his people.

Summarizing the Old Testament, David announces, "[The saints] shall speak of the glory of thy kingdom, and talk of thy power; to make known to the sons of men his mighty acts" (Psalm 145:11–12 KJV). In the New Testament, Peter and John boldly assert that they "cannot help speaking about what we have seen and heard" (Acts 4:20). While these proclamations centered on the gospel, in context they were announcing to Israel's rulers that a man lame from birth was healed by them near the temple in the name of Jesus (see Acts 3:1–10; 4:5–12).

This book resides squarely within this great mission. We are proclaiming the good news of Jesus by pointing to the mighty acts and miracles he has done—and continues to do today. So take a deep breath, strap on your boots, and get ready for an exciting adventure. Let's go witnessing!

Chapter 1

WHY SO MANY WESTERNERS ARE EMBARRASSED BY MIRACLE STORIES

During an appointment with my Christian doctor, our conversation turned to the topic of miracles. As we talked, I asked him if he could recall an answer to prayer that he knew—without a doubt—was miraculous. He thought for a bit and then shared (in his own words) this story with me:

> Our daughter, Ashley, was about ten years old at the time. She had two parakeets, and one of them had just died. So she told her mother she wanted to get another one so she would have a couple again. Her mother, however, had had enough of pets for the time being, and she told Ashley that we weren't going to get another parakeet right now. Ashley had a mind of her own though. She said she was going to pray to God for another parakeet. And she did.
>
> The very next day, Ashley was playing outside with her friends when one of the kids saw a bird in the tree. They all knew that Ashley had just lost her pet. And it turned out to be a parakeet—even the very same color as the one she had just lost! We asked around, and no one could remember ever having seen a parakeet in the neighborhood before. Keep in mind, this occurred the very next day after she began to pray. You

11

can imagine her sense of triumph as she brought the bird—an exact duplicate of the one that had just died—into the house on her finger and announced that God had answered her prayer!

Was this just an odd coincidence? Perhaps, but a very unlikely one. As we'll see in this chapter, there are good reasons to believe that God had intervened and responded to her prayer. I will show why it is unreasonable to take this incident as a serendipitous coincidence. In fact, this story shows God's love for children and his concern for the "little things" in our lives, and it also strengthens our faith—our confidence and trust—that God is real and still intervenes in today's world. Who among us does not need his intervention!

The primary purpose of this book is to help us flourish as maturing Jesus followers by strengthening the hope, faith, courage, and comfort that come from *knowing*—not merely believing—that God is real and still performs miracles today. I'm especially writing for those of us in Western cultures who have been raised with a worldview that downplays the reality and existence of the supernatural. I hope that each of us will gain confidence in and awareness of the supernatural realm and learn how to see miraculous interventions in and around our lives. I believe that God wants to see his church experience a renewal of Christian living that flows from a thoughtful, confident, bold acceptance of an explicitly biblically based *supernatural* Christian worldview. After all, this is our birthright as Christians.

At the core of a maturing Christian life lies the intentional, steady development of confidence in God and the Bible that is based on knowing *why* we believe these things. There are several ways to strengthen our faith, but a crucial aspect of such growth is the bearing and receiving of credible eyewitness testimony to divine intervention in our lives. And as I shared in the introduction, these testimonies facilitate our attachment love for God.

MIRACLES IN THE EARLY CHURCH

Testifying to the miraculous was a key emphasis of Christian believers during the first four centuries of Christianity. Speaking of the early church, Michael Green observed:

> It was the Spirit who gave his followers remarkable spiritual gifts. Prophecy, tongues (and interpretation), healing and exorcism were the most prominent in apostolic and sub-apostolic days alike. People did not merely hear the gospel; they saw it in action, and were moved to respond. The Western church has grown too dependent on words, and not nearly dependent enough on the power of the Holy Spirit. The Enlightenment induced much embarrassment about divine activity in today's world, and this tendency has outlived the demise of the Enlightenment. Instead of being a community demonstrating the Lord's power, we have become one which talks incessantly. We need to remember that the "kingdom of God is not talk, but power."[1]

For example, Tertullian (AD 155–230), when writing to defend Christians against Roman persecution, pointed out the foolishness of the Romans in persecuting Christians: "But who would rescue you [if Christians were to withdraw] from those secret enemies that everywhere lay waste your minds and your bodily health? I mean, from the assaults of demons, whom we drive out of you, without reward, without pay. Why, this alone would have sufficed to avenge us—to leave you open and exposed to unclean spirits with immediate possession."[2] In other words, Tertullian was pointing out that Christians were doing something unique and helpful—they were engaging the spiritual world and driving out the demonic. In this, they were providing a much-needed service to the Romans who were persecuting them.

Later, in addressing the Roman official Scapula, Tertullian mentioned what was public knowledge regarding the healings of several well-placed Roman citizens: "For, the secretary of a certain gentleman, when he was suffering from falling sickness caused by a demon, was freed from it; so, also, were the relatives of some of the others and a certain little boy. And heaven knows how many distinguished men, to say nothing of common people, have been cured either of devils or of their sickness."[3]

This is just one example, but it demonstrates that miracles were central to the early church's growth in faith and their power in evangelism. Sadly, this centrality of miracles is no longer the norm today. Instead of actively engaging with the world in this way, many believers are struggling to develop a vital, confident Christian life.

THE SECULARIZATION OF CULTURE AND THE PRIVATIZATION OF CHRISTIAN TEACHING

Western Christians have absorbed more of a secular worldview than we like to admit, and many of them find miracle stories hard to believe or even embarrassing. As Christian anthropologist Charles Kraft observed, "In comparison to other societies, Americans and other North Atlantic peoples are *naturalistic.* Non-Western peoples are frequently concerned about the activities of supernatural beings . . . The wide-ranging supernaturalism of most of the societies of the world is absent for most of our people . . . Our focus is squarely on the natural world, with little or no attention paid to the supernatural world."[4]

Kraft went on to add that this is true even in the Christian church in the West:

> In the present day, however, Evangelicals tend to believe
> that God has stopped talking and doing the incredible things

we read about in Scripture. Now we see God limiting himself to working through the Bible . . . plus an occasional contemporary "interference" in the natural course of events. What we usually call a miracle—the power God used to manifest in healing—has been largely replaced by secular medicine. The speaking he used to do now comes indirectly through rationalistic reasoning in books, lectures, and sermons—similar to the process used by the secular sciences.[5]

Kraft may have been overstating matters to make a point, but his claims likely hit close to home for most American Evangelicals. Many Christians today are embarrassed by the miracle stories in the Bible, and the secularization of American culture, especially of cultural elites like university professors, those in the media and entertainment industry, and many politicians, has led to widespread ridicule toward and skepticism about all things supernatural. A Christian worldview used to be the default position of most people in America, even many unbelievers. There was minimally a belief in God, a respect for Jesus and the Bible and prayer, and a belief that miracles, though rare, still happened. Since the 1930s, however, the default worldview has increasingly shifted toward a more naturalistic one. We believe science tells us what is real—and indeed *all* that is real, and thus the only way to know reality is through the hard sciences.

On September 10, 2004, I debated atheist Eddie Tabash on Lee Strobel's weekly television program *Faith under Fire*. Our topic was "Is the Supernatural Real?" For decades, Tabash has been a successful Los Angeles lawyer. He is a lifetime member of the American Atheists, as well as a strong supporter of the Internet Infidels (an organization of atheists on the internet devoted to promoting atheism and attacking Christianity), and he has served as the chair of the board of directors for the Council for Secular Humanism. During the debate, with great verve, Tabash asserted dogmatically that there is absolutely no evidence that any supernatural being has ever intervened in our law-governed, physical universe.

Tabash is an intelligent and well-educated man, but as we will see in the coming chapters, his assertion is simply ignorant and foolish. I cite Tabash as one influential example of the contemporary hostility toward miracles and the supernatural. And like it or not, this skepticism has rubbed off on many people in our churches. While most Bible-believing Christians retain a mild doctrinal belief in the supernatural and miracles, they live as practical atheists, with very little expectation of seeing the miraculous.

A few years ago, two graduate students from Africa—one a Nigerian and one an Ethiopian—came to my office to express a concern. Having been in the States for about a year, both had observed that the American church no longer believes in the supernatural world. I asked them to elaborate on what they meant. They shared that all of the churches back in their home countries have a time at the end of their services for healing prayer and demonic deliverance. Both of them had seen numerous miraculous healings and demonic deliverances. But they were puzzled as to why the churches in America don't seem to leave room for the supernatural. They had observed that for Americans, everything is cared for through medicine or therapy. In their day-to-day lives, American believers don't *really* believe in the demonic. Hearing them share their observations was painful, but I had to agree that what they said was largely true.

As the late Dallas Willard observed, "The crushing weight of the secular outlook . . . permeates or pressures every thought we have today. Sometimes it even forces those who self-identify as Christian teachers to set aside Jesus' plain statements about the reality and total relevance of the kingdom of God and replace them with philosophical speculations . . . [because] *something has been found out* that renders a spiritual understanding of reality in the manner of Jesus simply foolish to those who are 'in the know.'"[6] Embarrassment is a very painful emotion. Can you remember a time when you were embarrassed and felt foolish? Remember how you could feel the redness creep into your face? Doing a Houdini disappearing act seemed to be the only way out. Have you ever been embarrassed about being a Christian? Let's be honest. Intellectual embarrassment—looking stupid or coming across as ignorant—may be the worst kind of embarrassment. That's one reason that people are deathly afraid of public speaking. We want to avoid looking ignorant at all costs.

If being a Christian is identified with being ignorant or backward—as the term *Fundamentalist* is clearly meant to imply—we will fear witnessing or sharing our faith with others. We will struggle to stand up for our faith without coming across as defensive. And we will also lose our expectation of the miraculous. Not only will this way of thinking dilute what Christians *actually* believe, but it will also drain the power from our witness, making us increasingly ineffective in a secular culture that is slouching toward Gomorrah.[7] We all sense this secular encroachment, especially in our universities, media, and governments.

EIGHT WAYS TO INCREASE OUR EXPECTATION OF THE MIRACULOUS

Many people today understand the word *faith* to mean a blind choice to believe something in the absence of any good reason to make that choice. Faith is viewed as a privatized expression of emotion. But this view does not reflect a biblical concept of faith; in fact, it represents practically the opposite of biblical faith. Biblical faith is *trust or confidence in something that is based on knowledge or good reasons.* Think about a choice to drive a car. If the engine makes odd noises and the exterior is rusty and the car just doesn't appear to be well cared for, you may hesitate to put your trust in it to get you from one place to another. However, if you are borrowing it from a friend who takes care of his things and it's a relatively new model with a good reputation, you may drive it without a second thought. The more you know about a car, the more your trust in it will be appropriate or warranted and, if the car is actually a good one, rightly strengthened. Similarly, our faith is not opposed to reason or knowledge; it is built on reason and knowledge.

We cannot choose to believe something we don't believe. That's why bare, unsupported exhortations to believe are harmful and guilt-producing, since people do not have it in their power to respond. Suppose someone were to offer you $500 if, right now on the spot, you would actually believe that unicorns are real, that there is a flying spaghetti monster right above your head, that George Washington never existed, or that $2 + 2 = 98$. Motivated as you are to get the $500, the best you could do is fake a belief in those things. You cannot simply *choose* to believe them.

Now suppose you wanted to believe something you did not truly accept, say, that God and heaven are real. You could come to believe these things by studying Scripture and other sources that support that belief or asking others how they came to believe the idea or concept in question. You could wisely investigate the topic, seeking ways to experience it more fully. Or perhaps you'd look more closely at why you struggle with this belief and seek to remove potential barriers—perhaps emotional or intellectual barriers or early childhood trauma that negatively shaped your perspective and prevented a clear understanding.

We are not transformed in our thinking by choosing to believe harder in the midst of a vacuum. No, as Paul writes in Romans 12:1–2, we are transformed by the *renewing* of our minds. Why is this so? Because as our minds grow in understanding what we are to believe and why we should believe it, our beliefs change.

They are strengthened. Beliefs are formed or strengthened indirectly, depending on what we do with our minds and experiences. So it's not enough to ask ourselves whether or not we believe something. It is also important to examine the strength of that belief. There was a time in my life when I believed with a confidence level of 60/40 that God answers prayer. I decided to embark on an investigative journey to strengthen what I already believed, and I will honestly say that I'm now closer to 85/15 in my belief that prayer actually works. For comparison, as a philosopher, I'm only about 90/10 sure the external world is made of matter!

With all this in mind, I offer eight suggestions that have bolstered my own confidence in Christianity and my expectation of the miraculous. Where I've recommended that you read something (besides this book), be sure to consult the select bibliography at the end of the book, where you'll find a number of handpicked books geared toward helping you fortify your faith and expectation.

1. Read a book that gives reasons for how we know that God exists or that the Bible is reliable, or that addresses a problem you may be having in believing some specific aspect of Christianity.
2. Face your intellectual doubts honestly and with integrity. Put them down on paper. Once you've done this, be tenacious about looking for satisfying answers. Ask knowledgeable people for answers, read books and articles, go to apologetics websites, and so on. Doubt your doubts! Be patient, but don't stop until you are satisfied.
3. Emotional doubts tend to be vague feelings that God is absent and Christianity isn't working, and we may feel disoriented in our thoughts about God. In my experience, such doubts are often due to attachment issues—a lack of being intimately connected to or nurtured by our

family members in early childhood, traumatic events that have distressed us, and related matters. These issues can dampen our ability to feel close to others and be in touch with our own feelings. We experience God as absent, maybe even nonexistent. In this case, we need to process our issues and cultivate emotional intelligence. I suggest you see a good Christian therapist for help, listen to uplifting worship music, or read books on developing your ability to feel and to draw close to others and God.

4. Make a donation to the JESUS Film Project and receive the monthly newsletter. My wife, Hope, and I can hardly wait to receive ours each month. It reads like the book of Acts and never fails to build our faith and expectation. Or pick up a book that contains credible stories of the miraculous. These books remind us that we live in a supernatural world, even if we may not be experiencing it at present.

5. Make it a habit to ask others about what they've seen and heard. Ask them questions such as, "Have you recently experienced or do you know someone who has experienced something supernatural—a specific answer to prayer, healing, divine guidance or the audible discernment of God's voice, an angelic or demonic manifestation, or a near-death experience?" Or "Since you've become a Christian, what have been some of the most dramatic, memorable supernatural interventions in your life or in the lives of those you know?" Also, share with others what you've seen and heard, as the Bible urges us to do. Through it all, our motives are to honor God and strengthen our brothers and sisters.

6. Talk with your church leadership about the possibility of setting aside a time weekly, biweekly, or monthly for persons to share from the pulpit a short testimony in the Sunday service about a miracle they have seen or heard.

7. When hearing about a miracle, err on the side of trusting it instead of doubting it. We want to avoid two extremes— gullibility and skepticism. Obviously, if it is clear that a miracle has happened, we should trust the report. And if the report just isn't credible, we should not believe it. Harm can be done to the cause of Christ by believing something false or failing to believe something true. But because we have good reasons to believe that Christianity is true, we should choose belief instead of doubt when it comes to events we experience or about which we hear, if an alleged miracle could go either way. After all, the problem for many of us is that we are naturalists deep down. Thus, for borderline cases, we should place the burden of proof on disbelief, not on belief. For example, if we experience something that seems like divine inter-vention but also realize it's possible it isn't, unless there is harm in accepting the experience as a miracle, we would do well to conclude it is a miracle.

8. Be honest about your disappointment with God. Like you, I experience long periods when God seems utterly absent or uninterested and when I don't knowingly expe-rience something supernatural. Sometimes I get angry, or at least very disappointed, with God. There's no point in hiding our feelings from an omniscient Being who already loves and forgives us completely. So face up to your disap-pointments, tell God what you are thinking and feeling, and ask for help.

One way to begin to work on these ideas is to pause your reading, look over the list, and pray, asking God to draw your attention to one of these ideas that could help you in growing in your faith in God. He may lead you to one in particular or to something that's not on this list. Write the idea down and come back to it in the coming days. When you do, one fruitful action point may be to meet with a good friend or family member, go over the list, and talk about the ones that are especially important to you. You may wish to ask the person if they have that problem too and find out how they handle it.

I Am Speaking as if Insane

The church in Corinth was messy and hopelessly divided. Some claimed to follow a church leader named Apollos, others the apostle Peter, and still others Paul. Many did not accept Paul's teaching because they either did not believe he was an apostle or, at the very least, thought he was an inferior one. In 2 Corinthians 11, Paul does something that, on the surface, seems to lack humility (see Philippians 3:1–6 for a similar tactic). To take this approach was difficult for him to do, so much so that he says, "I am speaking as if insane" (verse 23 NASB).

What was this crazy, insane thing that Paul did? He boasted. He listed his credentials as an apostle and trustworthy follower of Jesus. And why did he boast? Because the situation warranted it. He had important things to say to the Corinthians—apostolic-level teaching—and he needed to establish his authority so the church would accept his teachings.

I mention Paul's "boasting" because I want to close this chapter by speaking "as if insane." Since my conversion in 1968, for more than a half century I have consistently wanted to know the real truth—the evidence for and against the things I believe. I am convinced that God called me to this task, and so I obtained three graduate degrees—one in theology and two in philosophy—with my PhD in philosophy. I did this to increase my skills to know the truth and to competently examine the quality of the case for and against my beliefs—in Christianity and its specific doctrinal claims.

In this specific sense, you could say that my commitment to truth has been greater than my commitment to God or a particular doctrine. In other words, I knew that if I ever found out that one of my beliefs was false, I would abandon it. This is how I have lived my life for more than fifty years. The things I believe and teach matter to me, so I try to get them right.

Further, with God's co-laboring help and favor, I have earned a solid reputation as a trustworthy, fair-minded, faithful, and informed Christian intellectual. Through teaching, speaking, and writing, I have sustained a public ministry for many decades. As a result, many people throughout the world have watched me live out my life as Jesus' bondservant and give careful attention to the things I write and say. Many see me as a role model and are encouraged and strengthened as Jesus followers by my example.

Honestly, I would rather have the Lord take me home than risk failing to finish well, hurting those who look up to me, or losing my integrity. I was raised by blue-collar parents and taught to stay grounded, keeping what I say and do accessible and down-to-earth. My family and friends will tell you that I'm just an ordinary Joe as I interact with them day to day.

I share this because I desperately want you to be encouraged, strengthened, and confident in what you hear from me. I have nothing to gain and much to lose if I choose to make these things up or exaggerate them. God doesn't need my help to convince you of the truth. He is fully capable of doing that on his own. I say this because some of what comes later will strike some readers as "spectacular." It may fall outside of your own experience and be difficult to believe. But I give you my word, for whatever that's worth, that every miracle story I share from my own life is true and not exaggerated. I was an eyewitness to some of these events. Other stories relate miracles that occurred in the lives of others, and in these cases, I have vetted these accounts carefully in three ways: (1) I selected most of the cases from people I have known well for many years, those who have a wide reputation in the church for integrity and Christian maturity; (2) I've interacted personally with each person whose story I've included to verify the factual details, checking to see if others could vouch for the miracle's credibility, so I could assure myself that the person was being completely honest; and (3) whenever I cite a case from a book, I've done everything I could to contact the publisher, the author or editor of the book, or the person whose story I share.

The chapters that follow focus on five different kinds of miracles. I invite you to open your heart, focus your mind, and feed your soul on what follows. But before we start the journey of looking at various kinds of credible miracle accounts, we need to ask some key questions. That's where we'll start in the next chapter.

- Can we actually know that a miracle has occurred, and if so, how?
- How do we tell the difference between a genuine miracle and a mere coincidence?

Chapter 2

MIRACLES: WHAT THEY ARE AND HOW TO RECOGNIZE THEM

Years ago, my friend and colleague Professor Klaus Issler prayed each day before class for a student named Jason Lanker.[1] Jason was in his second semester of doctoral studies, and he and his wife, Heather, had asked God to provide for his tuition bills as an indication of God's guidance as to whether he should continue his schooling. "That way," Jason said, "if the finances ever dried up, I would know God was leading me in a different direction." When the payment came due for the next semester, Jason and his wife found they didn't have the money to make the payment. So they began petitioning God to provide for them—the *exact* amount of the tuition bill, $2,117.60, which was due on the coming Friday. By Friday's end, no funding had arrived, and Jason was angry, dismayed, and confused. "How could the God who had made his will so clear just one semester before have left me out in the cold? My disbelief was palpable and by Monday morning the anger that had been brewing all weekend boiled over in a two-day tirade against God."

Tuesday evening before class, Dr. Issler and other class members united to pray for the needed $2,117.60. And while Jason was driving home after class, his angry heart was softened. He listened as God reminded him that Jason had been the one who had put out the fleece about financial provision being a sign that he should remain in the doctoral program. Now when the funds had failed to come in, Jason was upset. He was rejecting the apparent direction that God's answer seemed to indicate. As Jason listened, he found that God's voice was not shaming. Rather, it reminded Jason to wait on the Lord and to refrain from setting up demands dictating how God needed to work.

Then a miracle happened.

The next evening, while cleaning her grandmother's home, Heather was rummaging through piles of old letters her grandmother had written to her but had never sent out. She was shocked to discover several bank bonds her grandmother had made out in her name, which amounted to $2,000! The following day, she and Jason deposited the bonds in the bank, and guess what? When the bank added the interest earned on the bonds, Heather and Jason received *exactly* $2,117.60! When he realized this amount was—to the penny—exactly what he needed, Jason wept. He knew this was a specific answer to prayer, and he praised God for not only the financial provision but also the guidance to continue his studies.

As you read this story and other accounts like it, I remind you of this book's primary purpose: *to help you grow as a Jesus follower by strengthening your hope, faith, courage, and comfort.* That strength comes from *knowing*—not merely believing—that God is real and that he still performs miracles today. I want you to gain confidence in and awareness of the supernatural realm and learn how to see more miraculous interventions in your life.

Confidence in God and his Word lies at the core of a maturing Christian life. This confidence grows when we know *why* we believe what we believe. Sharing and receiving credible eyewitness testimony to divine intervention in our lives is a crucial way we strengthen our faith. But before we read more of these testimonies, we need to be clear about what a miracle is. How do we know that a miracle has occurred and that it's not just a coincidence? Did Jason and Heather really experience a miracle?

Let me give you fair warning—the next section may be a little heavy for some readers, though I truly wish it were not so. But I assure you that grasping the remainder of this chapter will be beneficial, even if you have to read it twice! So let's begin in earnest, ready to learn.

HOW CAN WE REALLY KNOW A MIRACLE HAS OCCURRED?

We first must look at the question, what is a miracle? I define a miracle as an event or intervention that is caused by the special action of God or some other supernatural being that is an exception to the ordinary, law-governed course of nature for some specific purpose.[2] I will give special attention to miracles that involve specific answers to prayer, healing, the audible discernment of God's voice, angelic or demonic manifestations, and near-death experiences (NDEs).

Our goal is to formulate answers to these two questions:

- Can we actually know that a miracle has happened, or can we at least have more reason to believe than disbelieve that some event is a miracle?
- How can we tell the difference between a genuine miracle and a mere coincidence?

In the next section, we'll unfold three important points that will help us answer these questions.

WHAT DOES IT MEAN TO KNOW SOMETHING?

First, we need to get clear about what knowledge is. There are two kinds of knowledge: (1) knowledge by direct awareness or experience, and (2) *propositional* knowledge. The first type of knowledge is achieved by directly experiencing something— being aware of it. For example, a little child can experience the color red while looking at an apple, even if the child has no concept of redness or ability to use the word *red*. Thus, the child can be aware of red without being able to form the thought *this is red*. Knowledge by direct awareness goes well beyond the five senses. For example, I have direct introspective awareness of what is going on in my mind or emotions, or a direct aware- ness of wisdom and love and other concepts or feelings. As we will see, people often know that God, a demon, or an angel is present by being directly and experientially aware of the being in question.

The second type of knowledge is propositional knowledge. We have this knowledge if *we have a true belief about something based on adequate reasons or grounds*. For instance, I know my foot is hurting now because (1) I believe it is hurting, (2) that belief is true, (3) and I have adequate grounds for holding to the belief (that is, I feel the pain and throbbing in my foot or I can see it is swollen and inflamed). I know Jesus rose from the dead for a number of reasons, but among them is adequate evidence. Thus, I believe Jesus rose from the dead, that belief is true, and my evidence for this belief is more than adequate for it to count as knowledge.

Once we grasp that there are two kinds of knowledge, we must understand a second point, though it may sound confusing at first: *one can know something without knowing how they know*. Let me explain. My field of philosophy has a subbranch called epistemology that studies the nature of knowledge or reasonable beliefs, along with the ways we gain or possess such knowledge and beliefs. Most experts in this field accept the idea that there are clear cases in which one can know something without know- ing *how* one knows it.

KNOWING WITHOUT KNOWING HOW

There are at least two reasons for widespread acceptance of the idea that we can know something without knowing how we know it. First, this idea is consistent with many things all of us know. I know I had coffee this morning, even if I don't know how I know that. If you say I know it because I remember it, then I can ask how we know that my memory is reliable in this case. The truth is that I just know I had coffee, and that's it. I don't need to know any more than that.

Second, if we reject the idea, we end up in trouble. Here's how. Suppose we think that to know something, we must know how we know it. As an example, let's assume I know P—say, that the lemon on the table is sour. Well, if I know P, then I must know how I know P. Suppose I know P because I know a principle Q: if something appears a certain way to my senses, then I know it. Since Q tells me how I know P, P passes the test.

But wait a minute. How can I use Q to justify my claim to know P unless I know Q is a correct principle? I can't. But to know Q, I need to know how I know Q, and so I must have a second principle R that tells me how I know that Q is a correct principle. You can see where this is going: We're off on a vicious, infinite regress and cannot know anything on the assumption that I always have to know how I know something before I can know it. At some point, the regress must stop at a place where I just know something without knowing how.

Don't get me wrong. Knowing how one knows something—for example, that a certain interpretation of a biblical text is the correct one—is typically necessary. I am making the mere point that it is not *always* necessary, and there are clear cases where we know something without knowing how. This matters because, as we'll see in upcoming chapters, we sometimes know that God spoke to us, that an event was an answer to prayer, or that a demon was present without knowing *how* we know these things. We just do.

Consider the parakeet story at the beginning of chapter 1. It doesn't take a rocket scientist to know this was an answer to prayer. How do I know this? Well, in this case, I just do. More will be said shortly about another way of knowing this was an answer to prayer, but it's important to realize that specialists in the field of knowledge widely agree that one can know without *knowing how one knows,* and there is no good reason not to apply this to our knowledge of at least some supernatural miracles.

Following on this second point, the third point is the notion that *one can know something without being absolutely certain that one is right.* Remember, propositional knowledge is a true belief based on *adequate*—not completely certifying—grounds. What counts as adequate grounds for something to be a genuine claim to knowledge will vary from field to field, differing in literature, chemistry, history, art, mathematics, ethics, and theology—even in the "field" of hearing God's voice. One size does not fit all! The reasons for believing a demon is present will be different from those that justify the idea that dogs are mammals, yet both claims can be knowledge claims.

We can know something—say, for example, that our son left his room a mess—while at the same time admitting we might be wrong. We may even have some unanswered questions or doubts about what we know. This happens often and when it does, we still have knowledge. This means we can know something is supernatural while admitting we might be wrong and still have unresolved questions. In such a case, the possibility we are mistaken does not discount the solid grounds we have for claiming knowledge.

To illustrate, suppose a true belief needs a certainty of 80 percent to be counted as knowledge. If your question is, "Did God really speak to me when I was praying?" you would need enough reasons for your belief to be 80 percent confident it is true. But let's further suppose that you only have a 60 or 70 percent confidence in your belief that God was speaking to you. Should you reject that belief? Of course not. While you would no longer be able to say you *know* it was God's voice, it is still more reasonable to accept that it was God's voice than to reject the idea.

This simple conceptual tool brings relief and freedom. I've had many, many times in my life when I did not know *for certain* that an event was an answer to prayer—or whether a demon was involved in someone's problems or whether it was God who was directing me. But so often in those very cases, I was 55 percent, 60 percent, or 75 percent sure these were supernatural occurrences. And in those cases, I *should* have believed them to be just that.

GENUINE MIRACLE OR MERE COINCIDENCE?

Philosopher, mathematician, and theologian William Dembski has presented a clear, successful way to determine when it is legitimate to conclude that some phenomenon is the result of a purposive, intelligent act by an agent and when such a conclusion is unwarranted.[3] Among other things, Dembski analyzes cases in which insurance employees, police officers, and forensic scientists must determine whether a death was accidental (there was no intelligent cause) or brought about intentionally (it was done on purpose by an intelligent agent).

According to Dembski, whenever two factors are present, investigators are rationally obligated to draw the conclusion that the event was brought about intentionally for a purpose by an intelligent agent:

- The event was a very unlikely one; it had a small probability of happening.
- The event is capable of independent characterization. In other words, it is capable of being identified as a special occurrence besides the simple fact that it did, in fact, happen. Some independent description of the event itself implies that if an event satisfies that description, then the event is a special one.

To illustrate these two points, consider a game of bridge in which four people receive a hand of thirteen cards each. The winner gets $500. To simplify matters, let's focus on just two of the four players—person A and the dealer. What would you think if on the first deal person A gets a random set of cards, while the dealer gets a perfect bridge hand? If that were to happen, everyone would infer that the dealer had somehow cheated. But what justifies our suspicion?

It cannot be a matter of probability since person A and the dealer have the same number of cards (thirteen) and each hand is equally improbable. So the small probability of an event is not sufficient in itself to raise suspicions that the dealer cheated. Still, small probability is *necessary* to be confident that the result (the dealer getting a winning hand on the first deal) was brought about on purpose.

To see this, suppose that person A and the dealer were the only two players in a different game. In this game, each person is dealt three cards, and the winner must have at least two black cards out of the three dealt to him. Person A gets two red cards and one black card. The dealer gets a winning hand, with two black cards and one red one. If this happened, no one would suspect the dealer of rigging the deck. Why? Because getting two black cards and one red card does not have a small probability of occurring. In fact, it is fairly likely, and thus it can easily be explained by pure chance.

By itself, the small probability of the dealer in the bridge game getting a perfect hand is not enough to charge him with cheating. Highly unlikely coincidences happen all the time. Something else is needed to infer intentional agency, and the second criterion makes this clear: *the perfect bridge hand can be described as special independently of the fact that it happened to be the hand that came about, but this is not so for person A.* Person A's hand can be described as "the improbable hand person A happened to get." Now this specification applies to all hands and does not mark out as special any particular hand that occurs. Thus person A's hand is no more special than any other random deal.

But this is not so for the perfect bridge hand. This hand can be characterized as a special sort of combination of cards by the rules of bridge, quite independently of the fact that it is the hand that the dealer received. It is the combination of small probability (this particular arrangement of cards was quite unlikely to have occurred) and independent describability or "specialness" (according to the rules, this is a pretty special hand for the dealer to receive, which we know independently of the fact that it happened to be the hand the dealer got) that justifies us in accusing the dealer of cheating. To sum up, *small probability + independent specialness = done on purpose by an intelligent agent.* Let's call this the "intelligent agent principle" (IAP).

Here's another example. If a spouse happens to die in a car accident, even though her car was in good shape, she was a careful driver, and the driving conditions were excellent, would this be an accident or the result of some malicious act done on purpose? Given the conditions, the event was very unlikely to happen, so the probability of her death being an accident is very low.

Still, if that was all we had to go on, the accident could have been a sad, unlikely mistake of some kind—a coincidence.

But the situation changes dramatically if the car "accident" occurred just after the husband took out a large insurance policy on his wife and had purchased two tickets to Hawaii for himself and his secretary, and the marriage was heading toward a divorce that would ruin the husband's reputation in the community. In this case, the two factors satisfy the IAP (low probability and being a special situation independently of the fact that it happened) and could justify an arrest for murder. The "accident" was actually the result of an intentional act by an intelligent designer!

What does any of this have to do with distinguishing between a genuine miracle and a mere coincidence? Let's recall what we've learned about the intelligent agent principle (IAP): *small probability + independent specialness = done on purpose by an intelligent agent.* If the agent is God (or a demon or angel), we have a miracle (or some sort of supernatural event, if we prefer not to call acts by angels or demons "miracles"). The IAP is almost never wrong, and you can be assured that if some event or phenomenon satisfies it, it is miraculous. Small probability alone is insufficient.[4]

Clearly God can perform miracles by bringing about an event that is likely to occur without God's intervention. One prays for rain; there is already a 40 percent chance it will rain, and it does. This *could* be a miracle. *Maybe* God intervened and redirected the weather front. But in this case, one could not know, or even be reasonably justified in believing, that it was a miracle. And the occurrence of a highly improbable event might be a miracle since, unbeknownst to us, God may have a specific purpose for the event that would give it "independent specialness." But again, we would not be able to *tell* whether or not it was a miracle. In any case, the use of the IAP allows us to distinguish a real miracle from what, to all appearances, must be judged a mere coincidence.

Let's apply the IAP to another case. Shortly after my

conversion in November 1968, I heard a talk about learning to pray for things specifically, and I wove that instruction into my prayer life. After graduating from college, I joined the staff of Campus Crusade for Christ (now called Cru) and was assigned to work at the Colorado School of Mines in Golden, Colorado, starting in the fall of 1971. After a summer of training in Southern California, I drove to Colorado alone to start looking for a place to live with one roommate for that year. I had already begun to pray specifically that God would provide me and my roommate with a white house that had a white picket fence and a grassy front yard two to three miles from campus and costing no more than $115 a month (this was 1971!).

After two weeks of daily prayer for this, I arrived in Golden and looked for three days for a place to live. I must have visited fifteen different places, but I found nothing at all in Golden. There was a two-bedroom apartment located ten miles away in Denver for $130 a month. Frustrated, I told the manager I would take it. She informed me that the apartment was the only one left and that a couple had looked at it that morning and still had the day to decide to move in. If they didn't take it, it was mine. She called me around 5:00 p.m. to inform me that the couple would be moving in. I was back to square one.

That evening, I received a call from a fellow Crusade staff member, Kaylon Carr. Keep in mind that no one, not even my roommate, knew anything about my prayer request. Kaylon asked if I still needed a place to live, which I clearly did. She went on to share how that very day she had gone to Denver Seminary, looked at their bulletin board, and spotted a pastor who wanted to rent a house in Golden to a Christian. I met the pastor at the house the next morning around 9:00 a.m. And would you believe it? As I drove up, I saw a white house with a white picket fence. It was located two miles from campus and was available for $110 a month! My roommate, Ray Womack, and I lived there for the year, and it was the perfect home for inviting students over as part of our ministry on campus.

Was this a miracle—a specific answer to prayer—or a mere coincidence? To answer this question, we no longer have to rely on mere commonsense intuition, as helpful as that can be. Now we have a scientifically tested and proven way to tell the difference. The IAP will do the job. Was the discovery of that specific sort of house (white with a white picket fence, and so forth) highly improbable? Yes, given all the specifications for the house mentioned in my prayer. Was the discovery of that specific house special, independently of the fact that it happened to be the house we rented? Wow, you bet! Prior to finding the house, I had been praying for some kind of house that satisfied a certain description—white house, white picket fence, grassy front yard, two to three miles from campus, available for no more than $115 a month! And it was perfect for meeting our ministry needs. This specific house was highly improbable and independently describable or special. So it is safe to assume its provision was brought about by an Intelligent Agent.

Just for fun, you might go back to the story about Ashley and the parakeet in chapter 1 and apply the IAP to it. Or apply it to the story I shared about Jason and Heather. What do you find? Remember, the IAP provides us with an objective, evidence-based way to answer questions like this in our own lives and in the lives of those we love. The IAP has been tremendously helpful to my own growth; it has strengthened trust, helped me to know and not merely believe, and given me courage for my more than half a century as a Jesus follower. It brings reassurance that when some event or phenomenon satisfies the IAP, we have solid grounds for claiming to know that the event or phenomenon was miraculous. We are not—I repeat, *not*—engaging in confirmation bias (the tendency to look at and accept only evidence that confirms what we already believe while disregarding disconfirming evidence).

DEFUSING THE ATHEIST'S TRUMP CARD[5]

A friend of mine, Craig Keener, once debated a skeptic at a scholars conference on the historicity of the New Testament. During the exchange, the skeptic raised an alleged trump card. He admitted that no one denies that the New Testament documents clearly pass the ordinary tests for historicity. However, he argued that a significant difficulty overrides this fact: *the New Testament includes extraordinary miracle claims, and ordinary evidence isn't adequate to justify believing such incredible assertions.*

This objection is frequently made by agnostics and atheists. Michael Shermer, founder of the Skeptics Society and editor of the society's journal *Skeptic*, boldly asserts the same idea: extraordinary, highly improbable claims require extraordinary evidence.[6] To see Shermer's point, suppose your friend Carlos said that he saw his pastor at the grocery store and they chatted for a while. But what if Carlos claimed that on the way to the store, he saw a flying spaghetti monster. The former claim—meeting up with his pastor and chatting—is quite ordinary. It would not require much evidence to believe Carlos. But the second claim is a very improbable, extraordinary one, and you would need a large pile of evidence to warrant accepting it.

Extraordinary claims require extraordinary evidence.[7] Miracle claims, especially those in the Bible, are, so the argument goes, quite extraordinary. So the strong evidence for New Testament reliability would be more than adequate *if the New Testament were bereft of the miraculous.* But according to skeptics, this "ordinary evidence" is woefully inadequate to substantiate belief in the extraordinary claims in the New Testament. It allegedly follows, then, that "ordinary" evidence presented in this chapter and in books defending New Testament historicity fails miserably.

How should we evaluate this argument? Initially, this

argument appears to be quite strong. But upon further reflection, we must judge it to be a complete failure. Here's why.

When we read and study the Bible, we learn that the biblical God is not primarily concerned with convincing people to believe he exists. Romans 1 teaches that the knowledge of God's reality is evident to all, so evident that people suppress it (Romans 1:17–23). People have to work hard *not* to know that God is real. And God has other concerns. His fundamental project is forming a community of people who have freely, noncoercively chosen to enter his kingdom from now through eternity. Kingdom people will grow in the love that characterizes the relationship among the members of the Trinity, and they will focus this love toward God and each other. Moreover, God's people will rule with him by co-laboring and co-exploring in the work to which he has called them and the creation he has made.

To fulfill this purpose, God hides himself so people have the distance from God to noncoercively and lovingly make the choice to enter God's kingdom and to grow in it. For those who want to be a part of this kingdom, they will see the adequate evidence that God is real. But for those who don't want to know God or be part of this plan, God is hidden enough for them to successfully block God out of their minds, employing their intellect to justify what they desire to be the case. They wish to rid themselves of the cosmic authority problem.

In a moment of rare candor, atheist philosopher Thomas Nagel was speaking of the idea that the mental realm (our thoughts and the like) is a fundamental feature of reality—instead of matter alone:

> The thought that the relation between mind and the world is something fundamental makes many people in this day and age nervous. I believe this is one manifestation of a fear of religion which has large and often pernicious consequences for modern intellectual life.

In speaking of the fear of religion, I don't mean to refer to the entirely reasonable hostility toward certain established religions and religious institutions, in virtue of their objectionable moral doctrines, social policies, and political influence. Nor am I referring to the association of many religious beliefs with superstition and the acceptance of evident empirical falsehoods. I am talking about something much deeper—namely, the fear of religion itself. I speak from experience, being strongly subject to this fear myself: I want atheism to be true and am made uneasy by the fact that some of the most intelligent and well-informed people I know are religious believers. It isn't just that I don't believe in God and, naturally, hope that I'm right in my belief. It's that I hope there is no God! I don't want there to be a God; I don't want the universe to be like that.

My guess is that this cosmic authority problem is not a rare condition and that it is responsible for much of the scientism and reductionism of our time. One of the tendencies it supports is the ludicrous overuse of evolutionary biology to explain everything about life, including everything about the human mind. Darwin enabled modern secular culture to heave a great collective sigh of relief, by apparently providing a way to eliminate purpose, meaning, and design as fundamental features of the world.[8]

In more than fifty years of interacting with atheists and agnostics, I have come to see that the desire to live in a state of being free of any divine authority underwrites much of their rejection of a divine father figure. For these people, their fundamental problem with God is not a lack of "extraordinary" evidence that he exists; it is their habituated approach to life, the urge to let autonomous desires control them, and such an approach necessitates using their mind to make the world safe for their lifestyle by killing that father figure.

I believe a properly developed rational case for Christianity should begin by defending the existence of God, followed by defending miracles and the historicity of (especially) the New Testament to show that Christianity is the most reasonable form of theism. This sequence is not merely chronological; it is also rational. I would not appeal to miracles primarily to support God's existence. Instead, given the adequate evidence for a personal God (which will not be defended in this book; see the bibliography for works that accomplish this), we can use theism to see if God has revealed himself, such as through miracles, in a more specific way in human history. Given that God exists and is a Person, the only way one can say that a given miracle or miracles in general are improbable and extremely unlikely is to know God's mind. And I have no idea how an atheist can claim to know that, much less know what God is supposed to do or not do if he were real.

Here's the atheist's problem: *people don't always act the same way.* Rather, they act freely when they judge it is appropriate, even if such actions are very small in number compared to all the acts people do in their lifetime. Suppose Jaegwon gives his wife an extravagant trip for their fiftieth wedding anniversary. This onetime action is highly improbable compared to the set of all of Jaegwon's actions throughout his life. But this doesn't matter. The most rational thing to do is to examine the evidence for the trip rather than dropping such an examination from the start on the grounds that it is improbable. Whether or not a free agent does something must be judged on a case-by-case basis, and the improbability of an act does not require extraordinary evidence. Free agents—whether God or finite persons—do improbable things all the time. That sort of flexibility is part of what it means to be free.

This same reasoning applies to divine miracles. We should examine them on a case-by-case basis, yet without knowing

God's purposes in a specific case, we have no idea whether or not the event is improbable. Maybe a given miracle is improbable compared to most events in world history, or even compared to most events in a given person's life, but wholly likely, given certain circumstances and God's intentions.

It is plain ignorance of the facts to believe that miracles seldom occur. Over the years, I have interviewed around one hundred church leaders and countless Christians to find out whether they have experienced a miracle or know firsthand from credible testimony about a miracle. The numbers are staggering. So many individuals have experienced stunning answers to prayer, undergone miraculous healing, heard specific words from God that later came true, or had encounters with angels or demons that were clearly real, given the evidence.

As I suggested earlier, read the monthly JESUS Film Project email newsletter, and you will be shocked. Or read Craig Keener's massive documentation of the outbreak of miracles in the last fifty years or so.[9] I will share more about the supernatural later in this book, but for now I simply note that it is demonstratively false to claim that miracles are improbable or "extraordinary" or to suggest that almost no one experiences them.

In addition, let's consider what would happen if we apply the standard we are considering to other areas of life. If we adopt the principle that "extraordinary, improbable events require extraordinary evidence," it follows that many things we should believe (since they are rationally obligatory, given the evidence) we will have to reject. Stated more formally, my counterargument runs like this:

1. Premise 1: If we accept the principle, then we rationally should not believe in x, y, or z.
2. Premise 2: But we rationally should believe in x, y, or z.
3. Conclusion: Therefore we should not accept the principle.

Interestingly, experts in probability theory have decisively refuted this principle.[10] According to William Lane Craig, "It was soon realized that if one simply weighed the probability of the [highly improbable] event against the reliability of the witnesses to the event, then we should be led into denying the occurrence of events which, though highly improbable, we reasonably know to have happened."[11]

Craig goes on to provide a helpful example. Suppose, he says, that the morning news reports that last night's lottery pick was 7492871. This is an extremely improbable event, one out of millions. So even though the accuracy of the morning news is 99.99 percent, we should (apparently) never believe this news report. Why? We are told that the improbability of this extraordinary event swamps the probability of the news being accurately reported. Yet we all know that we should believe the news report.

Remember, the news did not report that the lottery pick was some number or other. The probability of this happening is 100 percent. After all, the lottery pick actually happened, so some number or other had to be chosen. To make clear why this is a result that is 100 percent guaranteed, consider this example with the additional fact that the night before, a news reporter predicted that when the lottery pick took place tomorrow, some number or other would be chosen! It would be trivial to predict that some number or other would be picked. No, the report specified that 7492871 was picked. The choice of that specific number out of the millions of numbers available has a probability of almost zero. To see this, consider that if someone predicted the night before that 7492871 would be picked, everyone would know the selection was rigged.

What has gone wrong? We all rightly believe the report that 7492871 was selected, yet the fact that this very number was chosen is an extraordinary event with almost no chance of occurring. Remember, the idea that some number or other was picked is very different from the idea that 7492871 was selected. This extraordinary event does not require extraordinary evidence for us to be justified in believing the report. Why? The atheist principle is simply wrong: rational thinkers do *not* simply weigh the probability of the event (which is close to zero for that specific number) over against the reliability of the witnesses. The probability of the evidence for and the reports of the event staying the same must also be factored in, given that the event did *not* occur. The likelihood of the report being intentionally false, all relevant parties lying, and so forth overrides the improbability of 7492871.

This correct way of evaluating things defeats the atheist principle and can support the idea of improbable miracles. In this proper evaluative context, it is rational to acknowledge an extraordinary event without needing extraordinary evidence! If we follow the atheist principle, there are many things we should not believe (the report of the selection of 7492871) that we all know we should believe.

Finally, by using the insights from IAP—*small probability + independent specialness = done on purpose by an intelligent agent*—the problem of being extraordinary and exhibiting small probability is no longer an issue. Independent specialness solves the problem of small probability.

I realize that these last two chapters may have been difficult to wade through. You may want to come back to them in the future to make sure you grasp the concepts I've shared and, more importantly, to review the ways they provide practical help in evaluating miracle claims. Now that we've paved the way for a thoughtful assessment of such claims, it's time to enter the supernatural world of miracles!

Chapter 3

CLEARING UP SOME UNPRODUCTIVE MISUNDERSTANDINGS ABOUT PRAYER

Helen Roseveare (1925–2016) was born in England, lived and served as a physician in Northern Ireland, and later served as a medical missionary in the Congo and its surrounding region for many years. Here is an eyewitness account she shares about a hot water bottle:

> One night, in Central Africa, I had worked hard to help a mother in the labor ward; but in spite of all that we could do, she died leaving us with a tiny, premature baby and a crying, two-year-old daughter. We would have difficulty keeping the baby alive. We had no incubator. We had no electricity to run an incubator, and no special feeding facilities. Although we lived on the equator, nights were often chilly with treacherous drafts.
>
> A student-midwife went for the box we had for such babies and for the cotton wool that the baby would be wrapped in. Another went to stoke up the fire and fill a hot water bottle. She came back shortly, in distress, to tell me that in filling the bottle, it had burst. Rubber perishes easily

in tropical climates. ". . . and it is our last hot water bottle!" she exclaimed. As in the West, it is no good crying over spilled milk; so, in Central Africa it might be considered no good crying over a burst water bottle. They do not grow on trees, and there are no drugstores down forest pathways. "All right," I said, "Put the baby as near the fire as you safely can; sleep between the baby and the door to keep it free from drafts. Your job is to keep the baby warm."

The following noon, as I did most days, I went to have prayers with many of the orphanage children who chose to gather with me. I gave the youngsters various suggestions of things to pray about and told them about the tiny baby. I explained our problem about keeping the baby warm enough, mentioning the hot water bottle. The baby could so easily die if it got chilled. I also told them about the two-year-old sister, crying because her mother had died.

During the prayer time, one ten-year-old girl, Ruth, prayed with the usual blunt consciousness of our African children. "Please, God," she prayed, "send us a water bottle. It'll be no good tomorrow, God, the baby'll be dead; so, please send it this afternoon." While I gasped inwardly at the audacity of the prayer, she added by way of corollary, ". . . And while You are about it, would You please send a dolly for the little girl so she'll know You really love her?" As often with children's prayers, I was put on the spot. Could I honestly say, "Amen"? I just did not believe that God could do this. Oh, yes, I know that He can do everything: The Bible says so, but there are limits, aren't there? The only way God could answer this particular prayer would be by sending a parcel from the homeland. I had been in Africa for almost four years at that time, and I had never, ever received a parcel from home. Anyway, if anyone did send a parcel, who would put in a hot water bottle? I lived on the equator!

Halfway through the afternoon, while I was teaching in the nurses' training school, a message was sent that there was a car at my front door. By the time that I reached home, the car had gone, but there, on the veranda, was a large twenty-two-pound parcel! I felt tears pricking my eyes. I could not open the parcel alone; so, I sent for the orphanage children. Together we pulled off the string, carefully undoing each knot. We folded the paper, taking care not to tear it unduly. Excitement was mounting. Some thirty or forty pairs of eyes were focused on the large cardboard box.

From the top, I lifted out brightly colored, knitted jerseys. Eyes sparkled as I gave them out. Then, there were the knitted bandages for the leprosy patients, and the children began to look a little bored. Next, came a box of mixed raisins and sultanas—that would make a nice batch of buns for the weekend. As I put my hand in again, I felt the . . . could it really be? I grasped it, and pulled it out. Yes, "A brand-new rubber, hot water bottle!" I cried. I had not asked God to send it; I had not truly believed that He could. Ruth was in the front row of the children. She rushed forward, crying out, "If God has sent the bottle, He must have sent the dolly, too!" Rummaging down to the bottom of the box, she pulled out the small, beautifully dressed dolly. Her eyes shone. She had never doubted! Looking up at me, she asked, "Can I go over with you, Mummy, and give this dolly to that little girl, so she'll know that Jesus really loves her?"

That parcel had been on the way for five whole months, packed up by my former Sunday school class, whose leader had heard and obeyed God's prompting to send a hot water bottle, even to the equator. One of the girls had put in a dolly for an African child—five months earlier in answer to the believing prayer of a ten-year-old to bring it "That afternoon!"[1]

What should we make of this? From what we learned in chapter 2 about the IAP, combined with some good old common sense, we can see that the events described were certainly no mere coincidence! I can think of only two remotely plausible options—and one of them is ridiculous. Either Roseveare made this story up, or the Christian God is actually real and answered their prayers. If you look up biographical details about Helen's life, it's evident she was no liar. Therefore, the second option is the only reasonable one.

However, this incident raises some interesting questions about petitionary prayer, which I hope to answer for you.

QUESTION #1: WHY DID GOD SET UP AN ARRANGEMENT THAT INCLUDED EFFICACIOUS PETITIONARY PRAYER?

At first glance, the sheer reality of efficacious petitionary prayer (hereafter I'll simply refer to this as prayer) seems a bit odd. After all, God is an infinitely perfect, competent Being. Surely he could create the very best world without needing our help or making some things he does depend on us. But on closer inspection, the practice of prayer makes good sense. I'll focus on a few points that have helped me.

First, we need to step back from the topic of prayer and clarify the reasons God created the world—specifically, human history—in the first place. To answer this question, we must lay out the central purpose for history as it is presented in the entire Bible. While there are small differences among scholars about how to frame this, most would agree to some version of the following:

> The purpose of history is for God to build a community of people with the triune God at the center as the most

cherished and unifying Being (that is, to build the kingdom of God somewhere in his universe—namely, the earth) in which people (1) voluntarily join that community by meeting the conditions for entrance established by God; (2) progressively experience and grow in the kind of wise, loving, creative relationships (toward God, others in the community, and the created world) exhibited among the members of the Trinity; and (3) co-labor with God to defeat evil, rule over and explore creation with God, and with his help find goodness, truth, and beauty forever.

Admittedly, this is a mouthful, so I encourage you to read it one more time, noting two important points. First, human entrance into and continued participation in the community are purely voluntary, involving the exercise of commonsense free will. Given the centrality of love in the kingdom, if love cannot be coerced, free will is important. Among other things, this implies that our actions for good or evil, for God or against God, actually matter. We make a real difference; history is not a mere puppet show. Second, it's also crucial to grasp that God has graciously invited us to be his co-laborers in a variety of ways. We work together—God in his way, we in ours. This mission is why we get up each morning.

But *why* is this God's purpose for creation, history, and our lives? It goes without saying that, without creation, God was doing quite well on his own! He did not *need* us. But we also must remember that God is personal—indeed, tri-personal—and persons (created or divine) have the unique feature that by nature they love to share good things with others, *desire* to create other persons (that's why the desire to have children is a natural one and goes far beyond the desire for sex), and very much enjoy doing things with others, including working together. Since these traits also characterize God, and we know he is filled with joy, goodness, and love, we can conclude that creation and history are the result of an overflow of God's wonderful life. It's as though God was bursting at the seams with delight, so much so that he desired to share the joy of life with others and work together with them.

Persons can work together in many different ways, but a central aspect of working together is communication—talking to each other and asking for things and sharing things when there are needs. Communication is at the center of flourishing relationships, and this is what prayer is. Prayer is part of the deal, given the personal and perfect nature of God, the purpose for creation and history, and the unique way persons work together and build relationships.

QUESTION #2: WHY PRAY IF GOD ALREADY KNOWS WHAT WE ARE GOING TO ASK FOR?

One evening at our church, we hosted a special evangelistic event. Building up to the event, we were rightly urged to invite unbelievers and pray for God to spur many people to attend. When the time for the event came, the crowd was quite meager, embarrassingly so. One brother in the church who had prayed fervently for the event said to me minutes before it started that the size of the crowd didn't matter. Why? Because God was going to bring just the right people to the event, irrespective of our labors and prayers, and we could rest assured in that fact. I replied by asking, "If you really believe that, why did you work so hard and pray so faithfully?" According to this man's way of thinking, God already knew what we were going to pray and who he was going to bring, and our efforts or lack thereof didn't seem to matter. He didn't answer my question.

I believe there is something wrong with my friend's outlook. To grasp the importance of what that is, we must ask two questions:

1. If God already knows what will happen in the future, then it has to happen, whether or not we pray for it. So why pray?
2. Since God knows what we are going to ask him before we ask, how are we to understand what we are doing when we make our request to him? In our unreflective moments, it *feels* like we are informing God of a need, but this can't be right, can it?

Let's start with the first question, which has to do with the issue of divine foreknowledge. Medieval theologians made a helpful distinction between the following two sentences, which may help us solve this difficulty:

- A: It must be the case that if God foreknows that X will happen, then X will happen.
- B: If God foreknows that X will happen, then X must happen.

When we first read these two statements, we may think A and B are saying pretty much the same thing, but we must not let surface appearances fool us. They are very, very different. I agree with the medieval thinkers (and many still today) who say that A is true, yet it does not imply that God's foreknowledge determines the future. Conversely, I would argue that B is false, since it does imply that God's foreknowledge determines what must happen. That's the key question: Does God's knowing that a future event will happen make it so?

To deepen our understanding, let's look at statement B. We could rephrase it to say that if God foreknows on Monday that Alice is going to lunch at McDonald's on Wednesday, then when Wednesday shows up, she has *no choice* about what to do for lunch. She *must* go to McDonald's and has no other alternative open to her at lunchtime. If she didn't go to McDonald's, she would make what God foreknew on Monday turn out to be false. That would be bad news, to say the least.

But for those of us who believe Alice has commonsense free will on Wednesday, she didn't *have* to do anything. She could have gone to Burger King or not gone to a restaurant at all. Statement B implies the same thing about prayer. If I pray for such and such on Monday and God foreknows on Monday what is going to happen, then it *must* happen, regardless of whether I pray for it. Something is wrong with B for those of us who believe in genuine free will and the effectiveness of prayer. What are we to do?

The answer lies in statement A. It does not say, as B does, that if God foreknows X, then X has to happen, period. Statement A makes a different claim, yet one that is completely consistent with foreknowledge and the alterability of the future due to creaturely free actions. A says that it *must* be the case that if God foreknows that X will happen, then X will indeed happen. So far so good. If God foreknows on Monday that Alice will go to McDonald's on Wednesday, then this *will* happen. There is no doubt that God's knowledge is correct and accurate.

But when lunchtime on Wednesday arrives, Alice is completely free to go to Burger King. In fact, let's suppose she does. In that case, God would have foreknown on Monday that Alice would go to Burger King on Wednesday. Statement A implies that it is not God's foreknowledge that fixes a future event; rather, it is the fact that a future event will happen that explains what, exactly, God foreknows. If Alice goes to McDonald's freely, God would have foreknown that; if she had gone to Burger King, God would have foreknown that.

Let's apply what we've learned about prayer and God's knowledge of future events to Helen Roseveare's account at the beginning of this chapter. Recall that the hot water bottle and the baby doll were sent in the mail by Helen's former Sunday school class *five months before Helen and the others prayed for it.* Did these prayers make a difference and change things? You bet, and statement A explains why. Because the prayers were going to be offered at the time of need, God foreknew that the students would be imploring him on this matter. And he set in motion five months earlier the events that would lead to the timely answer to prayer. If the students had not prayed, then God would have foreknown they would not pray. Remember, the prayer request was an expression of their free will and the petitioners could have refrained from praying. In that case, he would not have set in motion the answer.

This very sort of thing has happened in my own life as well. My family was faced with a specific financial need, and we needed funds to pay a bill on a particular day. We prayed and prayed, and that very day the funds came in the mail. We knew they had been put in the mail two days before we started praying. But God's foreknowledge did not nullify the effectiveness of our prayers. Foreknowing we would pray for the funds, God influenced a person to give ahead of time. Had we not prayed, God would have foreknown that, and no funds would have been sent. God answered the prayer *because* we prayed, but not *after* we prayed!

Now you may be thinking, *Wait a minute! Since God knew the child needed the hot water bottle and he knew the Morelands needed the funds, why wouldn't God send them, whether or not prayers were offered?* I will address that issue when we look at our next question.

For now, let's set up the second issue by asking this question: If God already knows what we are going to ask for, what are we doing when we ask? When we pray like this, it doesn't seem that we are simply meeting the conditions that explain God's foreknowledge and what subsequently will happen. We have the intuitive sense that we are, in some way, informing God of our need, telling him something we want him to be aware of. But if God is omniscient, these intuitions must be nothing but projections of our own characteristics onto God and completely misguided. Or are they? Let's dig a little deeper into this conundrum.

We begin by looking at the attributes—the qualities, characteristic, and abilities—that things have. An orange, for example, has characteristics of sweetness, roundness, and so forth. I have various attributes. I'm five foot seven inches tall, have white skin, and possess a certain body shape. God has many attributes too—being a necessary being; being personal, omnipotent, omniscient, and so forth.

Attributes come in two different kinds. There are those that are completely present and fully actualized, and there are those that are capacities—abilities or potentialities that are *not* currently being employed or actualized. For example, the fact that I am a person who is five foot seven with white skin is an attribute that is completely present and fully actualized. These characteristics aren't waiting for anything else to happen to be manifested. By contrast, my ability to speak English is an unactualized capacity I have while sleeping. So is the ability to lift a certain amount of weight while sitting in my easy chair doing nothing, or my potential to learn German, which I do not currently know.

God has both kinds of attributes. Being personal and being a necessary being are examples of the first kind (actualized). Being omnipotent is an example of the second kind—a power, capacity, or ability God possesses to do anything consistent with his nature. Why is omnipotence not a fully actualized, completely present divine attribute? Because God has far, far more power than he is utilizing or actualizing. If God wanted to, he could be creating multitudes of universes or at the least creating our universe to be bigger than it is. But many things God *could* do he refrains from doing for his own reasons.

What about omniscience? Is this a fully actualized attribute or a capacity that, while not always fully actualized, is at his disposal at all times to tap into? Let me be clear on this point: God is completely omniscient. There is not a single truth that God does not know. There is not a single falsehood that God believes. But does God need to be aware, all the time, of everything he knows? Dallas Willard used to say that while God knows the total amount of snot in all the noses of all the sheep on earth, he doesn't have to be aware of that all the time. In one conversation we had, Dallas noted that God's omniscience does not override his omnipotence. If he wants to, God has the power to refrain from being aware of things he knows.

But why would he do this? One possibility is to allow us to bring things to his awareness through prayer that he already knows but wasn't focusing on. In such cases, God could bring these things to his awareness at will without relying on us. After all, he knows everything. But he does not have to be aware of all he knows, and this withholding of awareness allows us to genuinely inform God of things, not in the sense that he didn't already know them, but in the sense that he has condescended in such a way as to allow us to recall these things to his awareness. And such an act of recalling would bring with it a genuine, and not feigned, sense of fresh excitement and concern for the prayer being made.

An illustration may be of help here. Years ago, my daughter Allison came home from school very excited to tell me what she had learned that day. "Dad," she said, "I've been waiting all day to tell you about the three branches of government and what they do!" Now, I already knew all the truths she was about to share. But I wasn't thinking about them at the time and I decided not to recall them on my own. Instead, I focused on Allison and let her bring to my awareness what I could have done myself because I knew the topic. I was not attempting to be entirely aware of what I knew, and in a real sense, she genuinely informed me. I was sincerely excited and surprised, as we all are when we become aware of something interesting that we weren't attending to, yet I already knew what she shared. I'm suggesting this as a plausible way to understand what we are doing when we share our requests with God. Remember, God's omniscience does not override his omnipotence. Thus, while God's power cannot prevent him from being omniscient, including having foreknowledge of all future events, his power can, indeed, allow him to choose not to focus on or be aware of something he already knows and could recall to his awareness anytime he desires.

QUESTION #3: WOULDN'T A PERFECT GOD DO WHAT IS TRULY GOOD AND PREVENT WHAT IS TRULY EVIL, WHETHER OR NOT WE PRAY?

Here is another problem that has likely occurred to many of us.[2] God is completely, perfectly good, and he loves us unconditionally. Surely he would desire to give us any genuinely good thing that would be good for us and enhance our flourishing in the way he wants. In a similar way, he would refuse us anything that would genuinely harm us, especially anything that would hinder our well-being. God would do these things, whether or not we asked for them, wouldn't he? It would certainly seem, then, that prayer doesn't make any difference and as a result is pointless.

Here's a slightly different way to put what's at stake. If one believes in the efficacy of petitionary prayer, these two principles would seem to follow:

1. G: If a prayer for some good thing is efficacious, then without prayer, it would not have happened.
2. B: If a prayer against some bad thing is efficacious, then without prayer, it would have happened.

Principles G and B are clarified ways of saying that prayer makes a difference in the world. G involves asking for things that are genuinely good and implies that there are good things that God desires to provide for us or others, but he refrains from bringing about those good things if we don't ask him for them. B focuses on bad things and implies that there are bad things that God desires to prevent from happening that he will allow to happen if we don't ask him to keep them from occurring.

G and B seem to be critical assumptions we make if we believe that praying or not praying makes a difference when it comes to what does or does not happen. If we don't accept G and B, it is hard to see how we could engage in real petitionary prayer. Unknown to us, perhaps, when we think we are offering petitionary prayer to God, we are really doing something else. Perhaps we are bringing ourselves into alignment with what God is already going to bring about or will prevent from happening, regardless of whether we pray. Some people believe this. Yet while it is a good thing to bring ourselves into conformity with God's character and purposes, doing so simply is not genuine petitioning.

Unfortunately, G and B are in conflict with the problem we stated at the beginning of this section. We cannot have it both ways. Either we accept the description given above of what a perfectly good God who loves us would do and reject G and B (the efficacy of prayer), or we must go in the opposite direction. So what are we to do? How are we to think about this messy problem? Let's chip away at this difficulty and see if we can make progress toward resolving it.

First, we should acknowledge that some things we pray for are impossible for God to do, or at least they are things he is unwilling to do (for example, overriding the free will of his image bearers). In such cases, God cannot (or will not) grant our requests, even though we make them sincerely. Our prayers are not efficacious simply because we are asking God for something he cannot or will not do. Sadly, if our prayers for such things are not answered, we may walk away with one more disappointing example of prayer not working, and over time we will lose confidence in the efficacy of prayer. However, if we stopped praying for things that God cannot or will not grant, our sample of unanswered prayers would be smaller, and we would avoid mistaken discouragement about prayer by approaching it more thoughtfully.

In his contribution to *Contemporary Debates in Philosophy of Religion*, Michael Murray wisely notes that some goods are of equal value and the petitioner may be fairly indifferent as to which among those goods happen.[3] Usually, these are requests for things that aren't of great importance. Such cases are discretionary in that God would be willing to grant a request for such a good—for example, a specific kind of car—though no overall good would be lost if he didn't. I suspect we've all asked for things that we desired while recognizing that we would be fine without them. In these cases, God really isn't withholding a significant good by making our possession of it depend on prayer.

But what about really important goods? Why would a perfectly good, loving God withhold such goods, things like healing from a debilitating disease or opportunities to get out of poverty, if we don't ask for them? I believe that in some cases, if God grants certain goods without our request, we might be unable to receive the greater goods he wants for us. Additionally, God's purpose for history and our individual lives is bigger than making sure he achieves the greatest amount of blessings and the least amount of bad things possible. In short, God has bigger fish to fry than simply providing important goods and keeping various bad things from happening to us. God's purpose for history—and for you and me—is to secure us as co-laboring participants with him in the unfolding of his plan. This participation, along with our dependence on him, is facilitated by our need to ask and receive from God.

It may be that God has several overriding goods for us that we cannot obtain if he were to give us important, though lesser, goods regardless of our request. By making the reception of these lesser goods depend on our praying for them (and then withholding them if we do not ask), God is able to achieve things that are of extreme importance to him. For instance, God may want to cultivate our dependency on and gratitude to him. He may decide it is best to do this by having us ask for help and express excitement and gratefulness to him in light of his answers to prayer. He is helping us avoid self-sufficient idolatry.

Another "greater good" may be possessing a genuine friendship with God. Murray, citing Eleonore Stump, notes that there are two difficulties in cultivating a friendship with a perfect, infinitely glorious Being.[4] First, there is the possibility of being so overwhelmed and overshadowed by God that we lose our individual personalities and become frozen in the relationship. Think of what it would be like to suddenly find yourself right next to the person you esteem most in the world or someone who is incredibly famous or powerful—a world leader or a well-known actor or athlete. You may not know how to act, and in your shock and awkwardness, you may become passive and defer to the person to direct what should happen in the relationship. That would not be a true friendship. God is several orders of magnitude more impressive than the person who came to your mind just now. And petitionary prayer is one way to prevent us from being frozen and unable to grow in friendship with God. It prevents us from being overwhelmed as we see that God actually responds to us and we know we matter to him!

Second, if God were to shower us with good things all the time, whether we asked for them or not, we would likely grow spoiled, begin to feel entitled, and even take God for granted.

By making the bestowal of many of his blessings dependent on our requests, he allows us to avoid these problems.

We also must consider the provision of encouraging signs. Specific answers to prayer are signs that God is real and that he listens to us and responds to our requests. We should not underestimate the value of these signs! Such answers to prayer strengthen and build our faith, as well as encourage us and assure us we are not alone. Answers to prayer do this like nothing else. Who among us hasn't received a clear answer to prayer without being strengthened and encouraged?

Sometimes the Bible presents us with situations involving both a good and a bad aspect. Upon reflection, we are able to place the different possibilities associated with these situations in an order ranging from the best to the worst. For example, in Philippians 1:12–18, Paul observed that some were preaching the true gospel out of bad motives—selfish ambition, envy, and strife. His evaluation of the situation? He rejoiced because at least the true gospel was being proclaimed. This stood in stark contrast to Galatians 1:6–9, where some Judaizers, very likely out of good but misguided motives, were preaching a false gospel. Paul responded with, "Let them be under God's curse!" (verse 9). Comparing these two situations to their good and bad aspects, we can rank four possibilities, from best to worst:

1. Preaching the true gospel with good motives.
2. Preaching the true gospel with bad motives.
3. Preaching a false gospel with good motives.
4. Preaching a false gospel with bad motives.

From best to worst, we have $1 > 2 > 3 > 4$. Now let's apply this reasoning to a specific case of petitionary prayer. Suppose Andrew, a married man with two children, has struggled for a long time to provide adequately for his family. Consequently, he decided to go to college. He is one semester from finishing his degree, and once he's done, a good job is waiting for him. There's just one problem. Andrew is out of money and cannot pay for the tuition required for him to finish.

As before, let's rank four relevant possibilities, from best to worst as God sees them. There could be a different ranking in similar situations, but clearly the following must be true much of the time, and if so, it explains why God doesn't give us important goods if we don't ask for them but does provide them if we do ask.

1. Andrew prays, and God provides the tuition money.
2. Andrew does not pray, and no funds are provided.
3. Andrew does not pray, and God provides the tuition money.
4. Andrew prays, and no funds are provided.

Keep in mind this is just an illustration, so let's not quibble too much about the ranking. It would go on and on if we were to add more details—for example, tweaking possibility 4 to encourage Andrew to endure in prayer even when no answers are given. Focusing solely on the information provided in the four possibilities, we can see that 1 is the best possibility and 4 is the worst. The crucial insight comes from looking at the relative ranking of 2 over 3. Why would God value 2 over 3? After all, in both cases, Andrew doesn't seek God in prayer for help, but at least in possibility 3, Andrew and his family's needs are met.

The answer is that it is *generally* the case that God places greater value on our learning the connection between prayer and provision than he does on meeting the need itself. Put differently, the reason God often does not just meet our needs, regardless of whether we pray, is that he is more concerned to secure our dependency on him, to prevent idolatry, to enhance our friendship with him, and to foster our co-laboring with him than he is to meet what is a legitimate, significant need.

This is one reason our petitions, or lack thereof, make a real difference in the world. It also explains why recruiting several people to pray for something rather than going it alone makes a difference. Second Corinthians 1:10–11 provides a helpful explanation here. Paul expressed thankfulness that God delivered him and his companions from hardship and conveyed his desire that God would do the same in future difficulties. To increase the likelihood this would happen, Paul enlisted the help of the Corinthians, urging them to pray.

If God wants to provide protection, and Paul has prayed for it, why enlist the help of the Corinthians? To paraphrase verse 11, if God provides protection in response to their collective petitions, he will accomplish more than Paul's protection. The entire church will be encouraged as he answers their prayer and makes them part of the provision. Going it alone would mean that God would obtain one good (Paul's protection), but enlisting many means that God will secure that good *and* bring about a greater good—namely, encouraging the church. God would have even greater reasons to grant the request if offered by many than he would if the prayer was offered only by the person in need. Understanding this principle should motivate us to invite others to join us in praying for our needs to be met.

Before we move to the next section, we have one final question to consider: Why does God sometimes withhold important goods even when we pray? This is a vexing problem, and I don't want to address it with a simplistic slogan or with a serving of "Christianese." But I do believe there is a reasonable biblical answer to this problem that has comforted me in my own frustration with God when he doesn't respond to my requests. By way of explanation, I'll share a story.

My daughter Ashley and my son-in-law Beau got married in 2003. Shortly thereafter, they moved to Washington so Beau could be close to his family and finish college. After Beau's graduation, they moved back to Southern California, where my wife and I live, and both of them began looking for jobs. Our entire family prayed over and over for God to provide, and after months of prayer, God answered our request. We were especially grateful for his provision of a job for Beau.

However, after Beau had worked at the company for about eighteen months, his boss was replaced with the proverbial "boss from hell," and in the ensuing weeks, several employees got fed up and left the company. To his credit, Beau stuck it out so he could continue to provide for his family—they had two daughters at the time—and he stayed for another year and a half. During this time, he was treated horribly, and Beau and Ashley were understandably discouraged.

Our family sought God for his help, but even though we prayed for more than a year for a new job and Beau had looked long and hard for a good opening, nothing was available—*nothing!* It was as though God simply was not interested in the situation, though it helped me to recognize that God could not coerce an employer's free act to hire Beau. Finally, out of the blue, through an odd, highly unlikely set of circumstances, an opportunity was presented to Beau. He beat out significant competition and secured a really good job at a solid company.

Here's the punch line that helps me understand why God doesn't always seem to answer my petitions when I want him to. The reason Beau (and not others who had applied) got the new job was the fact that he had stayed at his old job for a long enough time to learn just the right skills needed for the new job! God withheld answering our prayers for relief at the old job because God, seeing the bigger picture and knowing the future, knew that granting our request would harm Beau and his family in the long run. In retrospect, we're thankful that God didn't answer our prayers.

Dallas Willard once told me he was glad that God didn't answer a high percentage of his prayers because he eventually saw that God's refusals turned out for the best. I don't want to sound cliché, but I sincerely believe that God sees the bigger picture that is inaccessible to us. And in light of that bigger picture, God will often refuse to grant a request that, for all we can tell, is an obvious one for him to answer. This fact has encouraged me to remember that I am so limited in my understanding that I need to trust in God's goodness, even when it *seems* like he doesn't care.

QUESTIONS #4 AND #5:
WHEN SHOULD WE STOP PRAYING?
WHY PRAY MORE THAN ONCE?

In the final section of this chapter, I want to address two closely related questions that often come up in discussions I have about petitionary prayer: First, when should we stop praying? And second, related to this first question, since God becomes aware of our request after the first time we petition him, why bring it up more than once?

When all is said and done, my answer to the first question— "When should we stop praying?"—is that I don't have a clue! Besides personal inadequacies and limitations, there are two reasons for my cluelessness. First, I don't think the Bible speaks clearly about this question, as I know of no extended discussion of the question within its pages. Yes, it is true, on the one hand, that in 2 Corinthians 12:7–10 Paul limited his prayers about a specific issue to three prayers. Yet on the other hand, throughout the Old Testament we have cases of God's people crying out to God for long periods of time (see Psalm 88) and the Lord says he has indeed heard the cries of his people (see, for example, Exodus 3:7; 22:23, 27). And the proper interpretation of Jesus' teaching in Matthew 7:7 includes the encouragement to keep on asking, keep on seeking, keep on knocking.

In addition, the "one size fits all" philosophy doesn't work when it comes to prayer. Different people at different times with different requests and different responsibilities should pray about something for different lengths of time. In my view, two rules of thumb can be helpful as general guiding principles (nothing more than that), which I suggest you use in tandem: (1) if a desire to continue to pray remains on your heart and you're growing in your relationship with Jesus—especially in dependency on him—I believe you have good reasons to keep on praying; and (2) if by continuing to pray you find that time for other important requests is squeezed out, you're distracted from other important responsibilities, your prayers morph into anxious obsessing (baptized by beginning with "Dear Lord" and ending with "Amen"), or you're dragged down and pulled away from God, then you have good reasons to stop. You can always return to the issue after an adequate respite.

But what about our final question? Since God knows my request after the first time I make it, why pray more than once? Recall what we learned earlier in this chapter. God wants us to learn what dependency on him means and how we can practice it. As finite created beings, we are by nature dependent on God for our very existence. And we were created to flourish and experience shalom in deep relationship with God, not by living on our own, and this relationship includes co-laboring. Given that we are unequal partners with God—to say the least!—we need to habituate by repetition our dependency, and ongoing prayer is a way to do that.

Another answer to the question of why we should pray more than once flows from the very nature of petitionary prayer.

I believe petitionary prayer is made up of two different types—what might be called *supplicational* prayer and *soaking* prayer.

Supplicational prayer is the petitionary prayer we typically employ when we beseech or entreat God to grant our request. Such a prayer is found in Acts 4:24–29, for example. If a supplicational prayer is offered for one thing, it most likely will last for a few seconds to a few minutes. If the request goes on longer than that, it is usually because several petitions are being brought before God. In such a prayer, our relationship with God consists of us coming to God as our superior with a request for him to consider granting.

A less understood form of petitionary prayer is soaking prayer. We can see an example in the historical account found in Exodus 17:10–13, where Moses raises his hands and God gives victory to the Israelites over the Amalekites. At first glance, the event seems a bit odd, but upon closer inspection, it expresses a profound insight. In soaking prayer, God and the believer work together on a problem that needs solving. Soaking prayer becomes a means for directing the power of God onto a problem—allowing it to marinate. In that process, though it is almost imperceptible over time, something is changed.

As one engages in soaking prayer and God's power is directed onto the problem, prayer itself becomes a *conduit* of the power of God. In the battle against Amalek recorded in Exodus 17, Israel prevailed as long as Moses' hands were lifted up. Once his hands dropped, Israel began to lose. Moses' lifted hands were an expression of prayer, a way of demonstrating the people's dependency on God. The act of lifting the hands itself became a conduit of God's power, *while Moses remained in that activity*. With Moses' hands raised, God's power was released and the battle was being won. But when Moses let his hands drop, the power was shut off and the tide began to turn against God's people.

Soaking prayer is a way to immerse a situation in the power

of God, and it is important to learn to stay focused in prayer for long periods of time or return to an issue over and over again. In such a prayer, our relationship with God is the means for God to unleash his power. God is the power source, and our act of praying is the conduit that unleashes and directs his power.

I hope your head isn't exploding with all of these thoughts. My aim here has been to bring before our minds some new ideas. So let's shift gears and move from concepts to stories.

Chapter 4

MIRACULOUS ANSWERS TO PRAYER

If you had to guess, what would you identify as the most prominent source of doubt in America? Is it insights from science, incredulity about the Bible, or intolerance of Jesus' exclusive truth claims? None of these are even close. In his study of doubt and defection from Christianity, sociologist Christian Smith claimed that far and away the chief source of doubt came from God's apparent inactivity, indifference, or impotence in the face of tragedy and the apparent lack of God's intervention in daily trials.[1]

For several years my wife, Hope, made a weekly visit to a shelter for women who have various addictions. As Hope was teaching the Scriptures and reaching out to them, a new resident at the shelter interrupted her by announcing she was an atheist. When asked why she held to this view, without hesitating the woman bemoaned that she had often called out to God, as had others she knew, and no one answered. Since no one had answered, she concluded that no one was on the other end of the line.

We can all sympathize with this dear woman. Yet while unanswered prayer is a genuine concern in our lives, the simple fact is that God *is* intervening all over the world all the time. Our problem is that we fixate on the unanswered prayers, forget the ones that were answered, or don't hear of real cases of miraculous answers in the lives of others. A major part of witnessing to and about God is giving testimony to what we have seen and heard.

In this chapter, I want to increase your expectation of what is possible through prayer by sharing credible, factual eyewitness accounts of real divine answers to prayer.

TWO IMPORTANT THINGS TO KEEP IN MIND

As you read, keep two things in mind. First, recall the intelligent agent principle (IAP): s*mall probability + independent specialness* (it was exactly what was prayed for, met a need, and built up someone's trust in God) = *done on purpose by an intelligent agent.* The IAP is used in various branches of science and is a solid, well-tested principle that does not depend on a prior commitment to Christianity for its authority.

Second, if the eyewitness testimony satisfies a set of criteria for judging credibility, then it should be accepted. Modern detective work has been around for two centuries, and during that time, detectives have refined their skills. Especially relevant to this chapter, detectives have developed tools and techniques for assessing the credibility of an alleged eyewitness's report. J. Warner Wallace is a leading figure in this area of expertise,[2] a cold-case detective for several years with the Los Angeles Police Department who has appeared frequently on *Dateline NBC* and other programs. According to Wallace, when certain criteria are met, a strong case is made for trusting the eyewitness's testimony:[3]

1. How well could the witness see, hear, or otherwise perceive the things about which the witness testified?
2. How well was the witness able to remember and describe what happened?
3. Was the witness's testimony influenced by a factor such as bias or prejudice?

4. How reasonable is the testimony when you consider all the other evidence in the case?
5. What is the witness's character for truthfulness?
6. Is the witness known for his or her integrity or engaged in other conduct that reflects on his or her believability?

Points 1 and 2 are easy to answer in the affirmative for all of the cases I'll be presenting in this chapter. The witnesses themselves both knew they had prayed for something (or had a pressing need of some kind) and saw the events with their own eyes. Often, other people were praying and were direct witnesses. And most of the cases I share are so incredible and wonderful that the people who received God's answers would never forget something like this.

The same thing can be said for points 5 and 6. Some of what follows are things that happened to me personally, and I, along with my family and friends, was nearby when prayer was offered and answered. Thus we were able, willing, and qualified to tell the truth, and we have credibility among our friends and our local church for being honest and mature believers. Other accounts below are offered by people I have known well for a long time, and I have vetted each story by asking the witness or witnesses a set of questions to ensure they are accurately presenting the truth.

Regarding point 4, it is often the case that the answers to prayer were publicly verifiable, as will become evident upon reflection on the cases. Other people knew of the need and the specific prayers being offered—often they were joint prayer partners for the situation—and they saw what happened as a result. So these are not private cases; they were known publicly. They are not invented fables or lies, and the people who bear witness to them are not the sort who would deceive others. The only thing a skeptic can raise with any legitimacy is the claim that miracles in and of themselves are not credibly believable. Recall that I rebutted this claim in chapters 1 and 2, and I'll leave it to you the reader to investigate the stories that follow to see if they seem credible.

This leaves us with point 3: Was the witness's testimony influenced by a factor such as bias or prejudice? Skeptics often claim that believers are plagued with confirmation bias, the tendency to search for, notice, and recall only the things that confirm our previous beliefs, while disregarding or failing to notice disconfirming evidence. They will say that believers only notice and remember the times when their prayers "were allegedly answered," and fail to notice and remember all the times when prayer was impotent.

I have already addressed this claim at the end of chapter 2, but two things should be stated in response. First, the skeptic's claim is beside the point. When the intelligent agent principle (IAP) has been satisfied, the alleged bias of the believer is irrelevant. In and of itself, the satisfaction of the IAP is sufficient to show that a divine intervention has taken place. The principle is so reliable that it is almost impossible for its application to generate a false positive (taking an event to result from the action of an intelligent agent when it did not).[4]

Second, to put it bluntly, the skeptic needs to hang around with a different group of friends! Anyone who has been around genuine believers will know that one of the big challenges Christians face is their tendency to notice and remember all the times when their prayers *were not answered*! Indeed, this problem is one of the reasons I'm writing this book. Around 25 to 30 percent of the psalms in the Bible are laments or complaints against God for being indifferent to requests and not doing anything. Many of the Christians I know are honest about life and fully aware of the times God does not seem to show up. Confirmation bias? If anything, it is the skeptic who engages in naturalistic confirmation bias and projects that bias onto believers.

CREDIBLE EYEWITNESS ACCOUNTS OF MIRACULOUS ANSWERS TO PRAYER

God Listens and Cares about the Little Things

As Christian parents, we love our children with all our heart and want them to grow up loving Jesus and obeying his commands. While we don't want to shelter or isolate them, we want to keep an eye on them, their friends, and their social interactions. This is especially true for children who are entering the middle school years, when social influence begins to get significant and sometimes harmful. We preferred our children to have their friends at our house (so we could keep an eye on them!) rather than somewhere else.

In 1989, Hope and I, along with our precious daughters Ashley (ten years old) and Allison (eight years old), were living in Virginia when I received an offer to teach at Talbot School of Theology at Biola University in Southern California. I accepted the offer, and in June 1990 we moved to Southern California and purchased a small house in Yorba Linda, one block away from a good public elementary school. The house was 1,550 square feet and had a two-car garage. Hope and I knew that raising our girls in the culture of Southern California was a risk—they would be more susceptible to the influence of worldly values. So we committed ourselves to keeping a close eye on the girls and the friends they would make in the coming years.

In 1992, with the help of my parents, we had our garage transformed into a nice recreational room with a television and a foosball table. Ashley was in middle school and Allison was just behind her, so the new rec room increased the chances they would play with their friends and have "parties" at our home and not someplace else. In the summer of 1993, the girls asked if we could get a pool table so the room would be even more fun for friends (including, ugh, guys!).

I told them I thought it was a great idea, but we didn't have the money to purchase one at that time. The only way we could honor their request, I told them, was if God provided one for free. Thinking that was the end of the matter, the girls responded by saying that we should ask God for it, so we gathered in the living room, formed a circle, and held hands. We each prayed for the table, but I wanted a good one, so when it was my turn to pray, I asked the Lord, specifically, for a free pool table—like the good ones you find in a sports bar. And that was that.

Allison was on a soccer team that involved about fifteen families we didn't know very well. Two weeks after our prayer circle, a father I had never spoken with walked up to me during a game—literally out of the blue and for no apparent reason. After about a minute of chatting, he asked me if I could use a pool table. Only our immediate family knew we were praying for one, and when he asked me this question, I almost fell over! I was astonished, so I asked him why he had approached *me*—out of all the other people at the game. We didn't even know each other! He responded by saying that he was a Christian, and he had simply sensed that the Lord was nudging him to approach me.

He went on to say that he had been renting a house to four college-aged guys, and for the past few months they hadn't paid their rent, so he had evicted them a few days earlier. They had left behind a pool table in pretty good condition, just like the ones found in sports bars, and he needed to get rid of it. When I told him I was a believer and that my family had been praying for two weeks for this exact kind of pool table, it was his turn to practically keel over! It meant so much to him that this was a God thing, and that afternoon, he and three other men brought the table over and installed it in our recreation room.

Not only did having that table accomplish what Hope and I had wanted—our home became *the* gathering place—but our young girls came to know by personal experience that Jesus is real and that he answers prayers. In the years since, we've all had many times when God has *not* answered our prayers, but this one event has helped all of us—especially Ashley and Allison—never to lose our conviction that God does grant requests.

And this was only the beginning. Our backyard was fairly small, and it included a steep, 60-degree-sloped hill going up to our back fence, high above the flat area around our home. We didn't have a watering system, and the hill—no joke—was filled with bare dirt, ugly weeds, sagebrush, and gullies formed from the runoff when it rained. No one wanted to go into the backyard. It was small and ugly! In early August 1994, Ashley and Allison approached me again, requesting a swimming pool. After all, most of their friends had one, they said, so their friends had started gathering elsewhere most of the time, and a pool, along with the rec room, would really make our place popular once again.

No exaggeration, I was in agony. I desperately wanted to have a pool installed because I agreed with their rationale. Given their ages (fourteen and twelve), it was increasingly important for us to keep an eye on them and their friends. Ensuring that our house was a destination location facilitated our parenting. But installing a pool seemed out of the question. First, it was *way* out of our price range and too extravagant for our economic status. But even worse, I am the dumbest, most inadequate fix-it man you'll ever find. I'm not exaggerating when I say that if my wife couldn't fix a problem, we had to hire someone. And when we did, I was an easy target for being swindled, since I didn't have a clue about quality work or fair prices. Can you imagine my having to keep an eye on all the contractors who would come in at different times to put in a swimming pool? To this day, I break out in a cold sweat just thinking about it. There was no question we would end up paying far more for the work than we should. I felt frustrated and vulnerable and didn't know what to do.

So, once again, I told the family that it was out of the question, and unless God gave us one, we would have to do without. Well, duh, we decided to pray for it. We specifically asked the Lord to tell us what to do. If we were going to get a pool, two things needed to happen: (1) we needed someone we trusted to oversee the whole thing, and (2) we needed an affordable price. But I had no faith that God would answer. Over the next few days, I prayed several times a day that God would make his will clear and that he would provide if we were to get the pool.

Summer school had ended at Biola, and the campus was a ghost town during August, except for the last week as the campus began to prepare for the onslaught of students for the fall semester. On a Friday morning, I went to campus to check my mail and to have some quiet time to study. I heard a knock, and to my surprise, I opened the door to see a former student named Glenn standing there.

In his early thirties, Glenn had decided to go to college, majoring in philosophy. I'd had Glenn in a few undergraduate classes and liked him, but I didn't know him very well. Upon graduation, he moved out of state and had been gone for three years before deciding to return and enter our graduate program in philosophy. Glenn had called me to let me know his intentions to return, but in the months since that call, I had forgotten that he was coming back.

That Friday morning in August, I remembered Glenn was returning only after getting up to answer his knock! I invited him in, and he told me he was looking for a place to live and was excited to start our program that fall. He asked me how I was doing, and I don't know why, but perhaps since the pool was agonizingly on my mind, I blurted out my dilemma—my lack of guidance and the two problems I faced in going forward with the pool. My family will never forget what happened next.

Glenn asked me if I would let him take care of the whole

thing. I had no idea what he meant. He asked if I knew what he had done for a living before and during his undergraduate years at Biola, and I told him the truth—I had no idea. He went on to share that he had sold, designed, and overseen the installation of swimming pools for Curcie Pools. Now he had his old job back, and most of his former clientele were very wealthy people.

What he said next made my jaw drop. He said that if I agreed, he would design and oversee the entire installation. He would contract each company, oversee their work, and landscape the entire backyard, even arrange for the installation of a sprinkler system that included the hill! I would not have to do a single thing. Best of all, he could secure the whole job for less than half the price of what others would charge us.

But how? How could he offer me such a deal? He told me he was overseeing a new housing development with about a hundred homes, all of them with pools. As part of the project, he could offer various contractors the chance to work on that huge project—if they gave a deep discount on our pool.

Finally, Glenn said that if I'd agree, it would be an answer to *his* prayers. Before he had embarked for this latest trip out west, his Sunday school class in Tennessee had raised a nice chunk of money to help him with tuition, and they had asked just one thing of him: "We have given to you, so when you get to Southern California, we expect you to find someone you can serve." I was the person he had wanted to serve, but when he came to my office, he had no idea how he could do that. By providing the pool, he could keep his commitment to serve. The best part of all this was that Glenn let Ashley and Allison help design a waterfall!

Since that summer we have had an amazing pool with a jacuzzi, a waterfall, two streams running into the pool, a firepit, and tropical landscaping all throughout our backyard. The water is turquoise blue, and the whole thing is just paradise. I cannot tell you how deeply and profoundly this experience contributed to the ongoing spiritual growth of my entire family. Our trust in God grew through this answer to prayer, and it has stayed with us ever since. It wasn't completely cost-free, since we almost went into poverty feeding all the kids who were constantly at our house! But that was a good problem to have.

It would be irrational and stubborn for anyone who hears of these two events and the surrounding context to refuse to acknowledge them as miraculous answers to prayer.

God's Gracious Provision for a Retired Missionary Couple

Hope and I have known, loved, and deeply admired Ruth and Bill Henderson for fifteen years. The Hendersons have been active members of our church—the Anaheim Vineyard—for more than two decades and are respected for their love for Jesus, their faithful and untiring servant hearts, and their Christian maturity and integrity. The account I'm about to share is in Ruth's own words, and I assure you I thoroughly questioned her and Bill about the incident. This story was widely known by several church members when it happened, so there is no reasonable question about its validity. Their eyewitness testimony is an account of God's incredible provision of a specific house for Ruth's retired missionary parents.

This miracle was presented on CBN's *700 Club*, but I want to add a few details not shared on that show. As I was growing up, Dad would always say that God would take care of us, whatever we needed, and he always did too. As my parents got older, my dad would say, "If you give your youth away serving the Lord, he will take care of you when you are old."

My parents were missionaries for more than twenty-five years, part of that time working with Spanish-speaking people in the United States and part of that time overseas, first in Venezuela and then in Spain doing church planting. They returned to the States for health reasons in the 1980s, and my mom worked as a bilingual teacher in a school in Arizona and later in the San Diego schools. My dad pastored a small Baptist church, discipled pastors, and taught some pastoral courses in Spanish at an extension of Golden Gate Seminary. They lived in small apartments and were content, never really thinking they could ever own a house. After all, they came to the States with no retirement funds, and my father received little to no income in his retirement activities in the San Diego area. For all practical purposes, they lived on my mother's small salary.

Houses were quite expensive in the San Diego area and, humanly speaking, simply far, far beyond their ability to purchase or pay a mortgage. But deep in their hearts, they, especially my mother, wanted a house in which to finish out their lives. We knew about this and joined them in praying for God's provision. While still working as a teacher, my mom found a vacant house whose price had been lowered, and my parents went to look at it with a real estate agent. They loved the house! It was up on a hill, with trees all around and a big backyard overlooking the freeway.

They did not have a down payment and could not qualify for the $220,000 loan, so the real estate agent called and tried to get the owners to lower the price. As they were waiting in the empty house to hear back from the owners, there was a knock on the door. The person at the door just happened to knock on the door during the one and only short time period they were actually in the house. The man who knocked was going to all the houses on the street looking for a place to build a cell phone tower that overlooked the freeway! He was offering $10,000 per year for thirty years!

With that deal on the table the bank was willing to grant the mortgage loan so they could buy the house.

My dad is still able to live there, and the mortgage payments are $978 a month. The costs are paid by the developers of the cell phone towers in the backyard! Two towers were eventually installed, and they look just like palm trees. God has always kept his promise to provide! And he heard our requests to bless my parents.

Here was a couple who freely responded to God's call to live a life of near poverty and frugality as missionaries among the poor, who retired and continued to serve for little compensation, and whose hearts' desire was to have a home as they grew older. Humanly speaking, getting a house was virtually impossible. But their desire and faithfulness, along with the family's prayers, led them to find a house they loved. And they "just happened" to be at the house the very same day a cell tower representative was in that neighborhood, and they "just happened" to be at the house when the representative knocked at the door. By any measure, this occurrence was highly improbable and independently special (it exactly fit the prayers offered and met the desires of this faithful couple's hearts). In short, it is clear evidence that the Christian God is real and is still doing miracles today.

Hurricane Harvey and One Miracle after Another

On the weekend of November 9, 2019, I spoke at an apologetics conference in Port Neches, Texas, hosted by Dr. Jason Martin, the new pastor at First Baptist Church in that town. Port Neches is a town of about thirteen thousand people, located east of Houston and about twenty miles from the Gulf of Mexico. During the last week of August, a Category 4 hurricane named Harvey hit Southeast Texas, including Houston, Port Arthur, and Port Neches. According to records, Port Neches was one of the hardest hit towns. Fifty inches of rain dropped on the area in four days, affecting 80 to 85 percent of the homes and other structures in the town. In total, 1.3 billion dollars' worth of damage was incurred at Port Neches alone. At least four feet of water covered most of the small city, and as one observer put it, the entire town looked like a lake. Thousands of people had no homes, no food, and no place to stay. A large percentage of the gas stations were inoperable.

I had the honor of having lunch with Pastor Martin and his assistant (who were both present when the miracle occurred), and they shared an amazing answer to prayer. Pastor Martin also gave me contact information for three others who were part of the prayer team and who saw firsthand what happened. Again, I have vetted this account myself and have talked with several eyewitnesses who were present when it occurred. Here, in Pastor Martin's own account, is the eyewitness testimony:

Hurricane Harvey was a nightmare. I had only been at First Baptist Church in Port Neches for about three weeks when the storm hit. On the Monday before, we had a staff meeting and discussed being open to following God in meeting the needs—if there were to be any needs. The weathermen were saying this would only be a "rain event" and not a big deal. However, after the staff meeting, we decided to close our church office so each person could do what they needed to do.

That afternoon, my brother, Pastor Mike Martin of First Baptist Church in Huffman, called and said they were beginning to get flooding in their area. His church was an evacuation site, and people would start arriving shortly. He asked if my church could help get supplies to the church while the roads were still open. Being so new to FBC Port Neches, I had no idea if the church could do it. At the time I was heading to the local grocery store, and I saw Jeannette Harvey, our children's minister. I asked her what it might look like if we as a church could get those needed supplies in a short time to my brother in Huffman.

She asked if I was serious, because in the past, helping other churches had been discouraged. I told her that when a sister church calls and asks for help, we should help! She was excited to help, so I put her in charge of spreading the word. She began setting up our gym, and as she got the word out, items began to flood in: toothpaste, soap, diapers, canned food, and many, many other items. Stacks of clothing kept piling up, so we tried to stop people from bringing more. We had no space for these things and there was no clear need for these items.

On Tuesday afternoon, my brother called back and said the roads were now flooded and there would be no way to get to him now. All the while, supplies were still pouring into our church gym—*lots* of supplies—washcloths, towels, sheets, blankets, pillows, and clothes in all sizes. I told my brother we would get the supplies to other folks we could reach. Then I went to city hall and told them that if they needed our gym for an evacuation center, it was available. We didn't have cots for overnight stays—but that was about to change! I told Jeanette what I had done, and she said, "Well, let's get some cots!" She made a few phone calls, and before Wednesday we had more than two hundred cots, supplies overflowing our space, and more clothes than I could even think about. We wondered what was about to happen.

As the storm came closer, the rain got heavier and our neighborhoods began to flood. People were being rescued in johnboats, but no one was coming to the church yet. Then around 3:30 p.m., Officer Will Navaro stopped by and asked if we were an evacuation center. We said yes, and as we were talking, the rain began coming down even harder. He replied, "Get ready—you will be overrun with people." The "rain event" had turned into a horrendous human catastrophe.

For a few hours, no one showed up, and then at about 7:00 p.m., our first person showed up. Donna Smith, Lynn Jackson, Rob Jones, Jeanette Harvey, Larry Hinson, and many, many other church members greeted the folks who were arriving. We established a check-in location where we recorded names, addresses, phone numbers, nearest relatives, and so on. As people arrived, we also noticed they had nothing with them. The people were soaking wet, cold, and hungry. They had lost everything except what they had in their pockets. The water had risen so quickly, and many were just glad to be alive. Since they were soaking wet, we realized the clothes we had tried to keep from coming in were now very much needed! The towels we had said we didn't need were now a priority item. Several of our workers began to separate clothing into men's and women's and into various sizes. We told each person who arrived to get a set of dry clothes, and my wife ran across the street and began running our lone washing machine (it ran for many days after this, twenty-four hours a day). The clothes were just the first miracle of provision. The cots, the towels . . . all the rest followed.

By midnight on Wednesday night, we had around 250 people in our gym. Cots were lined up, and people were still arriving. A police officer told us that because our building was getting full, we no longer needed to accept evacuees. I remember standing outside and telling a family—soaking wet with a crying baby—that we were out of room. I still hate that moment! I have no idea who they were or where they are now. At about 4:00 a.m., I told Rob Jones, who was our youth minister at the time, that we needed to feed the people. I opened the refrigerators and freezers, and they were mostly empty. We had about three dozen frozen biscuits and some miscellaneous items, along with two gallons of milk. We cooked whatever we had, knowing there was no way this was going to feed all these hungry people, but we did what we could. We set out the food, and somehow we ended up with leftovers, even though there was clearly not enough when we started cooking! The babies were fed first, then the mothers, and then the men. Everyone who wanted to eat did so!

By Thursday, Lynn Jackson, who normally prepared our Wednesday meals, was working out a plan to feed everyone. Along with Donna and Jeanette, she got the word out that we needed food. And wow, the food began to show up! We also organized cleanup crews, bathroom crews, receiving crews, food crews, and other kinds of crews. By suppertime on Thursday, our 250 guests were all well taken care of. That Thursday evening, I was called to a meeting with the mayor, city manager, police chief, fire chief, and several others, and they told us that by Friday morning, our guests had to go. The people were all being transferred to Dallas. My head deacon advised me to share this info with the people, but to do it from the second floor—he was afraid of the way people might react to the news. But they took it well. No one liked it, of course. The city leaders had told us that on Friday morning there would be school buses to transport everyone to the local airport and then fly them to Dallas. As folks were being shipped out, our real work was about to begin. We began to receive phone calls asking our church to provide meals for people, and Lynn Jackson said she would do her best. The problem was that we didn't know what food we would serve or what kinds of plates and utensils we would use for it.

As the last of our 250 evacuees left, relief workers began to show up. The Cajun Army volunteer group arrived with folks from everywhere, and once again, our towels, clothes, and cots came in handy. But we had no way to provide showers, and so we began discussing this need. Keyla Poss, our financial secretary, said that her husband's company would loan us a hazmat trailer that had four showers and a washing machine and dryer (which was good since ours needed a break). The shower trailer arrived, and another church member said his company could donate an industrial generator. We hooked up the water and the generator. And then someone said, "Where are we going to get diesel for this generator?" I didn't realize the system needed fuel, much less diesel fuel, and gas stations were out of the question. So a group of us prayed that God would supply diesel fuel.

Just as we were finishing our prayer as we stood in a circle in our church parking lot, a man pulled into the lot. He had a trailer full of five-gallon containers of diesel, and he rolled down his window and asked, "Does anyone need diesel?" We looked at each other in shock. Here he was, offering us the diesel fuel we needed—within sixty seconds of our having finished our prayer! It was a clear miracle.

At this point, I was encouraging our staff to go home and sleep, since we had been working around the clock for multiple days. Folks were exhausted, and yet no one wanted to leave. Lynn Jackson was still preparing the meals. Lynn had been constantly feeding folks, and people had just kept on bringing in food. It was wonderful. She had just received another request to feed five hundred people in a neighboring town. I went outside to look at all the trash that was piling up, and Jeanette came out to tell me we didn't have enough food to feed those five hundred people. "We are running out of food," she said to me. So I told her, "Let's pray. 'Lord, You know the need. Amen.'" Just as we were finishing, the door opened and Lynn walked out. "I know my kitchen," she said, "and I know what is here. A few minutes ago, we had no food for this group of five hundred. Now our freezer is full of chicken tenders—more than enough to feed them." Jeanette and I just looked at each other and smiled.

There was another instance of this happening again later, when Lynn needed to feed about a thousand people in another town. This time she had the food, but we had run out of food containers. Jeanette and I were talking about some logistics when Lynn came up and said, "Food I got; what I don't have are containers." Before we could even pray, an 18-wheeler pulled up, and the driver said, "I have an 18-wheeler full of food containers. Do you guys have a need for them?" We still have a few of those containers today.

At some point during this crisis, the military began sleeping in our church. Jeanette saw them sleeping in a parking lot and told the commander to talk to me to see if they could use our church instead, and my answer was, "Yes, of course." The day before the soldiers were to arrive, a man came up to me and said, "The Lord told me to bring you a printer for a laptop. Here it is." I thanked him and set it on the floor by my desk. I was a bit confused. I went back to talk with the military guys and told them what was available for them to use. A lieutenant was setting up the command area for the group, and as we visited with him, I asked him if he needed anything. "Yes, sir, the funny thing is, we left our printer somewhere, and I need a printer really bad." I had him follow me to my office and handed him the printer that had just been delivered. It was exactly what he needed.

The stories I have shared are not earth-shattering. But they are perfect examples of how God meets our needs in answer to prayer—sometimes even before we know we have the needs! Jeanette can verify these stories and others like them, as can Lynn Jackson, Larry Hinson, and many others. Jeanette is now the executive director of the Hope Women's Resource Clinic in Beaumont, Texas, and she is always expecting to see miracles. Why? Because she always sees them. Her faith is great, but her Lord is greater!

Wow! What a story, right? And this account is from the person who saw it all firsthand. I hope you are encouraged to see that God is still actively answering prayer as he meets the specific needs we have. And if you think these specific answers to prayer are encouraging, wait until the next chapter! It gets even better.

Chapter 5

UNDERSTANDING THE
NATURE AND IMPORTANCE
OF MIRACULOUS HEALING

On Thursday, April 7, 2016, I was interviewed by a film crew for a documentary on miracles. The crew and the company they represented were not believers, but they were traveling to various places around the world to interview leading atheists and Christians to present a fair case to the public about miracle claims. Their aim was to present the best possible case for and against miracles. I was honored to be part of the project. To prepare, I gathered a few eyewitness accounts of miraculous healings, accepting only those for which I had several independent witnesses who could confirm the stories.

One story in particular was deeply moving—and its authenticity was beyond reasonable doubt. In 2004, our church—the Anaheim Vineyard—offered healing prayer every Monday night for anyone who needed it. Usually, around thirty people came each Monday. They would sign up at a greeting area, and the trained prayer team of about ten people would break into groups of three or four, take the next person on the sign-up sheet to a private room, and pray for twenty to thirty minutes for that person's healing.

On one particular Monday, a Jewish woman named Susan

Semegran showed up for prayer. She had been told about the Monday night healing prayer time from some of her high school students who attended our church. Aware that she was very sick, they had encouraged her to come. Susan had tried all the medical treatments recommended by the doctors, but nothing worked. Her condition worsened, and by the time she came to the Vineyard, the cancer had spread to fifty-one places throughout her body. The doctors had stopped treatment and sent her home on hospice to die. Medically speaking, she had no hope.

She came for prayer off and on for a while, but the final three consecutive Monday nights she received prayer were very interesting. Nothing happened for the first two weeks, but she felt loved by the care and bolstered by the prayer, and she decided to keep coming back. On the third Monday, something unusual happened. She shared that during prayer time, her entire body, starting with her head and descending to her feet, was filled with electricity and heat. Susan knew she had been healed, so she contacted her main doctor, who ordered a PET scan for a week later. In complete shock, the doctor brought the scan results, along with results from a previous scan. Susan looked at both of them, and the before and the after were quite clear—all the cancer that had been in her body was now gone. She was completely and utterly cancer-free! As a result, she gave her life to Jesus and became a Messianic Jew.

This story was confirmed to me by Brian and Ken Slezak—two members of her prayer team who were present that night. And just before my video interview for the documentary, Brian contacted Susan again, and I received an email from her confirming everything that Brian and Ken had told me. For twelve years (I haven't contacted her since 2016), she continued to be completely cancer-free and was walking faithfully with Jesus. Susan had been miraculously healed!

HEALING IN CHURCH HISTORY

If we were to remove all the exorcisms and physical healings from the Gospels and the book of Acts, we wouldn't have much left. We would have no coherent picture of Jesus' life and the spread of Christianity from his death in AD 33 to the end of Acts in 62. Moreover, it would be impossible to explain how the tiny Jesus movement ever got off the ground. After all, it began among "insignificant" people along the off-the-beaten-path shores of the Sea of Galilee. The founder of the movement was executed in an embarrassing way reserved for the very worst criminals, one among thousands of others caught in the crosshairs of Roman rule.

The Roman Empire was one of the most powerful regimes in all of human history. Yet within a mere thirty years after Jesus' crucifixion, his movement had spread all over the empire, even securing followers who belonged "to Caesar's household" (Philippians 4:22). This explosion of the early church took place amid a plethora of competing ideologies. By far the best explanation for Christianity's early success is that the miracles of Jesus and the early church (which were largely deliverance and healing miracles) really happened. These miracles included the grand miracle of Jesus' bodily resurrection. Nor were these miracles limited to Jesus and the apostles. The historical record indicates that ordinary Christians who were members of the newly planted churches had the power to perform miracles (see Galatians 3:5).[1]

Many people don't realize that we have conclusive evidence that the same sort of miracles we find in the New Testament continued on to the time of Augustine (AD 354–430). For example, Quadratus, an early second-century believer, said this: "But the works of our Saviour were always present, for they were true, those who were cured, those who rose from the dead, who not merely appeared as cured and risen, but were constantly present, not only while the Saviour was living, but even for some time after he had gone, so that some of them survived even to our own time."[2]

And in his most famous work, *Against Heresies*, Irenaeus (AD 130–202) confronts the followers of two false teachers— Simon and Carpocrates—on the grounds that they were unable to heal the blind, the lame, the deaf, the paralyzed, or the injured, or do anything to relieve the demon-possessed.[3] He goes on to say of related events in the late second century, "Wherefore, also, those who are in truth His disciples, receiving grace from Him, do in His name perform [miracles], so as to promote the welfare of other men . . . [Some] heal the sick by laying their hands upon them, and they are made whole."[4]

In addition, Origen (AD 184–253) notes, "By these [the names of God and Jesus] we also have seen many delivered from serious ailments, and from mental distraction and madness, countless other diseases, which neither men nor demons had cured."[5] Several other church fathers from the second to the mid-fourth century could be cited.[6]

After around AD 350, healings became increasingly rare. One of history's greatest intellectual giants was Augustine, bishop of Hippo in North Africa. In the early stages of his ministry training, he was taught (as was becoming increasingly customary at that time) that healing miracles had generally ceased and that he was not to pray for the sick but as a last resort was to send the sick to a shrine in the hope that they might be healed. Yet as time went on, Augustine changed his views about healing, mostly due to the fact that people were being physically healed in his church and he was an eyewitness to these healings.

Augustine started researching healing miracles and seeking rational validation of those that held up to examination. In 426, he wrote, "I realized how many miracles were occurring in our own day and which were so like the miracles of old and also how wrong it would be to allow the memory of these marvels of divine power to perish from among our people. It is only two years ago that the keeping of records was begun here in Hippo, and already, at this writing, we have nearly seventy attested miracles."[7]

For the remainder of church history after Augustine, the occurrence of miracles, especially healings, was something of a leaky water faucet. There were always occasional drops falling— periodic instances of healings or miracles—even when the faucet was closed tightly by the church authorities. And there were also periods when the faucet was wide open and the waters of miraculous healing poured out. In 1984, Yale professor of history and classics Ramsay MacMullen wrote an important book on the prevalence and importance of miraculous interventions by the true God, particularly covering healings and exorcisms.[8] Summarizing his research, MacMullen stated emphatically that, in spite of a plethora of competing ideologies and religions, along with the fact that most Christians were illiterate and uneducated, having come from the slave and working castes, Christianity had triumphed. Why? He pointed to regular miraculous interventions by the Christian God, especially manifested in healings and exorcisms.

Still, from around AD 400 to 1800 (with a few notable exceptions), miracles virtually died out in the Christian church. The faucet was shut tight, and despite a few leaks at times, it remained shut. But why? Why did miracles cease for more than one thousand years? Here are several possible reasons:[9]

- The New Testament teaching that healings are expressions of God's love and signs of Christianity's truth was reduced to the latter. As the church became triumphant, the need for miraculous proof died out and was no longer deemed important.
- The declining emphasis on miracles gave rise to a different way in which the church demonstrated its superiority

over rivals. Christianity regularly produces godly saints, and since suffering—which includes sickness—produces growth in sanctity and a reward in heaven, sickness came to be seen as a blessing. To pray against it undermined a person's chance to receive that blessing.

- As the church grew, a leadership class arose—the priests— and a clear line of demarcation formed between the priests and the laity, with the former being viewed as the only ones qualified to pray for the sick. Priests' prayers became formal recitations of composed prayers written down in liturgical books. Spontaneous reliance on the Holy Spirit by all Christians, with the opportunity to engage in healing prayer, became limited to a formal recitation given by priests alone, with reliance on the words of the prayer.

- The translation of the Scriptures into Latin—the Vulgate —by Jerome (AD 345–420) became the church's official Latin Bible. Jerome's translation of James 5:14–16 (about healing) turned the healing text into a salvation text (the Vulgate says the prayers of believers will *save*, not *heal*), which had a big impact on the church's growing neglect of healing prayer.

- Wanting to distance themselves from all things Roman Catholic, the Protestant Reformers—especially John Calvin—recognized that the ability to heal the sick (for example, through shrines and relics), was claimed to be proof that the Roman Catholic Church was the one true church. To undercut this claim, Calvin and others developed the doctrine of cessationism, the view that the New Testament miracles ceased after the death of the apostles so the preaching of the gospel would become the magnificent focus of the church.[10]

- The period of the Enlightenment (late seventeenth through eighteenth centuries) in Europe led to an increasingly secularized West, and consequently belief in miracles and demons waned, especially among the intellectual class. Doctrinal propositions replaced divine power and the Word replaced the Spirit, when really a both/and position should have been upheld.

In summary, as Francis MacNutt bemoans, "At one point, in the England of the 1520s, only *one* person held healing services: King Henry VIII. Even clergymen did not pray for people to be healed. A hundred years later, King Charles I even made it a crime for anyone else to pray for healing. The whole point was to show that the king was special—divinely anointed as no one else was."[11]

In sharing this whirlwind tour of church history, I want to highlight several crucial lessons for us today—in particular, for those who want to be strengthened in the conviction that God still heals and delivers people today. Here are three important points that relate to our understanding of the nature of miraculous healings, their role in Christianity, and our expectations.

First, it should be clear that miracles did not end with the death of the apostles or the formation of the New Testament canon. Miracles were intended by God to be a central, ongoing part of the Christian life and ministry, and their continued presence is well-documented in the historical record. While we may not know all the reasons, it seems likely that the "drying up" of miracles—with some notable exceptions—was largely the result of human error and not something taught in the Bible or an indication of God's desire. Healings and exorcisms are still occurring today, and they should be a regular part of a local church's usual ministry.

Second, there are two scriptural reasons that God performs miracles, including healings and exorcisms: (1) to express his love as he meets real needs, and (2) to provide signs and attestations that he is the true God. Both of these reasons are still at play today. This is power evangelism—approaching unbelievers, praying for their healing, and then communicating to them the gospel.[12] As one unbeliever frankly admitted after experiencing a miraculous event, "It only takes one supernatural encounter to shake you to the core and get you thinking."[13]

Finally, these examples from church history are good reminders that we need to take more risks, restore well-informed healing/ deliverance prayer to its proper place in our lives, and increase our expectations of what God can and will do. I hope to encourage you to accept this challenge in the remainder of this chapter. But first I want to raise a point I intentionally omitted in our tour of church history that will strengthen our ability to take risks and motivate us to have higher expectations for what is possible through healing and deliverance.

It is widely recognized by missionaries, leaders of missionary organizations (irrespective of their denomination), church growth experts, professors of missiology, and many informed Christians that since around 1970 there has been an exponential explosion of "book of Acts" type miracles—far, far beyond anything that has happened since the first century. Over the past five decades, miracles have been multiplying like loaves and fish, and as C. S. Lewis creatively said in *The Lion, the Witch, and the Wardrobe,* "They say Aslan is on the move"—with a power the likes of which we haven't seen since the time of Jesus and the apostles. Highly credible reports such as the ones we read in the JESUS Film Project email newsletter read like Acts 29 (Acts has only twenty-eight chapters).

I have talked to dozens and dozens of missionaries in the last fifteen years, and every single one has acknowledged this "outbreak" of miracles being done in Jesus' name. Many of these were miracles they personally witnessed, and they agreed the increase in miraculous activity is unprecedented. In his book titled *The Next Christendom*, Philip Jenkins, distinguished professor of history at Penn State, noted that the most significant changes in the world during the last decades of the twentieth century were not secular trends like fascism, Communism, feminism, or environmentalism.[14] By 1985, one-third of the world's population was living under Communist rule, and most of this expansive growth took place during the twentieth century. Yet, according to Jenkins, "it is precisely *religious changes* that are the most significant, and even the most revolutionary, in the contemporary world . . . We are currently living through one of the transforming movements in the history of religion worldwide."[15] According to Jenkins, the most transformative changes in the world are the product of religious beliefs. As evidence, he points to the explosion of the Christian church at unprecedented rates in the "Third World" or "Majority World."

Jenkins goes on to observe that for Majority World Christians (those in Africa, Asia, the Caribbean, Eastern Europe, Latin America, the Middle East, and Oceania), one of the primary causes of the explosive growth of the church in their communities is "the critical idea that God intervenes directly in everyday life," an intervention that is an expression of the power of God's kingdom.[16] This intervention in everyday life includes healings, exorcisms, and other miracles.

These global shifts are of critical importance for our own lives and the practices and health of our local church. If most of us who live in the United States or in the Western world derive our confidence in the miraculous from what we observe in our own church or from talking with other Christians we know in the West, we will have little to no expectation that God will respond when we pray for people's healing. But if we step back and take an informed look at the worldwide picture for the last half century, suddenly it becomes much easier to pray for a miracle *with expectation*. As a general rule of thumb, the greater our expectations of

God, the more of the supernatural we will see. But we can't just crank up an increase in expectations at will. That's called faking it. Far better to rely on accurate information—true stories of God at work that build our confidence. For now, I believe the simple fact that we have seen an explosion of miracles in the past fifty years should do us some good by increasing our faith in God's readiness to act.

FIVE BIBLICAL LINES OF EVIDENCE

Five biblical lines of evidence, if regularly taught and widely understood, will increase our confidence in and our expectations for healing, as well as spur the creation of more space in our worship services for these miraculous activities.

1. The Current Presence of the Kingdom of God

I am among those who anticipate a future form of the kingdom of God during the millennial reign of Jesus Christ. At that time the kingdom's presence and power will be fully manifested. However, I also agree with the majority of New Testament scholars in holding that when Jesus came the first time, he brought about a new form and greater presence of the kingdom than ever before. So before I define what I mean by the phrase "kingdom of God," I want to highlight a key axiom: *the kingdom is both now and not yet.* Remembering this simple truth will sustain our ministry of praying for the sick and demonized. It means that the kingdom of God is present in power right now—at this very moment—while affirming that a future form of the kingdom will exhibit even greater power in keeping with the full manifestation of the kingdom.

Applied to today, this means that the kingdom's power to heal and deliver, while very real and available, is not what it could or will be. We seek by faith to bring the kingdom's power to bear on a healing situation, but that power may be limited for reasons known only to God, and there are still the significant hindrances of the world, the flesh, and the devil. So we do not give up, but we learn from past failures and keep "doing the stuff," as some would say, with respect to prayer and healing. My friend and former pastor Nigel Morris told me that if I prayed for two hundred people, I'd surely see some healed, and he was correct. Through all of those prayers—some resulting in healing, others not—the "already but not yet" of the kingdom was a key truth that kept me from becoming discouraged.

So what *is* the kingdom of God? It refers primarily to the reign, rule, or authority of God himself and secondarily to the realm in which that rule is directly exercised, consisting largely in the laws governing the natural world and, more importantly, the individual and collective hearts of those who have bowed to God's rule.[17] The gospel of the kingdom is the news that the direct rule of God is now available to all in and through Jesus Christ. Among other things, the announcement of the kingdom brings to center stage the supernatural power of God over disease, death, and the kingdom of darkness.

2. Jesus' Ministry and the Holy Spirit

When I was saved in the late 1960s, I was taught that Jesus' miracles proved he was God because he did them from his divine nature.[18] In the years since that time, I have become convinced that this teaching was incorrect, and I now believe that Jesus' public ministry was done in his humanity, as a perfect man, doing in dependence on the filling of the Holy Spirit what he saw his Father doing. Theologian Thomas Oden notes:

> As a man, Jesus walked day by day in radical dependence upon God the Spirit, prayed and spoke by the power of the Spirit. In portraying Jesus as constantly dependent upon the Spirit,

the Gospels were not challenging or questioning his deity or divine Sonship. Rather, as eternal Son the theandric [divine-human] person already was truly God, while as a man, Jesus was truly human, bone of our bone, flesh of our flesh, seed of Abraham, whose humanity was continually replenished by the Spirit (Luke 4:14; Heb. 2:14–17). He did not walk or speak by his own independent human power, but by the power of the Spirit. Every gift requisite to the Son's mission was provided by the Spirit.[19]

It may be that some of Jesus' miracles flowed from his divine nature, yet there is a consensus among New Testament scholars that most, if not all, were expressions of his humanness. The implications of this shift in understanding are quite significant. As Gerald Hawthorne wrote, "Jesus is living proof of how those who are his followers may exceed the limitations of their humanness in order that they, like him, might carry to completion against all odds their God-given mission in life—by the Holy Spirit."[20] Practically, this means that when Jesus said, "Whoever believes in me . . . will do even greater things than these, because I am going to the Father" (John 14:12), he meant it in the ordinary way these words would be interpreted. In imitation of Jesus' ministry, the church is invited to exercise the miraculous power of the Spirit in the service of the kingdom.

3. The Availability of the So-Called Miraculous Gifts

Today there are four views about the miraculous spiritual gifts.[21] *Cessationism* believes there are no miraculous gifts today and that gifts such as prophecy, healings, and tongues ceased with the death of the apostles because their function of establishing the church was complete. The *open but cautious* position holds that cessationist arguments fail and the miraculous gifts are still present today, but their current employment is often flawed, unbiblical, and unhelpful and we should err strongly on the side of not using them. The *Third Wave* position believes all Christians are baptized by the Holy Spirit at conversion and subsequent fillings/anointings are received by faith. Though the gift of tongues is a reality, it is not emphasized or seen as evidence of the Spirit's filling, while other miraculous gifts, particularly those involved in healing, deliverance, and prophecy, are crucial for church life. Finally, the *Pentecostal/charismatic* position acknowledges the contemporary miraculous gifts and often endorses a baptism of the Holy Spirit subsequent to salvation with the evidence of tongues. This last position tends to place a greater emphasis on tongues than do Third Wave advocates, for instance.

In the concluding section of *Are Miraculous Gifts for Today?* theologian Wayne Grudem identifies some areas of agreement and disagreement among these positions:[22]

AREAS OF AGREEMENT

Dedication to Scripture, fellowship, closeness to God, and some similarities regarding miracles and the Spirit's activities. All imply (with different degrees of expectation) that God still heals, performs miracles, and guides believers, and that the Holy Spirit empowers us for life and ministry.

AREAS OF DISAGREEMENT

Degree of expectation for seeing and seeking supernatural manifestations of God; demons and angels; and differences regarding the extent to which church life in the New Testament—especially in Acts—is a pattern for today.

I personally hold to the Third Wave position, so I'll make two observations. First, while I have great respect for my cessationist brothers and sisters, the simple fact is that, over the last few decades, most biblical scholars have rejected this position in favor of one of the other three options. In addition and without question, the overwhelming majority of believers around the world are not cessationists.

Certainly we do not determine truth by counting numbers. Still, there are occasions when we need to consider that a large majority of well-informed people are moving away from one viewpoint in favor of a rival position. Cessationists owe us a fair-minded explanation for why an increasing number of Christian intellectuals, including many New Testament scholars, are abandoning cessationism. The ad hominem argument that people are abandoning propositional biblical truth for religious experience and feelings does not hold up. Even if this were true, it addresses only people's motives—not their *reasons* for changing sides.

Second, and more importantly, the debate about the miraculous gifts may be moot. Why? Because the current practice of healing/deliverance prayer, prophecy, and the other miraculous gifts is sustained largely by truths regarding the kingdom of God and the ministry of Jesus. In other words, even if cessationism were correct, these other lines of evidence would be more than enough to justify a change in the way we approach healing, deliverance, and prophetic words.

4. Healing in the Atonement

Some believe that physical healing was provided, or even secured, by Jesus' atoning work on the cross. If this is correct, it would provide another biblical reason for expecting healing miracles. The key text employed to support this idea is Isaiah 53:5: "and with his stripes we are healed" (KJV; cf. Matthew 8:17). Unfortunately, there is a problem with using this text and the claim that physical healing resides in the atonement. Several technical questions affect the interpretation of this text, resulting in a number of different yet legitimate ways of understanding it. Virtually no Old Testament scholar today holds that Isaiah 53:5 teaches that the atonement provided or secured physical healing. If this is correct, then the employment of this text, along with the teaching that physical healing is part of the atonement, is not good theology. At the very least, I think we are on shaky ground if we use the text in that way, but I include it because the understanding that physical healing is included in the atonement offered by Jesus can contribute to an increase of faith for healing.

5. Correct Interpretation of the Bible

The late Dallas Willard astutely observed, "If we are really to understand the Bible record, we must enter into our study of it on the assumption that the experiences recorded there are basically of the same type as ours would have been if we had been there. Those who lived through those experiences felt very much as we would have if we had been in their place. Unless this comes home to us, the things that happened to the people in the Bible will remain unreal to us. We will not genuinely be able to believe the Bible or find its contents to be real."[23]

He goes on to declare, "We must pray for the faith and for the experiences that would enable us to believe that *such things could happen to us*."[24] There is no good reason to approach Scripture in any other way. I am not suggesting that we are receiving biblical revelation today on par with what we find in the Scriptures, or that people like Moses, Elijah, and Elisha in the Old Testament, and Jesus and the apostles in the New Testament, were not special in many ways. But as Jack Deere has shown, miracles were done throughout biblical times in association with ordinary people like us.[25] And things stayed the same for the first four centuries of Christianity—and are again breaking out today in significant ways. Thus, there are good reasons to interpret biblical miracles as events that continued long after the apostles died and are happening today. The biblical miracles are still possible for us today, and we should learn to practice them.

AN OBJECTION: HEALING CLAIMS NEED BUT LACK MEDICAL VERIFICATION

In earlier chapters, I responded to skeptical arguments raised against miracles. As a reminder of what we covered, if one simply applies the intelligent agent principle (*small probability + independent specialness*) to an eyewitness case, the evidence speaks for itself. Still, there is a type of skeptical claim that I have not considered, even though I often hear it from atheists. They contend that only if miracle claims are medically verified by strictly controlled empirical experiments can they be accepted as rationally justified. Moreover, anecdotal reports about medical evidence are just that—anecdotal. And such reports fall short of the necessary scientific proof.

There are three ways to respond to this claim. First, the type of medical evidence for miracles that is being asked for does exist. Second, when properly understood, many of the anecdotal reports about medical evidence turn out to be the eyewitness testimony of doctors, nurses, and additional eyewitnesses to miraculous healings, and these are often recorded in the patient's medical chart. Third, if we were to accept this extraordinarily high bar for assessing the evidence related to an alleged event, then the majority of court cases, virtually all of history, and numerous other fields of study would have to be dismissed. This is an absurd requirement leading to a disastrous conclusion, and thus the skeptical declaration above is false since, if accepted, it entails a ridiculous conclusion.

Let's dig a bit deeper into these three replies. Regarding the first response, rigorous medical documentation for miraculous healing already exists. Consider a case published in the peer-reviewed medical journal *Complementary Therapies in Medicine*,[26] an article approved by the board of the Global Medical Research Institute, one of whose three authors is a member of the Department of Psychological and Brain Sciences at Indiana University. The authors share how the male patient at one week of age began to have intermittent cramping and projectile vomiting. He was taken to the hospital, underwent an entire battery of tests, and at two weeks old was diagnosed with gastroparesis (a chronic syndrome of delayed gastric emptying), a lifelong condition that is quite serious. The prognosis for recovery was extremely poor, and none of the standard medical interventions had done the baby any good. He was intubated with two different tubes, and for the next sixteen years, there was no improvement. His condition remained severe and refractory (resistant to treatment), and the patient was completely dependent on tubes for feeding and drinking for all those years. He never once ate or drank anything by mouth.

Raised in a Christian family and himself a Christian, on November 6, 2011, at age sixteen, he was taken to a church that believed in divine healing. He underwent proximal intercessory prayer (PIP) for less than fifteen minutes as a small group from the church laid hands on him and prayed to Jesus for his healing. During the prayer time, the young man experienced electrical heat running throughout his body (as is often the case during healing prayer; I myself have had such an experience when I was healed by prayer), and he was completely healed. Immediately, his intolerance to any form of oral feeding and drinking disappeared, and he started eating and drinking normally from that time on. Eventually, his two tubes were removed, and for the following six years up to the time the article was submitted for publication, he had no health problem and never took medicines or received any treatment for his syndrome. He didn't need medical intervention any longer!

The article concludes that his recovery after PIP was "remarkable" and could not be reasonably attributed to a placebo, since randomized placebo-controlled trials have shown that placebo effects have no impact on gastroparesis and gastric emptying. The article documents numerous cases of medically controlled studies in which healing occurred right after PIP and concludes that while proof of a miraculous healing is not possible, the case is quite favorably understood in this way.

At this point, a brief comment is in order. One does not need "proof," whatever that means, to know a miracle has taken place. Again, that sets the bar too high. Rather, all one needs is to show that it is more reasonable to believe a miracle happened than it is to reject that interpretation or to remain agnostic on the issue. When we then bring the intelligent agent principle (IAP) into consideration, it demonstrates beyond reasonable doubt that this was a genuine miracle.

Or consider another case, again published in a peer-reviewed medical journal, when after proximal intercessory prayer in the name of Jesus, a young woman who had been legally blind for twelve years with juvenile macular degeneration was instantly healed, and her eyesight remained intact for forty-seven years up to the time of the article's publication.[27]

These two articles contain references to a number of similar peer-reviewed articles. These studies are not hidden cases conjured up by charlatans. The evidence exists.

Regarding the response to the charge that anecdotal reports of medical documentation don't count because they are merely anecdotal, in my experience as a professional philosopher, I have noticed again and again that an opponent of an assertion will label it with a pejorative name as a substitute for a legitimate argument against it. Such a move is a conversation stopper that undermines rational dialogue about a topic. "Your view is racist!" is an example of what I mean.

The term *anecdotal* is another such example. The *Oxford English Dictionary* defines it as "(of an account) not necessarily true or reliable, because based on personal accounts rather than facts or research." Unfortunately, labeling something "anecdotal" and then rejecting it because of that label is not only a disingenuous way to win an argument; it is a false characterization of the real situation regarding reports of medically documented healings. Such reports express the eyewitness testimonies of doctors, nurses, and additional eyewitnesses to miraculous healings and their documentation in the patient's medical chart. Unless you start by assuming the self-refuting position that such eyewitnesses are all liars or don't have the sense to get their facts right, I see no reason to reject the numerous cases of these testimonies. And calling them "anecdotal" is surely not such a reason.

Finally, with regard to the third response to the skeptical claim, it is ridiculous to assert that *only* if we have tightly controlled medical documentation can we believe miracles have occurred. Ironically, during a debate I had with an atheist who practiced law, he made this sort of claim. I responded that if he was right, he could no longer practice law. The overwhelming amount of evidence used by a jury to reach a justified conclusion resides in eyewitness testimony or circumstantial evidence. Law, history, and other fields would not be able to meet an equivalent standard, as so many of the things we know in life depend on testimony. In chapter 2, I offered a rebuttal to the charge that extraordinary claims require extraordinary evidence, and we concluded that the credibility of eyewitness testimony is reliable unless there are overriding reasons in specific cases to distrust it.

HOW TO PRAY FOR THE SICK

Well, it's time to roll up our sleeves and get practical with what we are learning. Up to this point in the book, I've made an occasional suggestion or two about how to apply what we're reading. But for the rest of this chapter, we're going to dive into some specific and practical guidance on prayer for healing. I will take up the topic of demonization and deliverance in chapter 8, so for now I'd like to focus on praying for the sick. Obviously, there is no magic bullet here, no "one size fits all" approach, and no way to reduce healing prayer to some sort of formula. But that doesn't mean we can't learn from what others have done. Much wisdom has been tested and refined over the years by those who regularly practice healing prayer.

Before I get into specifics, orient yourself around three key points. First, do not promise someone they will be healed. Such a promise is presumptuous and can lead to disappointment if nothing happens. Second, remember that your first objective is to bless, love, and serve the recipient of prayer. If the person leaves feeling cared for, edified, hopeful, or closer to God, then something good has happened. Third, don't try to crank up more faith than you actually have—and don't be a fake. Give what you have, trust God as you are able, and be yourself. Honesty is the best policy. With these key points in mind, here are the steps I use when I pray for the sick:[28]

Step 1: The Interview

I begin by greeting the person and asking them how I can be of help. I will ask questions about what needs healing, how long they've had their problem, and what they think might be causing the problem or at least be related to it—such as other health issues, emotional issues, stress, spiritual issues, or relational issues. I want to get as much of the big picture as I can while making sure the person feels comfortable responding. While I am listening to the person, I open my heart and mind to hear the Holy Spirit in case he has something to say to me. If you are not good at discerning the Spirit's way of speaking to you, that's okay. Be yourself and do your best. Over the months to come, you will grow in this ability.

Step 2: The Invitation

Next, I invite the person to relax, close their eyes, and feel free to hold their hands in front of their body, palms up, in a comfortable position. I then tell the person simply to receive prayer and blessing, to open their soul to Jesus and not try to make something happen. I want the person to be completely relaxed and receptive.

Step 3: The Assessment

I then ask for permission to lay hands on the person where the pain or health problem resides, and if during the prayer time I could place my hand gently on the person's forehead or the top of their head. Obviously, you do not want to place your hand on an inappropriate place. If that's where the problem lies, I ask if I may place my hand on the person's shoulder. The laying on of hands is thoroughly biblical and very important.

I then pray out loud, inviting Jesus to come, manifest his presence, and speak to me if he desires. I tell the person that I want us to wait in quiet for a minute or so and see if the Lord has something to say. I have prayed for hundreds of people in this way, and I have been shocked at how often my mind will be given something to share—something I could not have known and is often very helpful to the person.

In chapter 7, I will say more about learning to hear God's voice. If I receive something, I share it, even if I'm not sure it came from the Lord. I may say something like this: "I seem to be getting [hearing, sensing] the idea that . . ." Sometimes the person will break out in tears. If that happens, I say, "Take your time, let go, and stay in the moment. We have plenty of time, so don't rush." I will then pray a silent blessing on what God is doing and wait. If nothing happens when I share what I seem to be receiving, I ask if what I said meant anything to the person. If they say yes, I pray out loud that God will use whatever was from him in the person's life and take away the memory of anything that was not from him. If the person says no, I simply thank them for being honest and move on. As I'm waiting on the Lord, I also seek to discern what to pray for.

Step 4: The Prayer

When speaking about prayer, Dallas Willard used to emphasize that *praying* and *saying* lie on a continuum. The continuum represents different ways to address or solve a problem by co-laboring with God. At one end lies prayer: asking God to grant the request, or being a channel of God's power in soaking prayer. At the other end lies speaking: as a member of God's kingdom and indeed as Jesus' kingdom ambassador standing with the associated, delegated authority, we speak to or against a problem.

Examples of petitionary prayer are common enough, so I won't go into this kind of prayer in detail. An example of *saying* is found in Matthew 21:18–22, the well-known story of Jesus cursing the barren fig tree. Two things are important in this event in relation to praying for the sick. First, Jesus did not ask God to make the fig tree barren. He spoke to the tree. He stood in the authority of the kingdom and expressed that authority through speaking. Second, when the disciples queried Jesus about how the tree had instantly withered, Jesus replied by offering a teaching about the need to pray in faith. In other words, his speaking *was* a form of praying, a direct employment of God's kingdom power and authority.

By way of application, when I pray for the sick person's healing, sometimes I ask God to heal, while at other times I soak the area that needs healing by staying at it for five minutes or so and, all the while, asking God in different ways to direct his gaze and power on the problem. And sometimes I speak directly to the problem and command the disease to leave, asking that the cells, brain chemistry, and so forth would be restored to health, all in Jesus' name. By using various ways to address the problem, we can engage in healing prayer for a longer period of time.

Step 5: The Evaluation

After a period of prayer, I will stop and ask the person if anything has changed. For example, whether they feel less pain or any form of heat or electricity in their body or some emotion or other. I ask if any thoughts are coming to the person's mind. Based on the reply, I will either ask if I can pray again or move to step 6.

Step 6: The Closing

When we are finished, I sometimes will give some direction that I hope is wise as to what the person might want to do or read next. I invite the person to come back for additional prayer, and I note that even Jesus prayed for someone in stages. For example, see Mark 8:22–26, where at first the person was only partially healed, but with additional prayer, the person received total healing from Jesus. I then note that some healing work may have just been accomplished, partial though it may have been, and it would be quite appropriate to ask for further prayer later. If nothing seems to have happened, I express my hope that the person felt loved and blessed by me and the Lord.

* * *

In praying for the sick, it is easy to get discouraged and lose confidence that anything will happen when you pray. As I mentioned in a previous chapter, when I began to practice healing prayer regularly in 2003, the advice I received was that if I prayed for two hundred people, I would surely see some stirring miraculous healings. As it turned out, the advice was correct. Still, in my experience and that of others I've spoken with, the percentage of people who get completely well, or at least experience some improvement, is somewhere between 5 percent and 25 percent, the latter figure being rare. So in the rest of the chapter, I want to address two issues that, if properly understood, can help us sustain our motivation and expectation. First, why do people not get healed? And second, how do we increase or maintain our expectation that God will move? Before we turn to these subjects, I share a word from Jack Deere that is good to ponder:

> If you haven't seen any truly miraculous healings, ask yourself how often you pray for these things . . . When I ask you how often you pray for miraculous healings, I am asking how often do you go into a hospital room and pray for the sick and suffering to be miraculously healed? How often do you lay your hands on the sick in your church and pray for them? . Most of the people I talk with who have never seen a miracle are people, by and large, who never take the trouble to go and lay their hands on sick people in believing prayer. Conversely, I have yet to find anyone who regularly lays hands on the sick in believing prayer who doesn't see at least some miraculous healings.[29]

FOURTEEN REASONS WHY PEOPLE ARE NOT HEALED

While in some cases it may be possible to discern why healing prayer was ineffective, most of the time, at least in my experience, it is hard to know for sure. Nevertheless, the following list provides solid reasons why people are not healed. If you get discouraged because you're praying and not seeing anything happen, reflecting on this list can be encouraging.[30]

1. There is a lack of faith. The Bible is clear that the presence or absence of faith can make a difference in healing prayer. To be sure, we should never try to crank up more faith than we actually have, and later in the chapter I'll suggest ways to increase our faith in this area. Two quick points here: (1) the lack of faith may be on the part of those who are praying or on the part of the one receiving prayer, and (2) during or shortly after the prayer time, it's almost never a good thing to tell the person who was not healed that it was because of their lack of faith, which just adds insult to injury.

2. God is using the problem for redemptive suffering. The Bible usually distinguishes sickness from suffering, and in general, we should assume that God always wants someone to be well unless there are overriding reasons to the contrary. With that being said, it is still true that there are times when God is using the suffering that comes from the sickness for a greater good—possibly for the person's sanctification or as part of a larger plan that is at work.

3. A false value is attributed to the suffering that comes from sickness. The flip side of the previous point is the fact that almost everyone today thinks that the suffering resulting from sickness is God's will and is therefore a good thing. While this is sometimes true, we can assume that God hates sickness and does not want us to be affected by it. Of course, God can work in the sickness for good, but that doesn't mean he wants us to be sick. Again, our default belief should be that God wants the recipient of prayer to get well, while we also acknowledge there may be cases where this principle does not apply.

4. Sin is connected to the sickness. Clearly Jesus taught us, on the one hand, that sickness is not *always* a result of sin (John

9:1–3). On the other hand, he asserted that in some cases, sickness *is* a result of sin (John 5:14). Today science has demonstrated there is a deep body/soul connection such that our health is affected by what we believe and do. Biblical teaching has been verified once again as accurate and true. There are times when the real cause of pain and sickness is an underlying, unconfessed sin or an unbiblical, stress-filled approach to life.

If nothing seems to be happening during a prayer session, it may be quite appropriate to suggest to the recipient that they take a moment, search their conscience, and see if there might be something they're not bringing before the Lord to confess and turn from. This is a delicate issue, and while the person's confession may involve the need to seek reconciliation or to share the confession with a close and safe friend or family member, we who pray for the sick usually have not earned the right to be that intimate with a person. If they want to confess what is going on to you, that's fine. But if the person wants to confess privately, that's fine too.

5. We are not praying specifically enough. Can God answer general, nonspecific prayers? Of course he can—and he does. Yet for three reasons I suggest we should be as specific as possible in our prayers: (1) a specific diagnosis of the problem can provide additional insights that may contribute to healing; (2) a specific diagnosis enhances my role as a co-laborer with God by directing his focus and power on a specific problem, which better fulfills God's purpose of including us in his kingdom work; and (3) if a healing comes that is specific, its ability to serve as a sign to enhance people's faith is increased.

6. There is a faulty diagnosis. Our healing prayer may be ineffective because of a faulty diagnosis of the real problem. This matters for at least two reasons: (1) as I mentioned in the last point, an accurate, specific diagnosis accomplishes several important things as part of God's larger plan to work through our healing prayers; and (2) sickness is a multifaceted thing, and an illness can be due to sin, to demonic action (more on this in chapter 8), to psychological factors, or to an underlying physical problem causing the presenting symptoms. We want to do our best before we pray to work with the Spirit to get as much clarity as possible about what is really going on.

7. There is a refusal to seek medical help. God uses medicine to heal, and medical advances are a gift he has given us to use. Our attitude should always be miraculous prayer *plus* medicine, not one in opposition to the other. Nowhere has the Christian community promoted this false dichotomy between trusting God and using medicine more than in the area of psychiatric advice and the use of medications for anxiety, depression, or other mental health problems. Much harm has been done by the advice to refrain from medical help or psychiatric advice. Many people are shamed for "lacking faith" if they use medication to get well. I have addressed this issue elsewhere if you are interested in learning more. I encourage you to do some reading and thinking if you accept this false dichotomy between medicine and miraculous healing/trust in God, which can be quite damaging to those needing healing and help.[31]

8. Healing does not typically violate natural health practices. If a person has adopted a lifestyle of addiction to food as a source of self-soothing or is many pounds overweight, which has resulted in high blood pressure and heart problems, then praying for their heart condition to be healed may be a request God is unwilling to grant. This isn't meant to condemn anyone, as we all do things, knowingly or unknowingly, that are not good for us.

And while these types of choices do have an impact on our health, if we are ignorant that some habit is harmful, we are, at the very least, not actively rebelling against the way we know God has made us to function. In some cases, we may be doing everything we know to do to guard our health, but there are just some things we're not aware of. Given that we are not intentionally disregarding our knowledge of the truth, nor exhibiting an unwillingness to change with God's help, it seems to me that God is still likely to consider our requests for healing.

However, if we knowingly and deliberately behave in ways that aren't good for us, there may be consequences. It isn't that God is punishing us when he doesn't respond to our petitions for healing. Rather, if he doesn't allow us to suffer the natural consequences of our intentional actions, then for all practical purposes, he is sending the message that it doesn't matter what we do because he will bail us out anyway. Understandably, God simply hasn't set up the world to work this way, though he can manifest his grace at any time he desires.

9. The timing may not be right. For reasons that may be known only to God, now might not be the time God wants to heal the person. In some cases, a person may be instantly healed after the prayer session, while in other cases, the healing may be gradual.

10. God may want to use a different or a larger group of people. Oddly enough, it seems that some people are gifted in healing specific problems, and perhaps God wants to wait until the appropriately gifted person prays. Or another person may benefit more by seeing a healing than the one who prayed and discovered that nothing happened. Furthermore, God may wish to bless more people by a healing than simply those who were currently available.

11. There is demonic interference. In Daniel 10:12–13, an answer to Daniel's prayers was delayed by a fallen angel (called the prince of the Persian kingdom) for twenty-one days. So much more is going on in the unseen world than we can imagine, and there is no question that demonic interference can thwart our prayers or delay an answer. Consequently, when we pray for the sick, we need to take authority over demons as best we can. I'll have more to say on this in chapter 8.

12. A church environment of legalism, lukewarmness, or dubiousness toward healing prayer exists. After my conversion in 1970, for the next thirty-three years I attended what I'd call "Bible churches," a description that broadly refers to churches that emphasize the Word with little or no practical theology of the Holy Spirit's role and power in individual and corporate church life. In these churches, there is almost no training and no expectation that healing prayer works, except for a miracle now and then. Healing prayer is viewed with suspicion, and I take no joy in saying that for all the good such churches do, they tend to be spiritually dead, legalistic, and lukewarm. On the other hand, Spirit-oriented churches—Pentecostal, charismatic, Third Wave churches—can err by becoming doctrinally sloppy, biblically illiterate, and just plain goofy. We all need to work on growing in the areas where we are weak, and there is no room for judgmental finger-pointing on either side. But given the topic we're considering, I simply note that those who attend Word-oriented churches must develop room for practicing the Spirit and the supernatural. The late Clyde Cook, president of Biola University from 1982 to 2007, used to say that even though he had attended Bible churches his whole life, if he ever were to get sick, he would go to a charismatic church for prayer! His perspective is worth pondering.

13. The person does not really want to be healed. Surprising as it may sound, some people, perhaps deep down in the subconscious mind, don't want to be healed. Why? I really don't know, but it isn't hard to guess. Sick people can get a lot of attention. They feel special and cared for, pitied, and not responsible to do the things healthy people have to do. It would be dangerous to assume a person feels this way just because healing prayer did not restore them. But this is a real phenomenon, and it may well be a reason a person does not get healed.

14. Some things remain a divine mystery. Finally, we have to submit to God and trust that he is good, even when we don't have a clue as to why he is not responding to a real need. The toughest thing of all is when it looks like there are a number of good reasons—God will be honored; unbelievers will see God's power at work; the church will be edified; the sickness will be removed—for God to act, and then he is a no-show. These are not the times to offer simplistic platitudes. Still, we must keep in mind how finite and fallen we really are. And it's also good to remember all the wonderful things God has already done.

HOW TO GROW IN FAITH AND EXPECTATION

We can't create faith or increase expectation by trying directly to believe something more strongly than we do. If someone were to offer you money if you would believe that a pink elephant was standing in front of you, you couldn't really believe it, even though you might say you did. But you would be faking it, and you would know it.

Beliefs are not subject to the direct control of the will, so we cannot simply *will* to believe something on the spot. Thankfully, we *can* change our beliefs or their degree of strength indirectly. By study, meditation, risk, practice, willingness to learn from successes and failures, and in similar related ways, we can grow in faith and become more "naturally supernatural."

One of the best ways to grow in our faith is to *increase our exposure to credible miraculous healings and other supernatural phenomena happening today.* This is one of the reasons I've written this book, but there are other ways to grow in our faith as well. Start by reading the narrative portions of Scripture with new eyes, especially the Gospels and the book of Acts. Read the events as though they really happened—because they did! If you have doubts about the historicity of the New Testament documents, read a book selected from the bibliography that solves your doubts. And read the events as though they could happen today to you and your church, because they are happening all over the world.

You can also read credible books that recount miraculous events, including miraculous healings. These books will increase your awareness of the unseen world and the factual nature of current miracles. Again, see the books in the bibliography for suggestions on where to get started. My wife and I read books like this together about five nights a week, and no single practice has enhanced our expectations more than this one. You can also subscribe to the JESUS Film Project email newsletter, which I've mentioned several times already. It comes out once a month and reads like a modern-day continuation of the book of Acts. Credible eyewitness accounts of divine miraculous action pepper its pages. Your heart will be thrilled!

Consider having members of your church's mission ministry report on credible accounts of miracles they have seen or heard about—especially those from any short-term mission trips or from your missionaries. Also, create space in your services for a regular (biweekly or monthly) five-minute testimony of a miracle experienced by a congregant. Be intentional about regularly asking your Christian friends if they have seen or heard of something supernatural occurring. And be intentional about making space for testimonies in your home group or Sunday school class.

You can also *receive training in praying for the sick (and for deliverance)*. Do some research on credible churches in your area that are committed to an emphasis on supernatural ministry, especially healing prayer. Visit those churches, observe what they do, and find good training seminars in your area on these matters. Invite to your home group or Sunday school class a credible, well-known pastor or church leader who is skilled in supernatural ministry, and let them share stories and train your group.

Along with training, I urge you to *practice, practice, practice* (and take risks). Start praying for people. Find others to join you—perhaps in your home group or Sunday school class, or begin a healing prayer time right after the worship service—and just get started. Eventually, we have to take a risk and step out. Remember, we learn through our failures, and if we are teachable, we will grow over time.

This chapter has given us much to think about and do. It's now time to fill our hearts and minds with credible, true accounts of miraculous healings to help us grow more in our faith.

Chapter 6

ENCOURAGING CREDIBLE
TESTIMONY OF CASES OF
MIRACULOUS HEALING

Reginald B. Cherry, MD, owns and operates the R. B. Cherry Clinic in Houston, Texas. For more than twenty-seven years, he has practiced a combination of healing prayer and application of the best modern medical practice. He has treated thousands and thousands of patients and seen and testified to numerous miraculous healings following prayer. Dr. Cherry wrote, "When a supernatural healing occurs, it can be documented and will stand up to medical scrutiny. While we do not have to have scientific evidence that God is a healer, documenting medical healing . . . gives glory to God, and confirmed testimonies . . . give hope to others and instills faith in God as our Healer."[1]

I could not agree more, and in the cases that follow, I hope to grow your gratitude to our loving God and build encouragement and faith within you. I agree with Cherry's point that medical documentation is not needed to justify belief in an alleged divine healing. As I mentioned previously, there are different ways to know or reasonably believe in such healings—such as credible eyewitness testimony—besides employing scientific evidence. In the cases shared in this chapter, I will explain the evidence I have for their credibility. Enjoy, read with your head and heart, and worship when you desire. Be strengthened and encouraged!

CASES I HAVE PERSONALLY VERIFIED

My Own Healing

On February 20, 2005, the Sunday evening service at my church had just ended and I wanted to get home. I was really frustrated. I had been distracted during the entire service, and now I had to decide what I was going to do. In the middle of the afternoon on the previous Thursday, a virus had invaded my chest and throat, and in a period of less than three hours, I went from feeling fine to having the worst case of laryngitis I'd had in thirty-five years (since college). The next day I went to our walk-in clinic and got the bad news. The doctor said this virus was going around, that she had seen several cases in the last few weeks, and that nothing could be done about it. I just had to wait it out. The laryngitis would last at least seven to ten days.

"This can't be," I whispered to her. My main day of teaching at the university was Monday, and I was scheduled for a full day of lecturing. I couldn't afford to cancel classes because I had already hit my limit of canceled classes for the semester. To make matters worse, I was scheduled to deliver a three-hour lecture at a nearby church that Tuesday evening, and I didn't want to let the church down. But there was nothing I could do. The doctor said I wouldn't be able to speak either day, so I needed to make other plans. All weekend long, my throat felt like it had broken glass in it, and I was reduced to whispering. On Sunday evening, I whispered a few greetings to various church friends and even tried to speak normally, but it hurt too much. I just couldn't talk. After the service I planned to head home, contact our department secretary (I didn't have her home phone number), and cancel my classes for Monday. I planned to cancel my lecture at the church the next day.

As I was walking out of the sanctuary, two lay elders intercepted me. "Hey, J. P.," one yelled out. "You can't leave yet. Hope [my wife] just told us you have laryngitis, and we can't let you get outta here without loving on you a bit and praying for your throat!" One elder laid hands on my shoulders and the other placed his hand on my lower throat area and started praying. To be honest, I wasn't listening to a word they said. I had already left the church emotionally, and I wanted to get home to call my secretary. But then something happened. As the two men prayed gently for me, I began to feel heat pour into my throat and chest area from the elder's hand. *After no longer than two or three minutes of prayer, I was completely and irreversibly healed!* I started talking to the elders normally with no pain, no additional effort, and no trace that anything had been wrong. I never had to make that call to my secretary. The laryngitis never returned.

Five Stunning Interviews with Missionaries

A few years ago, I talked to a missionary couple working in Nepal in a very difficult area in which to evangelize. They related that they had recently led a poor Buddhist woman to Christ. Shortly thereafter, this woman's main source of economic hope, a little calf, became deathly ill and lay listlessly in a field near the woman's little shack for a day and a half. As a new Christian just becoming familiar with the miracles of Jesus in the Gospels, she gathered several of her Buddhist friends around the calf and announced that she was going to ask Jesus to heal it. And he did! Instantly the calf came to its feet in full health, and her Buddhist friends became Christians!

In 2006, I spoke at a Christian education conference. During lunch the first day, I spoke with an American teacher who taught in Brazil with the Association of Christian Schools International. He told me that two of his missionary friends had recently been called into a village to pray for a desperately sick little boy with a softball-sized hernia protruding from his abdomen. They laid hands on the boy and prayed, and before their very eyes, the hernia disappeared and the boy was healed. This event was not tied to evangelism. It was just an act of God's love for a family in need.

Not long after that, on a Sunday at church I met a missionary to the Congo who was home on furlough. He told me that he and his colleagues have seen numerous miraculous healings in recent months and also said that supernatural prophetic words have been of great help to the local believers. In addition, he testified to seeing demonic deliverances in significant numbers. Later that very week, I had lunch with a world-renowned American New Testament scholar. He had just taught a course for some twenty missionaries, and he had heard story after story about the display of the supernatural power of the kingdom from these missionaries. One man told him that for several years, every one of the many conversions to Christ he had witnessed came by way of the Lord having spoken or appeared to the person in a dream or vision.

In the summer of 2007, my wife and I attended a small gathering where we heard reports from a missionary couple who had returned after several years in China. I interacted with the husband, who had a PhD in chemistry from UC Berkeley but later decided to change careers and become a missionary. When I asked if he had witnessed any miraculous healings, he replied that he had seen so many medically inexplicable healings in the underground Chinese church that he didn't even know where to start. According to him, miracles were *the* main way the church there was expanding. He also referred me to a related newspaper article published a year or so before our conversation, and I tracked it down.

The Washington Times is hardly a conservative evangelical publication. Yet in 2005, they featured a story on the explosion of Christianity in China.[2] According to the article, the underground church alone contained at least 100 million believers compared to 70 million members of the Communist Party. In China, Christianity is a social revolution of staggering proportions. But *why* is Christianity growing this way? Here's the answer from the article: "One of the driving forces of Christianity's growth in China has been its association with healing powers, particularly in rural areas where basic health services are lacking." To illustrate this, the article cites the case of a young Christian woman who had contracted a virus doctors had never seen before. She was on a ventilator and everyone had lost hope for her recovery. But after being prayed for, she was healed and experienced a full recovery. As a result, "now her family [all Buddhists] follows Christ, too."[3]

A fifth missionary conversation happened in August 2005. Hope and I were visiting our dear friends Jim and Jeanie Duncan, who lived in Maryland at the time. During the visit, they introduced us to a missionary couple they knew very well—Joe and Kay Harding who were affiliated with the missionary agency SIM in Ethiopia. Joe lived in Ethiopia for ten years as a child and fifteen years with SIM, and after moving back to the States, he traveled to Ethiopia six or seven times a year during the next eighteen years. I asked Joe if he had seen any clear-cut miracles in their work, and whenever I ask a missionary that question, I usually get a "How long do you have?" Along with Kay, Joe told us a very encouraging story. On May 16, 2020, Joe sent me the following email to verify what he had told us in 2005:

> A village not far from where we lived was 100 percent Muslim, and a mosque was located right next to the home of a young man and his very sick grandmother. Teaching about Christianity was completely forbidden, so SIM Sports Friends leaders came up with a strategy: using soccer to build relationships and provide opportunities for the youth to consider Jesus. SIM Sports Friends started to train

Ethiopian soccer coaches who loved Jesus in 2002 to reach out to boys and girls and their families to coach and play soccer in the villages and towns, trusting God would use this strategy to open a door for the gospel where Christ is least known.

One day after practice, a young man who had been trained by Sports Friends as a coach approached me to inform me that he had to get home quickly. The young man's grandmother (who had lived with his family for a good while and had been sick for some time) was feeling unwell that day. Inquiring about the grandmother, I learned that she had been bedridden for many months, had a distended stomach, and was growing weaker by the day. I asked if I could follow the young coach home and pray for his grandmother. This was risky, but the young soccer coach was happy that these followers of Jesus wanted to visit his grandmother.

After I received permission to pray for her, I laid hands on his grandmother's stomach and prayed for her healing. Before our very eyes, her stomach shrank to normal, and the woman got out of bed for the first time in months. She had been completely healed. As a result, word began to spread and soon her family and many friends came to believe in Jesus Christ. The mosque next to their home soon became a place to worship Jesus. It was amazing to see and hear the grandmother share with joy her testimony of healing.

The Healing of a Young Man Legally Blind

For several years, I have traveled every September to a Christian study center in Pine Mountain, Georgia, called Impact 360 Institute, where I lecture for a few days. Ed Bort is a former graduate student of mine, a longtime close friend, and one of the leaders of the institute. Here in Ed's own words is what happened one year after I left:

In September 2011, Dr. Moreland was invited to our campus to teach about competing worldviews. The plan was simple. The students had read his book *Kingdom Triangle* and had written an essay about what they read. Now they had the opportunity to learn from the author. Dr. Moreland taught about the existence of God and how theism better explains the world than other competing worldviews. He also taught about the importance of loving God with our minds and the importance of the renovation of the soul, and on the third day he taught the students about the importance of relying on God's supernatural power.

When Dr. Moreland arrived, the mood on campus was one of anticipation and anxiety. The students were excited but intimidated to learn from him. Some of the students expressed doubts about their academic ability and some confessed that they were not sure that God really existed. A small group shared with me that their doubts ran so deep that if they didn't see God during their time with us, they were planning to leave Christianity and not look back. I was thrilled that these students were drawn to what was true and that they were not simply going to follow a religious system blindly. What the students didn't know was that God was planning to move in a significant way that would open their minds and their eyes to the reality of his existence and demonstrate his care for them as human beings.

Elise came to our program. She was a very thoughtful and sweet young woman who had a servant heart and a sharp mind. She was always asking for ways she could help and serve the staff and the other students. Elise is one of those students who stands out, but not for the typical reasons. She wasn't extroverted and flashy with a charismatic personality. Elise was a very intelligent young woman. And she was also born with only one hand. But this disability was not something that fazed Elise. She did everything the other students did and rarely even considered that she only had one hand. Other students would ask her about it, and I was always impressed by her gentle response and how she normalized the situation. It just wasn't a big deal to her. She was more focused on caring for others.

David arrived on campus with a bright mind, full of excitement for the year. He was very sociable and quick to get to know other students. He was more extroverted than Elise and was often seen interacting with other students, either joking around or deep in conversation. I fondly remember many wonderful conversations with David about a host of topics. David disclosed in his application that he was legally blind in one eye. Since birth, he had only been able to faintly distinguish dark from light. He wore glasses and had learned several ways to overcome his disability. Most people would never know he could only see clearly out of one eye. During that first week, as the students and staff were getting to know one another, David shared about his disability. All of this was leading us up to the week that Dr. Moreland came to campus.

As Dr. Moreland began teaching on the importance of relying on God's supernatural power, the students listened in amazement. He relayed accounts of angels, of people being healed of cancer, and many other miraculous events. As the students listened, some were in awe and rejoicing at what the Lord was doing in the world. The more analytical ones listened with a quizzical look on their faces. Could this actually be true? The class was mixed. Elise was one of the students who was fine thinking that God does small miracles today. She had experienced God doing small things like giving her some fatherly guidance, but she remained very skeptical about God doing bigger miracles in the present, like healing.

She was one of the students who listened politely but was not convinced that God still moves in the more miraculous ways that Dr. Moreland was describing.

After finishing his time interacting with the students on a Saturday morning, I drove Dr. Moreland back to the airport. At the very same time we were driving there, Elise began to pray. She was not convinced that God would still heal in these "big" ways, but she was also wrestling with things Dr. Moreland had shared with the class. So she took a risk and began to pray for a few of the students to see if God would act. One of the students she began praying for was David. She didn't tell anyone she was praying. She just started praying in some of the ways she had been taught.

The next day, Sunday, was a time for the students to attend church, to rest, and, for many of them, to catch up on reading for the week. That afternoon, David was in his room reading. After some time had passed, he grew tired of reading and set his book down. He removed his glasses and rubbed his eyes. With his glasses still off, he glanced over to a whiteboard that was in his room. On the whiteboard were various dry-erase markers of different colors. As David was preparing to go back to his reading, he put his glasses back on and then realized something significant. He was now able to see the colors of the various markers. But wait! How could this be? He was shocked. David began testing his vision, holding one hand over one eye and then the other—the eye in which he was legally blind—just as if he was in the office of an ophthalmologist reporting what he could see. When his roommates came into the room, he had them test him further by holding up one marker at a time for David to guess the color with the eye that had been legally blind. They were all amazed and began celebrating that David's sight was vastly and instantaneously improved. David and his roommates were excited to share this wonderful news with the rest of the students that evening when the student body gathered to talk through the next week.

At the gathering, one of David's new friends was so excited that he just started telling everyone the story. The students were excited, celebrating what the Lord had done. They joined in the fun of testing David's sight to see for themselves if he really could see the colors. In all of the commotion and excitement, Elise was incredibly overwhelmed and quickly left the room in tears to process what had just happened. One of the other women on campus went out to see how she was doing. This was the moment that all of the pieces began to come together. Elise came back into the room with all of the students and shared that since she had doubts that God still healed in these big ways, she decided to take a risk. She explained that she was praying the day before that God would heal David's eye. In that moment the students and staff realized that what happened was even greater than God healing David's eye. God had also opened Elise's eyes to see that he not only was aware of David's situation but that he also heard her prayers. He was communicating that he saw her too, and he wanted to demonstrate that he cared not only for David's sight but that Elise would see her loving heavenly Father in the correct light now: that God exists, he hears, he cares, and he still moves in big ways.

I have in my file independent emails from David and from Elise. Each of them tells the story from their own viewpoint, and both of them confirm Ed's account.

A Healing at Our Church of a Man with Near Total Blindness
In late April 2005, a group from our church traveled to Fresno, California, to teach at a healing prayer seminar and to

pray for the sick. Three friends of mine—Brian Slezak, Ken Slezak, and Stan Frisbee—and another person I've met—Ken Long (who works in an ophthalmologist's office fitting glasses and contact lenses and performing eye exams)—formed a prayer team and began to pray for people in need of healing at the home of John and Chris Wojdylak.

Among those they prayed for was a Vietnam veteran whose left eye had been completely blinded in the war. He had jumped in front of his commanding officer to protect him when a flash grenade went off. The shell had flash-fried his left retina. Two members reported that his eye did not move and had a white film covering it. After laying hands on him, they prayed for the eye's healing for about twenty minutes. Suddenly, the man started to freak out. His damaged eye was now completely restored.

As confirmation, Long tested the eye and acknowledged its complete healing. Team members told me they could tell he was healed since the eye moved and looked alive and normal. As one member put it, "His wife couldn't stop crying and hugging and thanking us." And Ken Long frankly acknowledged that "it is impossible for that type of healing to occur that quickly with that type of eye damage."

A Prophetic Healing of My Graduate Student

Not long ago, I met with a graduate student named Nathan shortly after class. While sharing with me about God's merciful healing, tears came to his eyes, and as I listened in amazement, my eyes filled with tears as well. At age thirteen, Nathan was diagnosed with GERD (gastroesophageal reflux disease), in which the valve between his esophagus and stomach wasn't working properly. He'd wake up every night gasping for breath and choking. He couldn't breathe because of the stomach acid that gathered in his chest and the severe pain it caused. As a result, Nathan developed insomnia and had to sleep sitting up. He said he hadn't slept through the night one single time for nine years. In 2002, Nathan got married, and his wife urged him to go to a doctor to investigate surgery. When he did, he was told he would need a series of five surgeries and would be on medication for the rest of his life.

The next day, Nathan and his wife went to a small group Bible study they regularly attended. That evening, a missionary couple from Thailand shared about their ministry, a ministry that included miraculous healings. No one at the Bible study knew of Nathan's illness. Before leaving for the study, Nathan had told his wife he was skeptical about the missionary couple, even though he had no good reason for his misgivings. However, in spite of his doubts, he went to the study that night, and something incredible and shocking took place. In Nathan's own words, "During the Bible study, out of the blue, the speaker stopped praying for another person, turned, and said, 'Someone in the room is suffering from gastroesophageal reflux disease.' This man had never met me, nor could he have known the disease's name." Nathan then told me how the missionary described a very painful event that had happened between the person with GERD (Nathan had not yet identified himself as the person) and his father when he had been diagnosed with the disease as a young boy. All of the details shared were unknown to anyone else, including Nathan's wife, and were accurately described.

Nathan raised his hand to identify himself as the person with GERD. When he did so, the missionary came to him, laid hands on him, and prayed for his healing. As emotion welled up inside him, Nathan relayed to me that at that very moment he was instantly and completely healed. From that night until the present time of writing (about three full years), Nathan has never had an incident and has slept through every night since that Bible study, and his doctor verified his healing shortly after the prayer meeting. I met Nathan's wife a few weeks ago at a student gathering and pulled her aside to ask about the incident. She confirmed every detail of the story to me.

God Is an Excellent Dentist

Tim Bayless is a former graduate student of mine who, along with his wife, Karen, has been a dear, close friend for many years. Tim is intelligent and well-educated—a no-nonsense kind of guy, the exact opposite of gullible. Recently, Tim sent me a story told to him by his boss—Tim Newell—which Bayless personally verified. Mr. Newell was kind enough to email me the account. Subsequently, I called him and was satisfied with its veracity. Here in his own words is Newell's account (edited for length):

> I was sitting in church on a Sunday night in the early spring of 1980. A guest evangelist was starting a few weeks of evangelistic meetings. I remember that her name was Sister Petri. She had a unique ministry gift of praying for people with dental problems, which seemed very strange to me, and with all that I had been reading and listening to at that time, I found myself being extremely skeptical.
>
> She had started her sermon and then abruptly stopped, saying, "There is someone back in that section of the sanctuary," pointing to the section I was sitting in, "who is questioning, 'Is this whole thing about divine healing really for today? Does God still heal?' God wants you to know that he hears you and loves you so much that he is going to answer that question once and for all. Although you did not come here tonight asking God to heal your teeth, in a few minutes you're going to feel a drilling sensation in your mouth and teeth like you're sitting in a dentist chair getting a cavity filled. God is going to remove a cavity and give you a new filling in its place." She went on to say, "When you feel that, I want you to go to the restroom and check, and you will find

a new filling in your mouth. When you do, come back and testify to what God did for you." Then she went on with her sermon. I immediately began laughing to myself, thinking, *What a joke! Now God is supposed to be a dentist.* At this point, I was more than skeptical.

And then, right there in my state of disbelief sitting there in the church sanctuary, and much to my surprise, I began to feel that drilling sensation in *my* mouth. I began to feel a sensation like I was sitting in a dentist chair getting a cavity drilled out. I said to myself, *No way! It's me, it was me she was talking about.* I immediately got up and went to the restroom to look in the mirror. What I saw blew me away. I saw not one but two new silver fillings in my mouth. Each of my rearmost molars on each side had a new filling that was not there before. I was overwhelmed. I went back into the sanctuary to testify to a truly divine and supernatural miracle that had just happened.

Much of the rest of what happened that night is a blur. But from that day forward, I have never had a doubt that our amazing, miracle-working God still performs miracles today. I have seen a number of undeniable miracles of healing in others, but the miracle of how God filled cavities in *my own mouth* definitely solved the dilemma I was having and the theological debate of whether our God still heals today.

About fifteen years after this miraculous healing event in my life, I needed to have dental work done on a tooth that got cracked off and needed a root canal. The dentist came back into the room after taking full-mouth X-rays of my teeth and inquired about the fillings in my back teeth. He was a teaching dentist, and he brought two dental students into the room with him. Putting the X-rays on the view box, he commented to them about the amazing work that the dentist who filled those teeth had done. He asked me to sign something, giving him permission to use the X-rays in a dental textbook he was writing. When I explained where and how they had happened, he responded with something like, "Well, I'm not sure what to say about that, but whoever did them did fine work." I am grateful that in the spring of 1980, God settled the question forever in my mind: God still does supernatural miracles today.

So far, every account I've shared is one that I, someone I know, or someone I personally interviewed experienced firsthand (except for the account in the *Washington Times*). These healings were experienced by ordinary folks in regular church or missionary activities. There are no superstars here! These things can happen today to and through you and your close friends.

FOUR MORE STAGGERING CREDIBLE ACCOUNTS

The four accounts to follow are among my very favorites due to my high confidence in their veracity and the virtually indisputable fact that these are miracles performed by the biblical God. Before you read them, may I suggest that you stop for a moment, express worship to God, and prepare your heart and mind to receive edification and courage in what you read.

Two Accounts from the JESUS Film Project

Perhaps the greatest, most impactful tool for the spreading of the gospel worldwide is the *Jesus* film. Film crews regularly put their lives at risk and enter extremely dangerous, remote places where they share the film—a retelling of the gospel of Luke—with people who know nothing about Jesus or have a distorted view of him as a result of their inherited religion. The crew members receive inadequate compensation, but they are radical disciples who regularly live, eat, and sleep in conditions that make me marvel at their integrity and commitment to Jesus. The entire organization is one of the most respected and most trusted in all of evangelicalism. The JESUS Film Project email newsletter, published monthly, is a highly reliable report of what numerous film crews from around the world are witnessing firsthand. Here are two of many stories that will thrill your heart.

The first is an April 1998 report from Paul Eshleman, former director of the JESUS Film Project:

> In the state of Bihar, India, there is a notoriously anti-Christian tribe called the Malto. When a crew with Campus Crusade's *Jesus* film attempted to schedule a showing there in 1998, they were strongly rebuffed. A few days later, a 16-year-old Malto girl died. But that evening, just as her parents were about to bury her, she came back to life. As an awed crowd gathered around her, she told them that the God of the film crew had sent her back for several days "to tell as many people as I can that He is real."
>
> The girl and her mother went searching, and the next day, they found the crew in a nearby village and invited them back for a showing. For seven days she told her story in every village they could get to, drawing large crowds for the film. Hundreds of people became Christians and started churches.
>
> After seven days the girl still looked fine, but she collapsed and died once again.[4]

Here is another report about a woman called "Paralyzed Anna." (In the article, there is a picture of her, bedridden, before attending the film.)

> They called her "Paralyzed Anna." She lived in a country quite hostile to the gospel. Anna could not walk, being

bedridden for three years. When Anna was told that a team of people was coming to her village to show a film in her language, she wanted very much to attend. So Anna's friends lifted her into a wooden cart and wheeled her to where the film team was setting up their screen and projector. Lying on her "bed of wood," Anna became transfixed by all she saw and heard. She watched Jesus perform miracles, give sight to the blind, heal diseases, and speak with love and divine authority. She was so intrigued.

It was then that Anna began to sense something strange . . . a sensation moving through her disabled body. Anna cried out to Jesus: "If You are God, heal me!" The film continued . . . ended . . . the invitation was given. The church-planting film team stayed to answer questions, pray for a few new believers (it was a restricted area where people are fearful of reprisals), and set up for follow-up. Everyone started home.

As they walked, there was the cart. But where was Anna? Everyone was stunned. She was in the departing crowd alright, but walking! The team went with Anna to her home and again explained the gospel. In restricted nations, *it can take multiple exposures to break through the misconceptions and spiritual darkness.* Anna believed. Upon witnessing this great miracle, her husband also became a follower of Jesus and gave up his liquor business in the community.

Anna began to share her testimony with family and friends, proclaiming all that God had done for her. A pastor who learned of her story decided he would use the *Jesus* film in their area. At last count, through the film, as well as the testimony of "Paralyzed Anna," five thousand people have been baptized with seventy churches planted—*where there had been none . . . in a restricted country.*[5]

The Averting of an Announced Suicide and Murder on Live Television

Tom Doyle attended Biola University as an undergraduate and completed a graduate degree at Dallas Theological Seminary. Tom was a pastor for twenty years, and along with his wife, JoAnn, he served as a missionary to Muslims in the Middle East for twelve years and now lives in the United States. He is an official tour guide for Israel, has written seven books, and has appeared on several television (such as FOX News) and radio (such as Focus on the Family) programs. Since 2001, he has worked with e3 Partners, a ministry focused on Muslim evangelism and church planting, as vice president and Middle East director.

In preparation for writing what follows, I contacted two leading figures in the world of missions, one who works exclusively in Muslim evangelism and discipleship, and both vouched enthusiastically for his credibility. One said to me, "Tom and JoAnn are awesome. Totally the real deal." On May 14, 2020, I contacted Tom and could immediately sense his warm, vibrant radiance for Jesus. I queried him about the account below, and he assured me it was completely true, without exaggeration.[6]

Hormoz Shariat (nicknamed "the Billy Graham of Iran") was born into a Muslim family in Iran and came to the United States in 1979 after the Islamic Revolution. He received a PhD from the University of Southern California and became a Christian during his graduate studies. In 2001, he founded Iran Alive Ministries, which utilizes satellite TV to reach millions of Muslims in Iran and the Middle East. His live daily program continues to this day, and it has seven to nine million daily viewers in Iran (10 percent of the population).

During the program, Hormoz receives live call-ins and answers their questions. Many of the calls are hateful, and in

2002, a woman he calls "Dina" called the show for her first time and announced, "You Christians are going to hell!" She thought Christianity was a fairy tale and was an extremely committed, radical Muslim. She was a ranking official in Iran's Female Secret Police (FSP), embraced strict Sharia law, and hunted down and tortured women who violated Sharia, even those who let as much as a single strand of hair slip out from under their hijab (Sharia violators received up to eighty lashes, along with beatings). Dina especially loved capturing Christians, imprisoning them, and watching them be tortured.

Dina regularly called Hormoz's show to condemn his program and express her hatred for Christians. However, Dina was also a single woman living with her dying, cancer-invaded, bedridden mother. One night, Dina was filled with emptiness and hopelessness after observing the corruption of Muslim leaders, and she made a dramatic announcement on the live program: "We are going to commit suicide right now, on your program."

This was no idle threat. Hermoz responded, "Since you're going to kill yourself anyway, why don't you give Jesus a week? If He doesn't answer a single prayer for you or do anything in your life in seven days, then go ahead and kill yourself. That's what you were going to do anyway. You have nothing to lose . . . But I'm sure you are afraid to try this—aren't you, Dina?"

Dina retorted, "I'm not afraid of anything you dare me to do! The Christian God is a false God. He is incapable of giving me anything I pray for, because He is not there! Only Allah can answer prayers." Hormoz chuckled. "I knew you were afraid." Irritated, Dina shot back, "Okay, then. I know you're just playing with me, but I accept your foolish challenge. What do I do for a week? Whatever it is will be a waste of time. I'll wait a week, and then come back and kill myself on your program—*if* you are brave enough to take my next call." Hormoz agreed on one condition: Dina was to pray daily and ask Jesus to be her Savior. Dina laughed at the suggestion but agreed to do it out of spite.

Early in the morning on the fifth day, Dina was in her room when she heard footsteps. She feared it was an intruder. After all, it couldn't be her mother because she couldn't walk by herself. Her mother's agony had been unbearable for months. Yet suddenly her mother peeked through the door with a peaceful smile on her face and said, "It's just me, Dina." Shocked, Dina asked how she had gotten out of bed. Her mother responded, "Dina, last night after you turned off my light, I thought, *I will die tonight.* It frightened me, so I wondered which imam I should pray to one last time. Then I saw His face. Right there in my room." Dina asked, "Which one was it, Mother?" "Dina," her mother replied, "it wasn't an imam. It was . . . Jesus."

Dina was appalled and grateful at the same time. Her mother continued, "I woke up a few minutes ago and realized I felt no pain. Not even a little. All of it was gone . . . Not only that, I could move comfortably and felt so peaceful that I decided to try to stand up. Dina, I could walk! I can hardly say it, but . . . I feel well again."

Dina melted in tears. She had told no one, not even her mother, about the prayer. Later, when Hormoz saw Dina's name on the screen as the next caller, his eyes widened, having no idea what was going to happen. Once her call was accepted on live television, Dina shared this: "Hormoz, last week I repeated the words you told me to say, but I didn't take them seriously . . . But God did. Tonight, my mother is with me again. She's *standing* here beside me! . . . I didn't want Jesus to be the answer . . . As for my mother, she's well, Hormoz. And so am I! Jesus is everything you promised."

Dina's mother remains healed to this day, and Dina resigned inconspicuously from the morality police, and as of this writing (2020), along with her husband (another Muslim convert to Christianity), she has been a radical disciple who discreetly shares the gospel. On May 16, 2020, I had a phone conversation with Hormoz Shariat. He said that Dina "has the spirit of a general," that she and her husband have planted hundreds of churches in many cities of Iran, and that they lead the largest network of underground churches in the country.

Hermoz told me that if Dina were caught, she knows she would be raped and executed, but as he emphasized, ever since her conversion, she would gladly give her life for Jesus. According to Hermoz, if you google "Padina's story," you'll find an account of her conversion on video.[7] Also, Voice of the Martyrs Radio has an interview with Dina herself about her story (this can be found online) and a film of about two hours online titled *Sheep among Wolves Volume II*, which tells the whole story in detail.[8]

There is a sequel to this story. A good while later, Tom Doyle and Hormoz traveled together to the Middle East, and while at a designated restaurant packed with Iranian believers, Hormoz introduced Tom to Dina and her mother. They both were filled with joy and loved the fellowship they enjoyed with these other believers.

One of the Most Amazing Healings I Have Ever Heard

Hope and I first came across the story of Barb Cummiskey (now Barb Cummiskey Snyder) while reading *Physicians' Untold Stories*, written by Scott J. Kolbaba, MD, and other physicians.[9] Each of the book's twenty-six chapters was written by a medical doctor about a miracle they witnessed in their practice. Barb's story is told by Thomas Marshall, MD, who had cared for her for over ten years, along with a number of other physicians. In what follows, we will read of the account as mentioned by world-renowned research scholar Craig Keener in an interview with Lee Strobel.[10]

I know Craig Keener personally and contacted him to ask about the case. On May 7, 2020, he emailed me back to say that since the healing took place in 1981, he would not expect to have full medical documentation (though I'm sure it was thoroughly documented by Dr. Marshall in Barb's medical records), but he did have some limited medical records about the case. More importantly, he had corresponded with two of her doctors and had interviewed Barb herself. Moreover, according to Keener, there are numerous independent witnesses to her condition and years of medical records. All of this confirms in detail my summary account that follows.[11] One of her doctors, Harold Adolph, a board-certified surgeon who performed twenty-five thousand operations in his career, acknowledged, "Barbara was one of the most helplessly ill patients I ever saw."[12]

In the late 1960s, at the age of fifteen, Barbara contracted progressive multiple sclerosis, a shocking diagnosis for someone so young, and she began a steady process of deterioration. In the early 1970s, she had two respiratory arrests, since the muscles she used for breathing were affected. Both arrests required emergency hospitalization. Shortly thereafter, she became unable to clear her secretions, and given the fact that her diaphragm was now paralyzed, Barbara was recurrently in the hospital for pneumonia and asthma. To make matters worse, she lost complete control of her urination and bowel functions. She had a permanent catheter placed in her bladder and an ileostomy created in her abdomen with a bag attached for her bowels.

Due to progressive loss of breathing capability, Barbara was referred to the Mayo Clinic in 1978 for a second opinion. At the time, she required continuous oxygen, and her muscles and joints were contracted and deformed due to inactivity. Unfortunately, Mayo agreed with the previous diagnosis of her condition and had no recommendations to help her.

As her condition continued to worsen, Barbara lost most of her vision and became legally blind (she saw objects only as gray shadows), to the point where she could no longer read. She could hardly move out of her bed. In 1980, she received a tracheostomy (a hole in her neck in which a breathing tube connected to oxygen was inserted to help her with her chronic shortness of breath). By this time, she was confined to bed; her body had shriveled into a permanent fetal position; and she had a feeding tube (she could no longer swallow), in addition to the tracheostomy, the catheter, and the ilium (the lowest part of the small intestine) sitting outside her abdomen wall, connected to an external pouch.

According to Dr. Marshall, "Her hands were so permanently flexed that her fingers nearly touched her wrists." By 1981, Barb had been unable to walk for seven years. Her feet were locked in a downward position. A while later, Dr. Marshall sat down with Barbara and her family to explain that she did not have long to live.

On Sunday, June 7, 1981, Barbara's aunt Ruthie came over to the house, and in the early afternoon, two of Barbara's girlfriends paid Barbara a visit. Suddenly, with only her two girlfriends in the room, Barbara heard a man's voice from behind her say, "My child, get up and walk!" Barbara informed her friends, "I don't know what you are going to think about this, but God just told me to get up and walk. I know he really did. Run and get my family. I want them here with us."

Before her parents got into the room, Barbara felt compelled to do exactly what she was told, so immediately, as Dr. Marshall told it, "she literally jumped out of bed and removed her oxygen." She was standing on legs that had not supported her for years. If fact, her leg muscles had been atrophied. And guess what! Her vision had been completely restored, her muscle and joint contractions were gone, and she could easily move her hands and feet.

As Barbara walked out of her room, she first saw her mother, who stooped down, felt her legs, which were distorted in shape and very thin due to atrophy, and cried out, "You have muscles again!" As everyone testified, muscle tissue had grown back instantly! After hugging Barb, her father took her for a waltz around the living room. As Dr. Marshall reported, the distressed occupational therapist attempted to restart Barb's oxygen, but when she saw what was taking place before her very eyes, she said, "This contradicts everything I ever learned in school."

But things get even more exciting! For years, her church friends at Wheaton Wesleyan Church had been praying for Barb faithfully. So on the day of her healing, Barb and her family went to the Sunday evening service. When she and her parents arrived, Barb "bounded up the front stairs," waited in the back until Pastor Bailie asked for announcements, and casually strolled down the center aisle to the front of the church. When parishioners realized who it was, they started clapping and broke out in song. Everyone had tears running down their faces. The rest of the service consisted of Barb's sharing of her story with the congregation.

The next day, Barb and her family went to see Dr. Marshall, who acknowledged:

> The greatest surprise was when I saw her in the hallway of our office, walking toward me. I thought I was seeing an apparition! Here was my patient who was not expected to live another week, totally cured.

I stopped all of her medication and took out her bladder catheter, but she wasn't quite ready to have the tracheostomy tube removed until another visit. No one had ever seen anything like this before. That afternoon, we sent Barb for a chest X-ray. Her lungs were now perfectly normal, with the collapsed lung totally expanded with no infiltrate or other abnormality that had existed before.

I have never witnessed anything like this before or since and consider it a rare privilege to observe the Hand of God performing a true miracle. Barb has gone on to live a normal life in every way. She subsequently married a minister and feels her calling in life is to serve others, which is what she did after her life was miraculously preserved by her Creator."[13]

And Barbara's other doctor, Dr. Adolph, flatly stated, "Both Barbara and I knew who had healed her."[14]

WHAT DO WE MAKE OF THESE ACCOUNTS?

I want to acknowledge that there are many, many times when God does not respond to our prayers or needs and bring healing. Moreover, there are times he does not heal, even though from our perspective it seems like the *perfect* occasion for God to show up and heal someone. Once word of that healing would spread, God would undoubtedly receive great honor, people would be drawn to the gospel, believers would be encouraged in their faith, and suffering and pain would be alleviated. Admittedly, these instances are head-scratchers.

Nevertheless, there are two encouraging lessons we can draw from this chapter. First, what is recorded here confirms that the

Christian God is real, and it is beyond reasonable doubt that he heals the sick today. And second, it means there are no completely lost, hopeless cases—no matter what the situation or how long we have prayed about it. So let's keep praying as we sense the need, and cry out with Jeremiah: "Heal me, LORD, and I will be healed; save me and I will be saved, for You are my praise" (Jeremiah 17:14 NASB).

Chapter 7

HEARING THE SUPERNATURAL
VOICE OF GOD

In a well-known quote, comedian Lily Tomlin gets to the heart of the matter: "Why is it that when we talk to God we're said to be praying but when God talks to us, we're schizophrenic?"[1] In the entertainment industry or the media, people who "hear from God" are almost always depicted as hucksters, deranged lunatics, or murderers. Even some Christians believe that God does not speak outside of his revelation in Scripture any longer. Yet the vast majority of Bible-believing Christians around the world do believe that, in addition to the Bible, God has specifically spoken to or guided them in one way or another.[2]

FOUR INITIAL CONSIDERATIONS

In this chapter, I will clarify the nature of how God speaks and give examples of six ways that God speaks directly to individuals or groups today (for example, church leaders). My purpose is not to defend each of these modes of divine communication, nor is this list intended to be exhaustive. Rather, I will give a brief perspective on each and share some real-life examples to build your faith in these supernatural interventions and enable you to seek God's voice more wisely and regularly. Before we dive into these examples, however, let's look at a few principles to guide us on our journey.

First, the inspired, inerrant Word of God—the Bible—is the ultimate standard for any alleged word from God. It provides us with the ultimate grounds for theology, doctrine, biblical ethics, and other matters on which it speaks. One way to learn how to recognize God's speaking is to read, study, and sit under the teaching of the Bible. Claims outside the Bible can reinforce Scripture, address topics not explicitly or implicitly in Scripture, or possibly contradict or in some other way undermine biblical teaching. Claims in this third category—claims that undermine or contradict Scripture—are to be rejected and argued against. Those in the first—those that reinforce Scripture—are to be accepted with a grateful heart. And we are free to accept or reject those in the second category, depending on the evidence for them. All alleged cases of extrabiblical divine speech or guidance should be handled in this way.

Second, there are a number of reasons God speaks to us personally. God speaks to us to sustain an intimate, conversational relationship with us (Isaiah 58:9–11). He may speak to correct wrong thinking or actions (Philippians 3:15) or to apply the words of Scripture to our specific life situations (1 Corinthians 2:13–14). He also speaks to provide encouragement and edification (1 Corinthians 14:3) and to give us needed guidance (Psalm 143:10; John 10:3–4, 16, 27).

Regarding the issue of guidance, while I know I may be wrong about this, I am among those who believe that sometimes God has specific things he wants us to do and sometimes he doesn't. Scripture and church history are full of examples in which God guided or spoke to someone about a specific thing he wanted that person to do. Yet when the prophet Nathan approached King David, rather than giving him direction from the Lord, Nathan said, "Whatever you have in mind, go ahead and do it, for the LORD is with you." (2 Samuel 7:3).[3] In other words, there are times when God wants to know what *we* want to do, and he promises to back us up. After all, we exist to make real choices that really matter.

Third, we should be aware of two objections to the reality of divine, extrabiblical communication. The first objection is sometimes phrased this way: "When God speaks, he doesn't whisper or speak unclearly." These objectors point to the fact that much of alleged extrabiblical divine communication comes in the form of ambiguous impressions or thoughts that can be interpreted in a variety of ways. And these impressions do not measure up to the perspicuous clarity we find in the way God speaks to us in the Bible, and so they should be rejected on that basis. In response, we should point out that many cases of God's speaking outside Scripture are crystal clear, so the objection is simply mistaken if raised against all examples of hearing God. In addition, the Bible does include some instances where God spoke unclearly to people.

The classic case involves the boy Samuel (1 Samuel 3), who did not understand or even clearly recognize that God was speaking to him until he finally received instructions from a wiser and more experienced mentor. There is also the example of the "gentle whisper" spoken to Elijah (1 Kings 19:12). The point of this passage seems to be that a standard way God speaks to people is not to bowl them over but rather to speak in such a way that someone must want to hear and listen carefully or they will miss what God is saying.

In the Old Testament we also read about "the company of the prophets" (1 Samuel 19:20 ESV, for example), or what some have called "the school of the prophets." And what do you think they were studying together? Well, among other things, they were learning how to prophesy. And to do that, one must learn to hear what God is saying. If God's speech is obvious and clear, why does one need training to discern what God is saying?

Finally, the Bible itself fails to live up to this extremely high standard. While there are clear texts in Scripture, many passages also have various different interpretations. Even though only one can be correct, in cases like these, different interpretations all do justice to the text and it is unclear as to which one is the truth. Indeed, God has allowed his children to differ on what books should be in the Bible in the first place. I accept the Protestant canon, but there are hundreds of millions of Catholic believers who adopt a different canon. If there is a dispute about the canon of Scripture, surely there can be ambiguity in some cases as to whether an alleged word from God is in fact such a word.

I want to make a crucial application of this last point. Take any belief whatsoever, say, the belief that the state capital of Missouri is Columbia. There are three rational perspectives one can take about this belief. One can believe, disbelieve, or be fifty-fifty about it. It follows that we believe something if we are 51 to 100 percent certain—perhaps mistakenly; after all, we all have false beliefs—it is true. It also follows that the strength of a belief can vary. At an early stage in my Christian life, I was 55 percent sure that God answered prayer. I believed it, but not very strongly. As time went on, my confidence in this belief rose to 90 percent. And for many passages of the Bible I have what I believe is a correct interpretation of the passage, but I may be 55 percent, 60 percent, or 95 percent sure I am right.

The same is true of alleged cases of God speaking to someone. We don't have to be 100 percent certain God was the one speaking before we should accept that he was. If we are, for example, 70 percent certain we heard from the Lord, that's not a bad percentage. Of course, the less certain one is about a biblical interpretation or a case of divine speaking, the less strongly we should act on our belief. Still, if we are 51 to 100 percent certain, then we *do* believe the topic under consideration. Of course, just as we can be wrong in interpreting Scripture, so we can be wrong about hearing God. But so what? Just because we *might* be wrong doesn't mean we *are* wrong. My advice is that if we believe we heard God correctly but our degree of certainty is low (for example, 55 percent) or the issue involved is very important, then we should ask God for extra confirmation that what we've "heard" was indeed from him.

A second objection is that Jesus is the unique, divine, messianic Son of God and as such is not a model for our hearing God speak to us. In other words, Jesus employed his divine prerogative when he did only what he saw the Father doing (John 5:19), but this does not apply to us mere humans. In response, I would say this objection is simply mistaken. New Testament scholars widely acknowledge that in the incarnation, Jesus did not utilize his divine nature but instead acted as a human being filled with the Spirit and living in constant communication with the Father. This is why we are exhorted to imitate him (1 Corinthians 11:1; 1 Thessalonians 1:6), something that would be impossible if he had lived his earthly life from his divine nature.[4]

Among the ways that God speaks to us extrabiblically, I will focus on six in the pages to follow: impressions; thoughts and feelings; prophecy, word of knowledge, and word of wisdom; dreams and visions; angelic visitations; and life circumstances.

SIX WAYS GOD SPEAKS TO US EXTRABIBLICALLY

1. God Speaks through Impressions

There are different ways to describe what I will call "impressions" as one of the ways God speaks to us. It can be a sudden urge to do something, or perhaps a nudge, a prompting, or a sense that God is directing us in a specific way. It may be an intuitive awareness of God's presence and direction. Mark 2:8 tells us that "Jesus [was] *aware [epignous] in His spirit* that they were thinking that way within themselves" (NASB, italics added) and this can be an example of this sort of knowing. It is a sense, an intuitive way of perceiving correctly something or other. The Greek word *epignous* (from *epiginosko*) means "to know experientially, to ascertain, to be directly aware of."

This is similar to Paul's prayer in Ephesians 1:18 that the eyes of our hearts would be enlightened or illuminated, that we would have "spiritual eyesight." The ancients believed, correctly in my view, that the chest area, especially the region where the heart organ is located, is a vehicle that human beings use to be directly aware or to sense or intuit invisible things, especially moral goodness and virtue. This is why in *The Abolition of Man*, C. S. Lewis bemoaned that today we produce "men without chests."[5] By this, Lewis meant that while people respond to their reasoning minds and their visceral bellies, they no longer are able to perceive moral wisdom and virtue with the heart located in the chest.

In Nehemiah 7:5, Nehemiah announces that regarding a certain task, "my God put it into my heart." This is another example of an impression—a nonverbal, intuitive awareness of what God wanted him to do. Before I illustrate this sort of speaking, here's a short word of application: when you get up in the morning and at different times during the day, invite the Spirit to help you be aware of and discern divine nudges or impressions that come to you throughout the day. Such awareness is facilitated by habit-forming practice in seeking God's voice and by an overall lifestyle with as much time for peace, silence, and solitude as possible, given your station in life.

Several years ago, I was preaching at a church in Southern California, and after my message, the pastor invited those who desired prayer to come to the front. We all stood as about ten people came forward. I was standing at the far left of the first row. As the pastor spoke some words to the congregation, my eyes kept being drawn to a young man near the back of the group, and I had the distinct impression that God wanted me to pray for him. It was just a sense I had, so I approached him to ask if I could pray.

Along the way, a clear thought had come into my mind from the outside: *Tell him not to leave his current ministry.* That was it. So after receiving permission to pray and lay hands on the young man, I said, "I have a sense that the Lord may be giving me a word for you—namely, you are not to leave your current ministry." His jaw practically hit the floor. He responded, "Dr. Moreland, I graduated from Dallas Seminary, and I don't believe in signs and wonders, including God's ability to speak outside the Bible. But I heard you were preaching at this Vineyard church, so I came to hear you. Here's the crazy thing—I'm a leader of a local parachurch ministry, and I've been struggling the last few weeks about whether or not I should leave and look for a new ministry. I have no idea how you knew this, but your words to me are exactly what I needed at this precise moment. May I call you at your home to talk further about this?" I agreed and gave him my number. And in the end he decided to stay where he was.

This example of hearing God began with an impression that I obeyed and turned into a series of thoughts that constituted a word of knowledge for this person. I'm sure you have had several experiences of the same sort. It may be edifying for you to attempt to recall some of them and share what you remember with a friend or family member. Remember, you don't have to be certain it was God, and if you choose to step out based on the impression and are wrong, that's okay—unless it's such a crucial matter that a mistake could do great harm, in which case it's wise to seek additional confirmation of the impression's authenticity. As you experiment with this, you'll find opportunities to grow.

2. God Speaks through Thoughts and Feelings

We read in Nehemiah 2:12 that after arriving in Jerusalem, Nehemiah arose together with a few other men, but he refrained from telling anyone "what my God had put in my heart to do." This sort of experience is not merely an impression or awareness of a divine nudge; it is a cognitive experience that centers on receiving a series of thoughts that come directly from God.

Here's an example from my own life. In 2003, my family and I were hit with an unexpected financial crisis. Shortly thereafter, as I was taking a morning walk, I told the Lord that I was at a point where I really needed to see him intervene for me. A thought suddenly came to me: *Why don't you ask me to do something for you today?* I wasn't sure if it was the Lord or my own thoughts, but I responded to what I thought was his prompting and asked him to bring my family $5,000 that very day. My faith was not particularly strong at this time. The mail came and went with no check. But at 5:40 that evening, completely out of the blue and totally unexpectedly, I received an amount *above what I had requested* ($5,200) from someone who knew me but knew nothing of my situation. It was simply incredible, and besides the wonderful provision from God, this answer to prayer created "God confidence" in my entire family and me.

This amazing event provided me with an occasion to learn more effectively how to discern when God was the source of a series of thoughts I might have. Since my request in response to what I thought I had heard (a specific invitation) was miraculously granted, I had external confirmation that it actually was the Lord who invited me to ask him for something that very day as a way of allowing me to see him intervene on my behalf. So I reflected carefully on the precise nature of the experience, and I learned several things: (1) In contrast to my talking to myself, the series of thoughts had a distinctive feel of dawning on me from the outside. (2) The statement was in the first person: *Why don't you ask me [not God] to do something for you today?* When I talk to myself about God, I use the third person (for example, *Why doesn't God do something for me today?*). Over the years, I have noticed that when God is the source of a series of thoughts, they are expressed in the first person. (3) The thought's texture was calm, steady, and matter-of-fact, with no nagging, no anxiety. (4) The thought had a feel of authority to it.

I think God speaks to us in ways we will understand, so one approach does not fit every person or situation. But by reflecting on cases in which we very likely heard God's voice, we can learn, through trial and error, to discern how God's voice sounds to us. We learn to interpret the Scriptures through trial and error, learn from our mistakes, and do better the next time, so why not use that method regarding extrabiblical divine speaking?

Here's another amazing example (names have been changed to protect privacy) that, miraculously, I was able to verify. About a year after Hope and I began attending Vineyard Anaheim in June 2003, a church friend named Brad Sweeney gave us a cassette tape (remember those?) and promised it would edify us if we listened to it. We listened, and what we heard was so wonderful that we both knew we would fervently seek to hear the Lord's voice for the rest of our lives. I hope my retelling of what we heard has the same effect on you.

The cassette contained a plenary speech from a conference on healing and hearing God, and from the crowd's applause, I'd guess there were five to seven hundred people in attendance. We listened to the plenary speaker, pastor Robert Reubens, PhD, and after a few minutes, he passed the microphone to his wife, Kathy Reubens, to share some things with the audience. Immediately, Hope and I both recognized some things about Kathy from the tone of her voice and her words. Clearly she was not used to being in front of an audience and was a bit sheepish in her presentation. But she had such a tender, warm, humble, and quiet spirit that it was hard not to feel love from and for this dear sister. Moreover, as unassuming as she was, Kathy kindly admonished the audience that when it comes to hearing God, we must be filled with the Spirit, utterly dependent on the Lord, and completely committed never to try to manufacture anything. You could tell Kathy lived what she preached.

Kathy shared that in a junior high class she taught, a girl named Kaitlyn became very special to her. At a young age, Kaitlyn had been abandoned by both parents and was being raised by her grandmother. Unfortunately, Kaitlyn's grandmother had endured a difficult life and was a hardened, bitter person. While at home one day, Kathy received a phone call from the grandmother, something that had never happened before. In a deeply troubled tone of voice, the grandmother shared that Kaitlyn had disappeared and had been missing for three days. The grandmother had called all of Kaitlyn's friends and done everything she could think of to find her, all to no avail. So even though the grandmother was not a particularly religious woman, she was desperate to have Kathy pray for Kaitlyn to be found.

Feeling burdened in her heart, Kathy agreed. She acknowledged to God that he was omniscient and that he knew at that very moment where Kaitlyn was, and she asked for revelation to help find her. As Kathy reports it, later in the day, two thoughts came into her mind: the name of a woman and the name of a local town. Kathy knew no one by that name and had no idea where the town was, except that it was in Southern California. Because it was highly implausible that these two specific names would come to her under these circumstances, Kathy called the grandmother and shared what she had received from the Lord.

After hanging up, the grandmother called information, asking for a listing under that name in that specific town. And guess what? There was one, and only one, such listing, so the grandmother immediately called the number. What was about to happen shocks me to this day. When a woman answered the phone, the grandmother asked her if she had found her granddaughter, Kaitlyn. The woman could not talk openly, because Kaitlyn was near her and she didn't want Kaitlyn to hear the conversation. So she chose to speak in broken sentences and managed to answer the grandmother's questions, beginning with a simple yes.

After a minute or two, Kaitlyn left the room and the woman could speak openly again, though she continued in hushed tones. She shared how earlier that day, while she was driving from Los Angeles to Palm Springs, she had spotted and driven by an attractive young girl walking on the side of the highway. As soon as she passed the girl, she sensed the Lord telling her to pull off the road and pick up the girl. She did just that, and the girl (who was Kaitlyn) had agreed to go to the woman's home for some food and a chance to freshen up.

The woman went on to tell the grandmother that she wanted to keep Kaitlyn for three days in order to lead her to Jesus and to guide her in the best way to return to her grandmother to work things out. Besides, the woman added, in three days, she had business to do in Los Angeles and, on her way, she would be happy to drop her off. The grandmother agreed, and after Kaitlyn returned to her grandmother's home, their relationship began to improve.

* * *

I don't know about you, but to me this account is incredibly supernatural and encouraging. It whets my appetite to hear God more clearly. Hope and I could tell from Kathy's presence that she was telling the truth, but there is a miraculous sequel to the story that involved my attempts to verify it. For some reason, I believed that the Reubens pastored a church in the Los Angeles area, specifically, near Pasadena.

Wanting to interview them, I made dozens of calls to 411 for directory assistance, trying to locate them in several towns in the greater Los Angeles area, including surrounding counties like Orange County. I had absolutely no luck. I wondered why God did not help me find them, but I would learn three years later that God had other plans.

I gave up my search, but in the mentoring group I led each semester at Talbot School of Theology, I played the tape for each group as an encouragement to their faith. As a result, the incident came to my mind four or five times a year, and each time, I prayed that God would somehow help me find the Reubens.

In July 2007, our church held a four-day training conference, with 2,500 to 3,000 attendees from all over the country. Hope and I attended the entire event, and on the second day, a friend at the conference asked me to go to lunch with him. He said he wanted me to meet a couple who were his close friends. He thought it would be edifying for us to meet each other, so we went to Keno's for lunch.

As it turned out, they were a pastoral couple at a church in Ohio, and after a few minutes, I started feeling odd. I didn't know what was happening until it dawned on me that I recognized the wife's voice (I didn't remember their last name at the time), and moreover, I knew she was the Kathy who had shared her testimony about Kaitlyn. I was able to interview both of them and came away with no doubt at all about the veracity of their testimony.

Now what were the odds of me going to lunch with, or in some other way meeting and recognizing, the Reubens, given that I had no idea they were in Ohio and that 2,500 to 3,000 people were at the conference? Even if I had met them, how would I have known they were the very people I had prayed to meet over the last three years? The intelligent agent principle provides the answer: *small probability + independent specialness* [I had prayed to meet and interview this very couple] = *an event brought about by an intelligent agent* [in this case, a miraculous, specific answer to prayer].

Besides a series of thoughts, sometimes God speaks to us by causing a bodily sensation in our bodies and, subsequently, giving us an impression of what it means. As Jack Deere notes, while this form of divine speaking can be abused, nevertheless, "Today it is not uncommon for God to speak to . . . people through bodily signs."[6] For example, one evening before I was speaking at our church, my friend Brian Slezak stood next to me and asked if he could pray for me. Little did he know that I was experiencing cramping in my stomach and a sense of oncoming diarrhea.

As Brian began to pray, suddenly he shared that a feeling of cramping and instability entered his stomach out of the blue. Based on past experience, Brian asked me if I was having troubles with my stomach. I was absolutely shocked he would bring up such a thing. After I acknowledged my problem, Brian prayed for healing, and—I am not exaggerating—the problem completely disappeared and did not come back. Honestly, I had been afraid I was going to have to run out to the bathroom right in the middle of my talk (and I feared I wouldn't make it there!). But after his prayer, the normal calmness in my stomach gave me confidence that the problem was behind me (pun intended), and I went on to enjoy the rest of the meeting.

3. God Speaks through Prophecy, Word of Knowledge, and Word of Wisdom

In 1 Corinthians 14:1, Paul admonishes us to "follow the way of love and eagerly desire gifts of the Spirit, especially prophecy." Gordon Fee observes, "It should be noted that the imperatives are directed to all, not to a select group of 'prophets.' One may assume therefore, that even though in reality not all will be 'prophets' (12:29), nonetheless prophesying is as available to all as [is] the command to pursue love."[7] According to Sam Storms, prophecy is "the human report of a divine revelation."[8] The phrases "word of knowledge" and "word of wisdom" are used only once in Scripture (1 Corinthians 12:8 NASB), and while the context helps us understand what they mean, there is no consensus on the matter.

As a working definition of these three concepts, I offer one given to me by a well-known New Testament colleague at Talbot School of Theology: "I would define prophecy as an inspired word or revelation from God for encouragement and edification, the word of wisdom as an inspired word from God characterized by wisdom (for example, giving perspective or insight into a situation), and a word of knowledge as an inspired word from God of a more factual basis in regard to a particular situation."[9] To save space in what follows, I will use "prophetic word" or simply "word" for all three.

Over the last seventeen years, I have received a prophetic word for someone approximately two hundred times, and the vast majority of these have been during times I was praying over and laying hands on that person. Many times the word was so clearly confirmed as being from the Lord that its presence in my life sustained and increased my intimacy with God. I acknowledge that I am fairly well-known as a speaker, professor, and author. But I assure you that when it comes to miracles, including receiving words from the Lord, I am very, very ordinary. The reason I have received so many prophetic words for people resides in my willingness to risk, to offer a word and be mistaken, and to regularly lay hands on and pray for people after church, inviting the Spirit to come and speak if he so desires. Here are a few of a multitude of stories I could tell. Let them encourage your faith and move you to risk more often while praying for the sick and hurting.

On July 6 and 7, 2007, I spoke four times at a global leadership development conference held at Vanguard University in Costa Mesa, California. Both days I was scheduled to speak at 10:00 a.m. and 7:00 p.m., giving lectures on apologetics for an hour and a half, along with a question and answer time. The conference was led by my Talbot colleague professor Ben Shin and a few others. The forty-day training conference focused primarily on twentysomething Korean Americans, with participants from thirty states and five other countries. I would guess around 100 to 120 Koreans attended the conference.

I was to deliver my second lecture on Friday night at 7:00 p.m., but when I arrived, I was informed that there would be a full worship time before I spoke, so my talk would begin around 8:30 or so. During worship, I sat at the back of the small auditorium. Moved by the worship, I asked the Lord if there was anything he wanted to say to the attendees when I spoke. I quieted my heart and mind, held my hands out with my palms up, and waited.

In less than a minute, these thoughts came to me: *There are people here who are demonized and unable to sleep at night or derive any benefit from the conference. I want you to cast the demons out of them. And there's a man named Mike who came to the conference right after a painful confrontation with his pastor. He's blaming himself for what happened, but it was the pastor, not Mike, who caused harm to the other. I want you to identify him and tell him he needs to confront his pastor about the truth of what happened so as to bring repentance for that behavior.*

I am not exaggerating what I received—not even one little bit. And based on the tone in comparison with other times I had verified words from the Lord, along with the oddness of the word that was given (it surely wasn't something that would bubble up from my unconscious mind—after all, I had never met a Korean American named Mike), I was about 70 percent certain it was truly from Jesus. At the end of my talk and after an extended Q and A session, I looked at my watch and saw that it was already 10:15 p.m. So I said, "Before I leave, I believe the Lord has given me something to share with you, so please close your eyes and open yourself to God." I went on to express what I had received earlier from the Lord. When I finished, I divided the crowd into groups of four or five people, had them close their eyes again, and prayed a deliverance prayer over the group, commanding any demon present to leave. When we had finished, I drove home and slept soundly.

On Saturday morning, I was to speak at 10:00 a.m., but I arrived at the parking lot around 9:15. The conference leader and three students were waiting for me, and the leader approached my car as I was getting out. I thought to myself, *Oh no! He was offended by what I did last night, and I'm not sure what's about to happen.* But I was dead wrong. The leader asked, "Do you know what happened last night?" When I told him I did not, he said, "After you left, the Holy Spirit's presence filled the room, and students stayed in their groups until 2:00 a.m., crying out to the Lord, confessing sin, asking for his help, and so on. It was incredible! And by the way, three students are waiting to speak with you. The first one is Mike." I honestly replied, "Are you kidding me? Is there really someone named Mike at the conference? I've never heard of a Korean American named Mike!" The leader replied—no joke—"There is one person here named Mike, and he needs to talk."

After introducing himself to me in the parking lot, Mike said, "You have no idea the importance of what you said last night. How did you know all that?" I said, "Well, I was only

70 percent certain it was from the Lord, and I just took a risk and gave what I believed he gave me to say." Mike went on: "Just before coming to the conference from my home on the East Coast, my girlfriend and I had an appointment with our senior pastor, who was rude and harsh toward us. Ever since that time, I've blamed myself for what happened since our pastor is a well-known Christian leader. I was unwilling to acknowledge to myself what I knew deep down—that it was really our pastor who needed to ask us for forgiveness. It has been eating me up all summer."

After I expressed my sadness at what had happened to them, Mike said, "There's one other thing I need to tell you. Part of this forty-day program is the chance to hear outside speakers like you. Next weekend, guess who's going to be the outside speaker? My pastor! The timing of what you said could not have been better. Now I know I need to admonish him next week for what he did, and I have a week to pray about it. Thank you for letting God use you."

After Mike walked away, two young women approached me. They hadn't really known each other and were staying in different dorm rooms, but each told me they had been experiencing a kind of darkness and sleeplessness ever since they had come to the conference (since around the middle of June). They both told me that as I had commanded the demons to leave the night before, a sense of darkness had left them that was replaced by a warm presence, and they had slept soundly Friday night for the first time since they arrived.

Here is yet another personal example with an important lesson as well.

In July 1999, our church hosted a five-day worship and training conference that brought about three thousand people from around the country. On the first evening, a dynamic time of worship was scheduled, and the sanctuary was packed to overflowing. While Hope and I were sitting in the front section waiting for the service to begin, I felt a tap on my right shoulder. Turning around, I saw a dear pastor-friend I'll call Aaron Smith from Northern California whom I hadn't seen in twenty years. We hugged, and he expressed his gratitude for being able to attend the conference and went to sit in the back in the sanctuary's upper-middle section.

After worship, an invitation was extended for those who wanted prayer to come to the front of the church. I'd estimate that about four hundred people responded. As I was sitting there, Pastor Aaron walked right by me on his way to the front. As he got on his knees to pray, I decided to join him, so I stood behind him, placed my right hand on his left shoulder, and silently prayed for Aaron. Suddenly, out of nowhere, a clear message came to me: *Tell him that I see him and that I approve of his ministry.* It was short and sweet, so I bent down and whispered, "Aaron, I believe Jesus may have given me a word for you: 'Tell him that I see him and that I approve of his ministry.'"

This is simply not the way I normally talk. I would usually say something like, "God is aware of your situation and is pleased by your ministry." But I've learned from experience to give the person exactly what I heard—nothing more, nothing less—so that's what I did.

Aaron began to weep uncontrollably from deep inside, so I asked him what had happened and how I could help him. I will never forget what he shared. "J. P., I've been going through a very dark, difficult time for several months. And while sitting in the upper section before the service began, I cried out to Jesus, 'Lord, do you even see me? Do you approve of my ministry?' I prayed the exact words you gave me, and I know it had to be from the Lord. My tears are tears of deep gratitude, relief, and love." I am so glad I spoke *exactly* what I was given to say.

Here is another very interesting case in which God used prophetic words as clear guidance for a couple. This account was shared a number of times from the pulpit at our church, and the man involved confirmed all of the following details to me on May 13, 2020.

Lance Pittluck was born in Long Island, New York, and was raised in a secular Jewish family. When Lance was old enough to live on his own, he moved to Southern California to surf. There he found Jesus, eventually graduated from Fuller Seminary, and became a leader at Vineyard Anaheim.

In 1984, Lance returned to his childhood neighborhood on Long Island, where he pastored a church and helped pave the way for other church plants until 1997. In the summer of 1997, Lance attended a Monday through Friday conference at Vineyard Anaheim, the church founded and pastored by John and Carol Wimber. During the conference, Carol pulled Lance aside and shocked him by saying that, based on a long time of praying, she and John believed that the Lord wanted Lance to return to Southern California to pastor Vineyard Anaheim. John was dealing with a cardiovascular disease and eventually died on November 17, 1997. Carol went on to say that Lance needed to hear this leading from God himself, and they were willing to wait to see what would happen. Lance told me he doubted the whole thing and simply dismissed the idea. He loved his ministry in New York and had no intention of leaving. But all of that was about to change.

According to Lance, from that Wednesday to Friday, completely out of the blue, he received thirty independent prophetic words from people all over the country (including one man who called Lance from New Zealand). None of them knew that any of the others had received such a word, and no one knew anything at all about what the Wimbers and Lance had discussed.

One person woke up in the middle of the night right after a dream in which he saw a map of the United States with a flaming arrow departing from New York, shooting across the country, and landing on Vineyard Anaheim church in Southern California. The Lord told the man that the dream was about Lance and that it meant he was to leave New York and pastor Vineyard Anaheim. By Friday, Lance shared with me that he had received these thirty prophetic words, and all of them were specific and clear. On Saturday while sitting at a coffee shop, Lance heard God say to him, "You know what you need to do." Starting in October 1997, Lance Pittluck and his wife, Cheryl, became the lead pastors of Vineyard Anaheim until 2017.

Here is another case involving my wife, Hope, in which God used a prophetic word to reach out to someone who needed prayer. I was there when this happened, along with Klaus and Beth Issler, who also witnessed the entire event.

One Sunday morning after the sermon, our pastor, Lance Pittluck, waited quietly for a bit before inviting people to come to the front to receive prayer. Then Lance proclaimed to the congregation that he believed the Lord had told him there was a woman named Sally who was present, that she was deeply despondent and needed hope, and that the Lord saw her and her situation that morning. He invited Sally (no one knew who she was) to join about seventy-five to one hundred people up front to receive prayer.

As soon as Lance shared this prophetic word, Hope prayed silently, *Lord, please let me be the one to pray for Sally.* We have a ministry team of about thirty people who are trained to pray for the sick, and after her prayer, Hope (who was on the ministry team) went forward and stood facing the congregation to see who, if anyone, would come to her for prayer. Hope noticed a particular woman who had come forward, and Hope approached the woman, asking if she could pray for her. Incredibly, the woman said, "My name is Sally, and I am the one Lance was talking about. I have lost hope that the Lord sees and cares for me." My wife responded, "Well, my name is *Hope*, and I prayed that I would get to pray for you, and here we are!" After prayer, the woman went back to her seat, obviously feeling encouraged and known by the Lord!

Here is another example of a prophetic word, this time being used in evangelism. The case is reported by John Wimber in his book *Power Evangelism*.[10] And as confirmation, on May 4, 2020, I had a long conversation with Carol Wimber (now Carol Wong), who vividly remembered the day when John told her the entire story as it had just happened to him. Carol said that in those days, this sort of thing happened often to John because he didn't know any better than to actually believe and act on the Bible!

Wimber founded the Vineyard movement, pastored Vineyard Anaheim, and taught in the church growth department at Fuller Seminary. He spoke at church growth seminars all over the country and frequently flew to and from conferences.

On this particular evening, having finished a grueling time of teaching at a conference in Chicago, John boarded a plane for New York in an exhausted, completely spent state of mind. He hungered to sit back, relax, and read the newspaper before attending another conference in New York. So John buckled up and waited for the flight to take off.

While letting his eyes wander around the cabin, John's eyes passed by a middle-aged man seated across the aisle. Suddenly John saw the word *adultery* written over the man's face. He rubbed his eyes and looked again, and it was still there. The word was visible not to the eyes but to John's spiritual awareness. Noticing that John had been staring at him, the man barked, "What do you want?" As soon as this happened, a woman's name came clearly to John's mind, so he leaned across the aisle and whispered, "Does the name Jane Smith [not her real name] mean anything to you?" According to Wimber, the man's face turned white, and he blurted out, "We've got to talk!"

The plane had an upstairs cocktail lounge, and as John followed the man up the stairs, the Lord put this thought in his mind: *Tell him if he doesn't turn from his adultery, I'm going to take him.* The following is both funny and realistic, given Wimber's exhausted condition, so I will let him tell you what he felt next in his own words: "Terrific. All I had wanted was a nice, peaceful plane ride to New York. Now here I was, sitting in the plane's cocktail lounge with a man I had never seen before, whose name I didn't even know, about to tell him that God was going to take his life if he didn't stop his affair with some woman."[11]

For a moment, put yourself in Wimber's shoes. It would have been horribly embarrassing if John had been wrong, so he must have been quite confident to go forward with this word. "Who told you that name?" the man asked. "God did," Wimber blurted out. Eventually, John shared the gospel with the man, and not only did he receive Christ, but all of his guilt and shame came gushing out and he prayed loudly the most heartrending prayer of repentance John had ever heard! Everyone in the lounge became intimately familiar with the man's sordid past! After the man received Christ, John told him he had to go back and confess to his wife. He did, and after a confusing time of turmoil, his wife also accepted Jesus. As they landed and exited the plane, John learned that the couple did not have a Bible, so John gave them his. And they went on their way.

4. *God Speaks through Dreams and Visions*

For millennia, people all over the world have rightly believed that some dreams and visions (dreamlike visual experiences that occur when one is awake) are cases of supernatural communication from God or from the evil one. Sigmund Freud (1856–1939) was the first psychologist to focus his study on dreams, and ever since, the growing tendency in Western culture has been to treat dreams or visions as thoroughly naturalistic events able to be completely explained by psychological analysis.

I have no doubt that many, perhaps most, dreams are natural events. And I believe much can be learned about ourselves from analyzing our dreams in a psychological manner. But I am not willing to cede this entire area of life to psychologists and naturalists, nor do I think it is rational to do so. Clearly some dreams and visions *are* from God, and as believers we need to pay closer attention to them and not dismiss out of hand the possibility that on a given occasion, God may be speaking to us. Of course, we should also recognize the need to ponder the dream or vision from a psychological viewpoint as we are evaluating the origin of the dream or vision.

A faculty colleague's wife often receives supernatural dreams, and my colleague always takes them very seriously. While we should remain balanced—neither skeptical nor gullible—we should not doubt that God speaks in these ways. With discernment, we should seek the Spirit's guidance. Many believers run around saying all the time that God told them this or that. These people need to calm down and seek wisdom. Others have provided guidelines for dream interpretation, but here's my advice: when you have a dream, pray the words of Psalm 139:23–24, ask God to make clear the dream's significance and meaning, and run it by wise, trustworthy friends or family members.[12]

As an example of a dream or vision, I begin with a supernatural vision that changed the course of an African nation. Hope and I have known Michael and Terri Sullivant for seventeen years and hold them, their marriage, and their family in high regard. In 2003, Michael gave me a prophetic word that changed my life permanently, and I owe him so much for that word and for his ministry to me over the years. I love him dearly—he's the real deal with a strong collection of supernatural gifts and a life of integrity and loving devotion to Jesus. Michael is the CEO of Life Model Works, as well as a church planter, an author, and a speaker. He has ministered in more than twenty-five countries during forty-five years of public ministry. Michael's latest book is *Thinking Biblically about the Life Model*.[13] Here is his story in his own words:

> Sometime in the late 1990s, I was suddenly swept up into a divine purpose and appointment. I served on the staff of a growing local church with a team of fellow ministers. We were, and still are, very devoted to asking God to move across our world in unprecedented ways in our generation. Many gifted leaders were attracted to our ministry in Kansas City in those years.
>
> Early one morning, one of my coworkers, David, had an unusual experience. He had a vivid image come to him, as in a waking dream, of an animated conversation between a wife

and her husband. They were in their bedroom, and David saw some of the specific pieces of furniture within it and the layout of their room. The woman was strongly encouraging her husband to put his trust in Jesus and to ask for God's wisdom to lead their nation. He overheard many specific words they were saying to one another, and he prayed that the husband might pay attention to the counsel of his wife. I cannot remember how, but he soon discovered that he had been allowed to see and hear an interchange between the president and first lady of a well-known African nation.

David had a friend from the United Kingdom who was a missionary to this nation and was able to get the official address of the presidential residence. He wrote a letter to the first lady and graciously reported to her the specific things he had seen and heard. It wasn't long before he received a letter from her that simply read, "When can you come?" So David came to me that very day and said, "Let's book flights to this nation right away. I want you to come with me." So we immediately did this and were soon on our way to East Africa. We arrived at the town outside the capital city where the airport was located, but no one was there to meet us. We booked two rooms at a nearby hotel and waited on the Lord in that place. We spent two nights there before a limousine came to pick us up on the third day, when we had been scheduled to meet the first family.

The time of waiting was providential. During both nights, my spirit was very alert and aware of the nearness of the Holy Spirit. I had multiple and repeated night visions in which I saw and heard messages that the president was called by God to share with various subgroups of the cultural leaders of his nation—lawmakers, educators, medical doctors, clergy, media leaders, social workers, and others. He was challenging them to put God first in all their fields of expertise and service. He also talked to them about human dignity, human rights, and the importance of protecting the freedom of religion in their nation, since loving God cannot be coerced. However, he said to them it could be inspired by their life examples and by the creation of policies and procedures that embody God's wisdom. I woke up both mornings and journaled my experiences. I had also felt led to bring two copies of *The Divine Conspiracy* by my long-distance friend (and mentor to Dr. Moreland) Dr. Dallas Willard to pass along to the president and his wife.

It turned out that the president had been called away from the capital during our visit due to a military conflict in the northern part of their country, so we did not get to meet with him in person. However, after spending ninety minutes or so with the first lady on the morning of that third day at their residence and office complex—which was exactly like David had seen in his vision and recalled to me before our trip, from the wallpaper, to the arrangement of things, to the nature and color of the furniture—she promptly cleared her calendar and spent the whole day with the two of us. Her limo driver escorted the three of us and her assistant to various places where she had invested herself for years helping the needy orphaned children of their nation. We had rich interchanges with her about the realities of God's great kingdom and shared about our mutual joyful trust in Jesus Christ our Lord. We were able to convey to her the things that God's Spirit had given to us for her family and for the nation, which she gladly and warmly received.

We left that nation a couple days later very confident that we had been sent on a special and timely mission to sow seeds of God's word and thoughts from God's heart into the lives of the leaders and people we met. The first lady welcomed us to return in the future, but so far, I have not been led to do more than continue to pray for this nation and its first family from afar.

One thing did happen a few years afterward that really encouraged me. I happened to see a video produced by George Otis Jr. called *Transformations II: The Glory Spreads.* In this video, I saw images regarding what God was since doing in this nation that captured exact images and words I had seen in my night visions while waiting on God! The whole experience taught me that God can easily and at any time take us from a place of obscurity and present us before the change agents he has raised up in places far from home for the honor of his Son and the furtherance of his good news among the nations.

Here is another example from someone I knew during my days with Campus Crusade (now Cru) in the 1970s. When I joined the staff in 1970, I was stationed for two years at the University of Colorado, where Marshall Rice was my roommate and trainer. Even though we live on different coasts and don't speak often, we have remained friends all these years. I had not heard from Marshall for many years when one day, he unexpectedly called me with great excitement in his voice. He had called to share a miracle story for my encouragement.

A young woman who worked for Marshall at Cru headquarters in Orlando, Florida, was also his good friend. The woman was short—a little over five feet tall—and timid. One day while in the grocery store checkout line behind a tall Middle Eastern man (whom she correctly took to be a Muslim), she noticed that he was leafing through a semipornographic magazine. Suddenly she sensed the Lord speaking to her: *Tell him to put down that magazine.* Well, that was the absolute last thing she was inclined to do, so she blew it off. But the word came a second time, and she knew it was the Lord. So she took a deep breath, tapped the man on the shoulder, and told him to put down the magazine!

Anticipating a harsh reaction, the young woman was utterly surprised by what happened next. He complied and repeated several times, "You are a holy woman! You are a holy woman!" Wanting to share the Lord with him, she asked if he would wait for her outside the store so they could talk further after she had checked out. The man agreed, and when they met, she took out a "Four Spiritual Laws" booklet and said, "I want to share with you how you can become a child of God." Now keep in mind, this approach is far from the ordinary way Cru staff are trained to introduce the booklet. Usually one would say, "May I show you how to know God personally?" or simply "Have you ever heard of the four spiritual laws?" But that wasn't what she said.

Instantly, the man dropped to his knees in front of several people entering or leaving the store and began to weep. *What in the world is going on?* the Cru staff woman wondered. So she asked him just that. She will never forget what he said: "Last night, I had a dream that I would meet someone today who would tell me how to become a child of God. And you are the one in my dream!" Obviously, the man gladly accepted Jesus on the sidewalk in front of a bunch of people. If this happened to you, wouldn't you do the same?

5. *God Speaks through Angelic Visitations*

In chapter 8, we will discuss contemporary angelic and demonic manifestations, but I must share one story now. The late Francis MacNutt (who lived from 1925 to 2020 and had a PhD in theology) and his dear wife, Judith, who worked as a psychotherapist for decades in private practice and in hospitals throughout Boston, are internationally known and respected for their integrative ministry called Christian Healing Ministries. If you google Judith MacNutt and listen to one of her talks, you will be immediately captivated by her genuine love for Jesus and people and by the deep learning she shares. Judith has a gift of discernment of spirits and often sees angels and demons. Two of her books are the best resources I've ever read on angels.[14] Here is Judith's heartwarming story of how God used an angel to communicate his love and care to a needy little boy. Be forewarned, you may need a tissue.

Several years ago, my husband, Francis, and I were leading a healing conference in a large church. The long day had been filled with teaching and lively discussion. We knew that everyone was excitedly anticipating the evening healing service, as many had already told us about their need to receive God's healing touch.

During the service, a young mother came forward for prayer, followed closely by her six-year-old son holding tightly to the folds of her skirt. Tearfully she told us of her deep heartbreak. She was recently divorced from her husband of ten years. The way she carried her body clearly showed her despair and loneliness. Her deepest concern, however, was for her young son, Timmy.

Since the divorce, Timmy had withdrawn more and more from life and had shown symptoms of depression. He missed his daddy terribly and felt that he was somehow to blame for the breakup of the family. A fearful mother's heart had brought her broken son to the Lord for healing.

Unlike most six-year-old boys, Timmy had a face etched with sadness. His eyes were deeply sorrowful. As we laid hands on Timmy and prayed, he began to cry softly. Suddenly, something drew my attention to the ceiling. I looked up, and there, sitting on a wooden rafter high above the cross, was an angel. A brilliant white light surrounded him, and his garment was shining—unlike anything I had ever seen before. His countenance was joyful, yet concerned as he watched us pray for Timmy. I had the distinct impression that he, too, was praying for Timmy.

After the prayer, Timmy tearfully thanked us and returned to the pew with his mother. Occasionally, I glanced at Timmy and noticed that he was looking in the direction where the angel was seated. Excusing myself from the healing line, I slipped into the pew beside Timmy. I asked him if he would mind sharing with me what had captured his attention. By this time he was staring at the angel, his eyes full of wonder.

He hesitated for a moment, and then he slowly said that he saw 'a large man sitting on a rafter.' He gave me a quizzical look, as if to ask, 'Do you believe me?' I smiled and assured him that he was seeing an angel of the Lord.

When I asked Timmy to describe the angel, he gave me an exact description of his hair, clothing, smile, and size. I asked him if he was bigger than my husband (who is six foot four), and he said, 'Much bigger.' I told Timmy he was greatly blessed to see this angel. A broad smile covered his little face. Excitement raced through his voice as he said, "I believe God wants me to know God sent this angel to always take care of me, since my daddy can't be around anymore."[15]

6. God Speaks through Life Circumstances

Most of us have discerned that God speaks to us through circumstances. Now, once we are equipped with the intelligent agent principle (IAP), we no longer have to guess whether such circumstances are serendipitous accidents or genuine divine miracles—a specific provision or communication from the Lord. If the circumstances are highly improbable and in some way a special situation apart from the fact that they just happened to occur, then we know the circumstances were brought about by an intelligent agent for a purpose. Remember, this principle has virtually no false positives (cases where employment of the principle falsely indicates the action of an intelligent agent). The "specialness factor" could be that the circumstances were just what one was praying for or just the thing required to meet an important need or bring a specific kind of comfort or encouragement. Here are some examples for you to consider.

In the summer of 2003, I experienced a series of anxiety attacks that led to a debilitating seven-month depression. Almost immediately after sinking into an emotional and spiritual abyss, I began to be plagued with doubts and self-criticism about my academic, scholarly work. My self-talk, which I believe was energized by demonic attacks, was filled with repeated accusations that I had wasted my life studying, writing, and lecturing, and that my intellectual endeavors for the cause of Christ had achieved very little by way of impact. This repeated thought plagued me for several weeks, plunging me deeper into depression. My work and life seemed meaningless. In the midst of this plunge, I went to Columbia International University in Columbia, South Carolina, to participate in a five-day lecture series. I live in Southern California and knew no one in Columbia, South Carolina, having never been there.

Before dinner on July 15, I came down with an extreme migraine headache. I can go five years without even a small headache, so this was a first for me. I took Tylenol, canceled my evening lecture, and went to bed. But things got worse. My head was wracked with pain. Around 6:00 p.m. I received a phone call from a conference attendee who lived in the area who knew my pain and said he was taking me to the emergency room. I slumped into the front seat of his car, and he drove me to a walk-in clinic about fifteen to twenty miles away in Irmo, South Carolina. I staggered in, left my driver's license at the front desk, and was whisked away to the emergency room. Immediately, two nurses hooked monitors to my chest and brain and began doing tests to find out what was wrong. My blood pressure was off the charts. They gave me an injection to alleviate the headache, which began to work quickly.

After about five minutes, the doctor who was on call that evening walked in the door. Holding my driver's license, he said, "Are you J. P. Moreland? The one who teaches at Talbot Seminary?" Taken a bit off guard, I nodded. "I don't believe this! There are nurses here who would give their eyeteeth if a movie star walked through those doors. In my case, if I could pick one person in the entire country to come in here, it would be you. Dr. Moreland, I can't thank you enough for what you have done in the intellectual world for the cause of Christ! I have read almost all your books, and hey, you know that book *Body and Soul* you wrote with Scott Rae? I teach ethics at a local community college, and I use that as a text. I can't believe I'm getting to meet you!"

It turned out that I had most likely eaten some bad shrimp at dinner the day before, and it took about twenty-four hours for the food poisoning to hit me. But as soon as this doctor shared the impact I'd had on his life, the Lord spoke to me: *I am well pleased with your academic work for my name's sake. You have done well. Keep trusting me.*

At the very moment of my need to be reassured about the value of my intellectual work, I met a doctor who "happened" to be on duty that evening in a city in which I'd never been who valued the very work for which I needed consolation during my depression. What a "coincidence"! What a special, unique event, given my need. It has been my repeated meditation on things like this in my own life that has reassured me that God knows about my needs and that I can trust him to act when he knows the timing is right.[16]

Another example comes from the life of Lonnie Frisbee

(1949–1993), who was a key figure in the early days of the Calvary Chapel, Vineyard, and Southern California Jesus movements in the 1960s. Lonnie was a broken man, but there is no question that he was fervent in seeking and serving Jesus, despite his inability to deal with some deep sinful tendencies in his life. Yet his worldwide impact can hardly be overestimated. He was a hippie who operated with a supernatural gifting few people have. Several books have been written about his life, and he was also the subject of a 2005 documentary film titled *Frisbee: The Life and Death of a Hippie Preacher.* Several people at our church—Vineyard Anaheim—knew Lonnie personally and remember him clearly.

I have had several conversations with Lonnie's brother, Stan, who has been with our church since its earliest days in the 1980s. Stan remembers the story I'm about to share, and it is also included in Lonnie's biography.[17] The events described below took place in the late 1970s and are about Lonnie and a friend, Peter Crawford. In the fall of 2018, I called Mr. Crawford (who didn't know me), and while he was driving, he spent about thirty minutes answering all of my questions and verifying before the Lord that all the events are true and actually took place.

> While on the staff of Calvary Chapel, Costa Mesa, California, in 1977, Lonnie heard the Lord say to him, *I'm going to send you to Africa. You're to quit your job and go to Africa.* Shortly thereafter, pastor Chuck Smith approached Lonnie and asked him point-blank, "How would you like to go to Africa?" Even though the church elders laid hands on Lonnie to commission his trip, a day or so later, Lonnie learned that he no longer had a salary from the church and that God would have to provide the funding.
>
> During the next five months, Lonnie's money ran out, so he moved into his grandmother's house and met two roommates, one of whom was Peter Crawford. Peter wanted

to go with Lonnie to Africa, but his financial situation was bleak. Still, Lonnie knew that God had called him to take this trip, so he and Peter prayed and went to Costa Mesa Travel. The travel agent told them they could travel around the world in one direction for a year for $1,900 apiece. With food and other expenses added in, the trip would total $5,000.

So Lonnie and Peter booked a nine-country trip, with South Africa at the halfway point and a final arrival on the East Coast of the United States, from where they planned to make it back to Southern California. According to Lonnie, when they got the tickets, he was "suddenly struck with terror" because they had virtually no money at all. As he recalls, at that very moment, he looked at the clock on the travel agent's wall, which read 10:00 a.m. It was a Monday morning, and they were responsible to pay for the tickets no later than three days from that day.

On the morning the money was due, Lonnie and Peter were discussing what in the world they were going to do when the phone rang. It was Dee, the church secretary, who said that a $25,000 check made out to Lonnie had just arrived at the church. It was from the owner of an oil company who wished to remain anonymous. After some sleuthing, Lonnie was able to find the man, and Peter, Lonnie, and this oil company owner had a meeting. The man told them a mind-blowing story.

On the Sunday evening before Lonnie and Peter first went to the travel agency, the host of a radio program named *Teen Challenge* needed a replacement, so Lonnie hosted the show that Sunday evening—the one and only time he was ever on the program. During the program, Lonnie shared his vision about the Africa trip. The donor reported that as he listened, the Lord told him to send a check for $25,000 to Lonnie Frisbee. The next day, the gentleman wrote and wired the check to Calvary Chapel, so it was there for Lonnie to pick up. But that's not all! At the very time Lonnie and Peter had been sitting at the travel agency—at 10:00 a.m. on that Monday morning—the man had been writing the check for their trip! God verified that the trip was his will by bringing it about through these confirming circumstances.

Does God still speak today? Yes, I believe he does—without a doubt. But there are other presences and voices all around us as well. As we learn to listen to the voice of God, we also need to learn how to be aware of and deal with this reality—the reality of angels and demons—in our daily lives.

Chapter 8

THE NATURE, REALITY, AND PURPOSES OF ANGELS AND DEMONS

I have never understood why some people believe that all of reality should be squeezed into a little box of things available only to the sense organs of Homo sapiens. In philosophy, many acknowledge that there is such a thing as "a priori knowledge"—knowledge that does not depend on an appeal to sense experience for its justification. The fields of logic, mathematics, metaphysics, ethics, and epistemology provide us with a knowledge of reality that goes far beyond the senses as well. I, along with many others, understand these fields to study things that *exist in a nonphysical realm*, things that are not capable of being sensed with the five senses. Furthermore, we know that our own knowledge of consciousness and our own self is made available through introspective awareness—a nonsensory form of awareness of things that are unobservable.

Angels and demons populate an unseen realm, but the sense-perceptible universe is a thin place. In other words, this "invisible" realm is never far away; it is very, very near to us. And it is not infrequent for angels and demons to manifest themselves on this side of the veil. But what more can we learn about this?[1]

ANGELS: THEIR NATURE
AND MINISTRIES

What are angels? Are they people? First, when we speak of a "person," we need to be clear that there is no such thing as a person plain and simple. There are only *kinds* of persons: divine persons, angelic persons, and human persons. If God had wanted to, he could have created Vulcans or other kinds of persons. And that's the best way to begin as we think about angels. They are a certain *kind* of person—angelic persons—and as such, they are pure spirits not naturally suited for bodies, even though they can temporarily manifest themselves in sense-perceptible ways or through spiritual awareness. They can even take on a body or something that looks like a body. At other times, one may simply sense an angel's presence. Some may "see" the angel as an ethereal sort of being, even while those around them are not permitted to see the angel.

So we can say that angels are people, but not human. But how does that work? Think about it this way. Person is to human as shape is to square as color is to red. If something is human, square, or red, then it is also a person, shaped, or colored, respectively. On the other hand, something can be a person *without* being a human (an angel, for example), a shaped thing *without* being square (being round, for example), or a colored thing *without* being red (being blue, for example). The lesson here is that being human is not the same thing as being a person. There are beings—angels—who are persons but not humans.

What do angels do for us? The Protestant Reformer John Calvin once noted, "Angels are the ministers and dispensers of the divine bounty towards us. Accordingly, we are told how they watch for our safety, how they undertake our defence, direct our path, and take heed that no evil befall us."[2] Yea verily and amen! Angels are our co-laborers in and for the kingdom of God, and precious, dear companions of believers. Here is a summary of several ways they aid us:

- They worship and obey God and serve us on God's behalf (Psalm 103:19–21).
- They minister to our needs and bring us comfort (Hebrews 1:7, 14).
- They protect us from harm (2 Kings 6:8–18; Psalms 34:7; 35:4–6; 91:11–12).
- They reveal messages from God to us (Luke 1:11–21; 2:8–12; the Greek *angelos* means "messenger").
- They guide us (Matthew 2:13; Acts 8:26).
- They often attend to believers at death (Luke 16:22).

This last point—attending to believers at death—may be new to you, so let me say something more about this comforting truth. Judith MacNutt, whom I introduced you to in the last chapter, remembers that as a child, she rode in the back seat when her parents would go somewhere. She often fell asleep on the trip home, but she always awoke in the morning safely tucked into her warm bed, carried there by the strong, loving arms of her father. He never left her alone in the dark, cold car. She concludes that when she dies, "I will go to sleep in peace and awaken in my forever home, carried there by God's angels."[3] Hospice personnel tell us that right before death, people often see angels who have come for them. Indeed, while in his hospital room, my own brother Bob saw an angel just before he died.

Do we have guardian angels? There is some controversy over whether we all have guardian angels assigned to us at conception who stay with us throughout our lives and facilitate our transition to heaven upon death. The controversy arises because there is only one text in all of Scripture that explicitly refers to guardian angels: "See that you do not despise one of these little ones. For I tell you that their angels in heaven always see the face of my Father in heaven" (Matthew 18:10). I must acknowledge that I myself am undecided on the matter, though I lean toward the view that we *do* have such angels.

The argument against guardian angels is that the case for them is based on one text and, moreover, that this text may justify belief in guardian angels for children but cannot warrant an extrapolation to lifelong guardian angels. The full case for the existence of guardian angels, however, is based on at least three considerations.

First, we need to understand the larger context of Matthew 18:10. Matthew 18:1–14 is about humility in the kingdom, as illustrated by the reference to children and the tremendous value of children over against the way society at the time placed them on the low end of the pecking order. Given this context, Jesus focuses on emulating their humble faith, not causing a little one to stumble, and caring about their final destiny. But surely these guidelines are not limited to children. We are to imitate adults as they follow Christ, not cause adult brothers and sisters to stumble, and care about everyone's eternal destiny. That said, it is reasonable to see Jesus using children as illustrations in his teaching, and if this is correct, we may interpret verse 10 in the same way. Jesus is not limiting guardian angels to children; rather, he is using children as an example to speak to what is true for all of us.

Second, the role of guarding human beings is a key role for angels more generally. Scripture is replete with cases in which angels guarded the people of God in a host of different ways, and in most cases, adults were the ones being guarded and protected. Given the broader scriptural case for angels as guardians, it makes sense that we would have individual angels guarding us throughout our lives.

One could respond correctly that this role might be fulfilled by different angels being sent to us at different times in our lives rather than by a set of angels assigned to stick with us as guards throughout our lives. The third and last reason addresses this response.

We know angels are not omniscient. They are curious and learn things, just as we do. So the idea that we might have specific guardian angels makes sense in at least two ways. For one thing, as time goes on, the angel learns more and more about us and is better able to work with us and anticipate what we may do next because they know us well. The angel learns where we are most vulnerable and so forth. Angels are not robotic beings who mechanically carry out their assignments. They are relational, and their love and concern for us are better facilitated if they are with us over the long haul.

While these three arguments seem reasonable to me, I acknowledge they are not knockdown arguments. So that is why I lean toward accepting guardian angels, but I cannot claim their denial is unreasonable.

ENCOURAGING CREDIBLE ACCOUNTS OF ANGELIC MANIFESTATIONS

For our own spiritual growth, it is crucial to see that we can actually *know*—not blindly believe—that the supernatural realm is real. Among other things, our knowledge of the supernatural is grounded in credible supernatural experiences. This claim may sound audacious, but I actually *know* that three guardian angels have been with me since at least the year 2005. And I want to explain to you *how* I know this. In what follows, I will refrain from using any individuals' real names to protect their anonymity. But all of the emails I mention are in a file in my office.

In May 2005, I spoke at a retreat for a church in Seattle. After my first talk on Friday night, a woman rushed up to me, and I could tell she was on a mission. After thanking me, she rather boldly shared that during my entire fifty-minute lecture, she had seen three angels surrounding me—a tall one behind me and two shorter ones on each side. Well, to be honest, I thought she was either crazy or simply seeking attention, so I thanked her but completely dismissed what she said. The pastor conveyed to me afterward that she was a very mature believer, but that didn't matter to me, since I had zero inclination to believe her and promptly forgot about what she had said—or so I thought.

Several months later, on August 24, 2005, Biola's fall semester began. Later the next week, I started experiencing some personal difficulties that I believed had a spiritual cause, and so one night in bed, I prayed for something I had never asked the Lord for in my thirty-seven years as a Christian. I remembered the woman who had shared about the angels on my visit to Seattle, and I told the Lord that I had no idea if those three angels in Seattle were real, but if they were; I wanted him to make sure they were still with me and protecting me. I also asked if he could somehow let me know they were present. I had never asked for angelic protection before. I went to sleep that night, and in the days that followed, everything seemed to be business as usual.

But as I was later to learn, things were not as they appeared. On September 21, I received an email from a philosophy graduate student named Joe in which he rather embarrassingly divulged that the prior week, while sitting in my metaphysics class next to the window in Myers Hall 109, about halfway into my lecture he suddenly saw three angels surrounding me. The scene lasted for about ten to fifteen minutes, and then it was over. He had waited to share it with me out of fear of looking foolish, but several other graduate students had urged him to do so.

The next day after sending the email, Joe came to my office at my request. He told me he was certain that the three angels had been there in the room and not just in his head. He shared how at first he had thought he was just seeing things, so he had started rubbing his eyes vigorously, but they remained there. He described them as wearing white robes, though he could not see their faces, and he also brought me a drawing of the scene he had made. A taller angel was behind me, and two shorter ones stood on each side!

As an aside, a few years later I described this incident while I was lecturing in Georgia. One person in that audience—Frank Waller—had been a graduate student in the same class on the day Joe saw the angels. Frank had sat two seats behind Joe, and he recalled to me one day early in the semester when he had noticed that Joe seemed extremely agitated and was rubbing his eyes in a way he had never seen him do, either before that time or after. Frank remembered the incident because he had almost gotten out of his seat to ask Joe if he could escort him to the restroom to wash out his eyes, but before he could do so, Joe had stopped.

Three days after meeting with Joe, on Monday, September 25, I was addressing a Biola student group, where I shared my two incidents with the three angels. That evening, I received another email from a student who had attended my lecture. After sharing her name, she noted that for years, she had been blessed with a gift of discernment and the ability to see into the spiritual realm. What she said next was a shock: "I had seen your three angels even before you mentioned it, and so when you did, I was shocked that you knew they were there." I never saw that student again, but she had no reason to fabricate the story and risk the embarrassment of being exposed.

There's more. Around ten years later, on May 2, 2015, I received an email from a lawyer who works in Ontario, California. Three years earlier, he had called me out of the blue—I had never met him or even heard of him. He shared with me that he suffered from severe anxiety and asked if he could meet with me at my campus office. We had a meaningful time together, and before he left, I asked him to get down on his knees. I laid hands on him and prayed over him for healing.

After our time of prayer, he left, and I never heard from him again until the email he sent me three years later. In the email, he said there was something he had wanted to share with me ever since our meeting but had been afraid to do so until now. He wrote that when he got down on his knees so I could pray for him, he sensed "presences" entering my office. Opening his eyes—and this is made rather emphatic in his email—he observed three angels surrounding me, one who was taller than the other two.

In response to my reply to his email, he affirmed that he was absolutely certain he had seen three angels in the room and that he had absolutely no knowledge of any of my prior experiences that I've shared with you above, and he added that the experience was life-changing for him. For me, this was solid evidential confirmation of the existence of my three guardian angels.

But there's still one more important event I wish to share. Marc Stephens, a good buddy of mine, traveled with me to an apologetics conference on October 26–27, 2018, in Beaverton, Oregon. I was a keynote speaker at the conference, and I gave an hour-long lecture on the existence of God that Saturday morning to a crowd of about 350 people. That afternoon, the conference concluded with a Q and A time with all the conference speakers, but there was a fifteen-minute break before that session. I was sitting at the book table in the lobby with Marc and two administrative assistants sitting right next to me when a woman in her forties approached the book table to talk to me.

After introducing herself, she noted that after being a Jewish atheist all her life, eighteen months ago she had given her life to Jesus. She expressed gratitude for the growth she had experienced from some of my books. Then she said this, and I'm paraphrasing a bit here from memory: "Dr. Moreland, I wanted to tell you that during your lecture this morning, I saw angels on the stage with you." When she said this, I interrupted her and asked Marc and the two administrative assistants to listen to what she would say next so I would have three eyewitnesses who could vouch for this incident. I asked her to tell me more, and whether she had any idea how many angels there were. She said there were three angels. I asked her if she knew where they were located in relation to me, and she replied with confidence in her voice that they were standing around me. I then asked her if she had noticed anything about their size. She responded that a tall angel was standing behind me and two shorter ones on each side. Marc and the two assistants already knew of my previous angelic encounters, and we were all amazed by the precise details this woman provided. But I needed to ask her one more question: "Have you ever come into contact with any information about me or heard of any previous experience I've had with angels?" She seemed genuinely puzzled by the question but said no. It was evident to all of us that she had no idea why I was asking this.

While I have never seen these angelic beings, I believe the testimonial evidence I have given about my guardian angels would stand up almost anywhere—even in a court of law! The truth is that the supernatural world is all around us. And please remember, there is nothing special about me. I hope the evidence I share will encourage you that God has sent angels to guide, protect, and minister to you too.

We are not on our own in this world![4] Angelic manifestations happen frequently and to all kinds of people. While they may be embarrassed to hear me say this, the late Christian philosopher Dallas Willard and his precious wife, Jane, have been giants in the way of Jesus, and they were like adopted parents to my wife, Hope, and me. I knew Dallas very closely for more than thirty years, and he would have been the last person on earth to make something up to draw attention to himself or to enhance his ministry. In fact, most often he did quite the opposite. He was a gentle, humble man who lived a life of quiet study and contemplation.

After Dallas's passing, I heard through the grapevine that he had mentioned to some people that he had seen angels (I heard he had seen four of them), so I contacted his wife, Jane, about the matter, and on August 28, 2014, she replied to my inquiry with this email:

> The timing was our last year at Tennessee Temple College—so Dallas was a senior and I had graduated and was on the faculty. The setting followed a meeting with the evangelist R. R. Brown, one of the four men to whom Dallas dedicated *Divine Conspiracy*. That incident is written up in the last paragraph of the *Christianity Today* (1996) article about Dallas . . . just a few sentences. Let me know if you can't find that and I'll try to fax it. I'm the one who told the writer about that. Dallas never told people unless they asked if he'd ever had an experience like that, then I would say yes and get him to tell it. But he told this only to me, and I don't know what use you want to make of it. But it was that night after the experience, we had gone to bed, and he said, "There is an angel at each post at the foot of the bed." In my mind, that was two angels. I didn't see them but deliberately pictured them there—only two, not four. Did he ever tell you about it?

Of course Dallas had never told me this himself. Sharing a story like this that might bring attention to himself just wasn't something he did. But I share this incident because I can't think of more credible eyewitnesses to an angelic sighting than Dallas and Jane Willard. My point is this: angels are real and people experience them. And that is that!

Here's a final case about angels that I find rather funny. I first read about it in *Encountering Heaven and the Afterlife*, a book written by James Garlow and Keith Wall.[5] Dr. Garlow has master's degrees from Princeton and Asbury seminaries and a PhD from Drew University. He is also the senior pastor of Skyline Church in San Diego and has appeared on CNN, FOX, NBC, and several other media outlets. He is heard daily on more than eight hundred radio stations and is a *New York Times* bestselling author. Keith Wall is a publishing veteran of nearly thirty years and has contributed to several prominent books.

Garlow and Wall had already carefully verified each of the accounts in their book, but before I was willing to include this case in my own book, I needed to verify it for myself so I would be confident of its veracity. I obtained the phone number of the woman mentioned in the account, Mayme Shroyer, and on February 9, 2020, I called her and we talked for forty to forty-five minutes. She personally affirmed the "100 percent accuracy" of the book's account while adding further background details not included in the published story.

While in her early thirties, Mayme had moved from Virginia to Oregon after a broken engagement (Mayme never married). She had a degree in electronics and was hired by Intel. At first she lived in apartments, but she wanted to purchase a home, which she did after a year of looking around. But there was just one problem—the only house she could afford was a lower-priced home located in a dangerous, drug-overrun neighborhood. The good news was that the neighborhood was next to a huge park with lots of trees. The bad news was that after the sun went down, groups of gang members gathered throughout the park and sold drugs.

Shortly after she moved into her new home, a drug-dealing "young kid" moved in with his grandmother two doors down from her home. Soon a stream of young men were purchasing drugs at the house, and according to Mayme, she was frequently awakened in the middle of the night by the sound of these men talking, doing drugs, and hanging out in her own front yard!

She desperately needed a security system, but they were too expensive for her to afford. She wrestled with the decision of paying $35 a month for a good system, but as she considered it, the thought came to her that for that same amount of money she could sponsor a child in another country through Compassion International. Immediately, she had a strong sense that God was speaking to her: *Feed a Third World child. I'll be your security system.* She listened, and that's what she did!

Working long hours each day, Mayme usually arrived home after dark. With a newfound confidence that God really was the one who had spoken to her, and weary of being a prisoner in her own home, she decided to start exercising outside again in the park, despite the significant danger. She laced up her tennis shoes and "hit the sidewalks that meandered through the tree-lined park." Suddenly, she sensed someone following her over her right shoulder. Glancing back, she saw a police car moving very slowly. Rolling down his window, the police officer asked Mayme if she had seen any suspicious characters in the area. After she replied no, the officer responded, "We have received several phone calls at the station from people living around the park. All of them reported seeing a tall black man, around seven feet tall, wearing a white muscle shirt and carrying a long sword."

Mayme concluded: "As the patrol car drove away, something struck me, and I couldn't help but laugh out loud with delight and gratitude. I'm sure the officer had just described my guardian angel."

This event happened years ago, but when I talked to Mayme in February 2020, I could hear the excitement in her voice as she relived her memories of that wonderful event. She was convinced that the tall black man was her guardian angel!

DEMONS: THEIR NATURE AND ACTIVITIES

Demons are fallen angels, and as such, they are malevolent angelic persons who, like persons in general, live in an ordered society in which some demons have greater power and authority than others. Many Christians hold that believers can be oppressed but not possessed by demons. Unfortunately, this view is terribly confused and false.[6] First, the distinction between possession (having a demon inside oneself) and oppression (being harassed by a demon from the outside) is not a biblical one and is based on an incorrect translation of the Greek word *daimonizomai* as "demon possessed." This was then contrasted with demonic influence or harassment (being oppressed).

But Scripture knows nothing of this distinction. The Bible uses two ways to describe a person's (including a Christian's) relationship with demons: *daimonizomai* ("to be demonized") and *echein daimonion* ("to have a demon"; according to a widely preferred interpretation of Ephesians 4:27, which reads [KJV], "neither give place [*topos*] to the devil"—where *topos* signifies a location, a stronghold rooted within the person). Thus, "to be demonized" and "to have a demon" are the biblical ways of referring to a believer's relationship to demons. In the New Testament, the Greek word for "possession" is never used in relation to demons but instead is limited to the fact that we are owned by God (Ephesians 1:14; 1 Peter 2:9).

People can have demons inside them, and with the rare exception of those who have repeatedly sought to give the devil control over them, believers cannot be completely controlled by demons. Even if they were under some control, with the indwelling Spirit's help, they retain a pocket of free will to make decisions that would lead to their liberation. Regarding the issue of control, many experts on demons rightly claim that for the believer, there are degrees of demonic influence, from mild harassment to significant control.[7]

One more thing I will add on this point. Christians make three common mistakes when it comes to demonization. The first two are paired extremes—acting like demons don't exist and, its opposite, seeing a demon under every tree. The biblical truth is somewhere between these extremes, a place of wisdom and balance. The third mistake is related—namely, ascribing all of our problems to "the enemy." Scripture makes it clear that there are *three* sources of attack on Christians: the world (that aspect of culture that is contrary to biblical teaching and wisdom; 1 John 2:15–17), the flesh (our own ingrained tendencies and habits to think, feel, and behave in ways contrary to God's will; Romans 7:14–25), and the devil and demons (1 Peter 5:8). Accordingly, we must keep *all three* potential enemies in view as we seek to grow and please God.

How should we think of demons if we wish to avoid these mistakes? Charles Kraft suggests we liken demons to rats. Rats need garbage to feed on and will leave when the garbage is gone. Similarly, demons usually gain entrance into our lives because of spiritual, emotional, or physical "garbage," and the demons fester and make worse what was already there, preying on our anxieties, fears, and sinful temptations. This means that once a demon has been dispatched or removed from a person, they often will still need therapy, discipleship, and assistance in making good choices to get rid of the garbage and leave no place for the demon to return.

FOUR WAYS WE KNOW DEMONS ARE REAL

There are four ways we can know demons are real creatures. *First, the Bible and Jesus clearly affirm their reality.* We have a host of good evidence, including (but not limited to) the testimony of the Spirit when we read or hear the Bible that it is God's very Word.

In its influence, Scripture is orders of magnitude above any other book (as is Jesus in relation to other significant people). The Bible has outlived its critics in the past, and it will do so again.

Second, we know demons are real because we have seen people experience relief after addressing them as demonic influences, even when nothing else works. There are clear cases in which a person has tried virtually everything to get rid of what is dragging them down, including adequate therapy and medications. In such cases, if a person is restored (and especially when instantly restored) through deliverance prayer and then remains that way for a good period of time (to show that something real happened and to allow for demons to attempt to return later), I consider this positive evidence that the demonic was an important aspect of that person's issues.

Third, we can know demons are real if the person's inner life and behavior comport with biblical descriptions of those for demonized people. Signs that an individual may under demonic influence include the following: they are apt to embrace false teaching (1 Timothy 4:1–2; 2 Timothy 2:25–26; 1 John 4:1); cannot accept the forgiveness of God and are filled with obsessive guilt, shame, and fear (1 Peter 5:8; Revelation 12:10); show resistance to spiritual things (Mark 5:7); cannot acknowledge that Jesus is Lord (1 Corinthians 12:3); do not love other believers (1 John 3:10, 14; 4:20); or respond in fear and disobedience to the name of Jesus. World-renowned missionary George Otis Jr. once told me that demonized people manifest similar behaviors all over the world (so these behaviors are not culturally conditioned) and do not respond to the name of any religious figure except Jesus, even in locations where the human people have no idea who Jesus is.

Fourth, we can know demons are real because we have witnessed explicit manifestations of supernatural phenomena. There are two strong pieces of evidence in this regard. First, there are instances when overt physical phenomena occur, such as moving objects.

A friend of mine (I'll call him Dr. Smith) has a PhD from one of the top ten universities in America and has published a technical monograph with one of the top academic publishers in the world while teaching at a well-respected university. Dr. Smith lives alone, and he told me recently that for a period of two months, he had seen overt demonic phenomena in his condominium. It began with a specific piece of furniture in motion in his living room, an event he witnessed with his own eyes. Next, his phone began to ring repeatedly, with no one on the other end of the line. Shortly thereafter, when he went downstairs for breakfast, he found a large wreath that had been hanging on his wall lying in the middle of the floor about twelve feet from the wall, as though someone had tossed it there. Note again that Dr. Smith lives alone and is quite certain no one had entered his home during the night, nor does he walk in his sleep.

Second, in addition to odd physical manifestations, there are instances during a deliverance session when a person will express private (usually embarrassing) details of the life of someone on the prayer team—details the demonized person simply could not have known. This happened to two friends of mine—on different occasions—who were embarrassed in front of others as a demon accurately accused each of a specific sin and went on to supply details.

In addition to people I personally know, New York psychiatrist Dr. Richard Gallagher says he has seen more than one hundred cases of genuine demon possession.[8] The following was published by Sheila Flynn in an interview with Dr. Gallagher:

> He says the demons exhibit extraordinary powers such as personal knowledge and near clairvoyance. On one occasion, a demon told him how his mother had died—ovarian cancer. That evil spirit also knew "how 15 other people's parents died, too. It wasn't just me."

On another occasion, a demon told him exactly what a priest was wearing though the clergyman was nowhere near Dr. Gallagher and the possessed person speaking. In a different case, Gallagher was also personally addressed.

"I had a demon say to me: 'How's that book going? It won't do any good' . . . that's when I was first thinking of writing a book. So I've had demons come and they've said they hate me, but again, I think they hate all Christians . . . they certainly put more of their energy in saying how they hate the exorcist. That's their real target, not me."

REAL CASES OF DEMONIC ENCOUNTERS

For the remainder of the chapter, I will share three clear cases of demonic deliverance in which I was personally involved. I share these personal examples for two reasons. First, since I was an eyewitness to each, I can say before the Lord that everything you are about to read is the truth, the whole truth, and nothing but the truth. And as you will see, others were involved in each case who can attest to what I say.

Second, I do not have a special gift of discernment regarding demons, nor am I in any sense especially gifted in this area. What I have going for me is that I have learned to see the world through biblical eyes and not through Western, naturalistic eyes. Thus, I am on the lookout for demonic presences and am willing to step out and help people who seem to be demonized. My point in saying this is that *you can do this too*. We start by asking the Lord Jesus to work with us to be able to better sense when demonization is taking place. I confess I still get it wrong and pray deliverance over someone who may not need it. But if I pray sensitively and nondogmatically (for example, "Let's be sure that no demons are trying to intimidate you or make your problems worse"), then even when I'm wrong, no harm is done.

Case #1 of Demonic Influence

The first case happened on a Monday night in the middle of February 2004. I was with about forty philosophy graduate students who had attended a talk I was presenting about the supernatural. After the lecture, I led the group in prayer when I suddenly sensed darkness and demonic presence in the room. I prayed in Jesus' name and on the basis of his shed blood that any attacking demon had to leave. The next morning during my office hours at the university, I was shocked to learn what had happened when I prayed that prayer. One of the students there that night—Michael Swanson—knocked on my door to ask if he could have a few minutes with me. Here is what he shared:

> This is a raw account of how God delivered me from demonization/spiritual oppression in 2004. It is a vulnerable story to share, but I share it in the hope that it might give someone hope who has lost hope in their life.
>
> But first, a bit about me, in case this will help you take my story seriously. I am a church planter and ordained pastor in the Anglican Church in North America. I was the founding dean of Southern California for the Diocese of Churches for the Sake of Others, led by Bishop Todd Hunter. I hold an MA degree from Talbot School of Theology, and prior to pursuing vocational ministry, I was a published philosopher. As an undergrad I was a student leader with Cru at Cal Poly San Luis Obispo, where I also led the Veritas Forum.
>
> In the fall of 2003, I began the MA Philosophy program at Talbot School of Theology. That semester, someone I loved dearly shared with me how she had been the victim of sexual abuse some years prior. Hearing this absolutely broke my heart. I was not only heartbroken because of the evil that had been perpetrated against someone I loved,

but I was also heartbroken over the effects I learned it was having in the present.

Initially, this led me into deep grief. But over time, I found myself in the midst of a major depressive episode. I also developed symptoms of secondary posttraumatic stress disorder. It was as though a cloud of darkness had descended over my life. My life became a waking nightmare. Things got so bad that many, many times I asked God to snuff me out, to take my life. I simply couldn't stand the pain any longer.

By God's grace, I never attempted to take my life. But in a 2004 journal entry, I wrote, "Black death has hovered on my doorstep for months now. What salve is there for this madness? Can anything bring healing?" I felt as though I was being tormented. And thoughts of doom would fill my mind, such as the thought that the same sort of violence my loved one experienced in the past would happen again, and there was nothing I could do about it. Thoughts of accusation against God would flood my mind as well, including novel arguments against God's existence and goodness. It was so bad that I lost all hope for my life, and I nearly lost my faith.

But there was a tremendous turning point in my journey that I want to share with you. Sometime in early 2004, I heard that Professor J. P. Moreland had just returned from sabbatical, that he had recently walked through a major depressive episode and was going to be sharing his story. So I was determined to attend.

When J. P. shared about his journey with depression, I resonated with everything he said. He talked about how as human beings we are multifaceted. Therefore, healing needs to address all the different facets of the self. For example, we are physical beings, so those with depression need to get adequate sleep, eat well, and consider psychiatric treatment. We are relational beings, and therefore we need community and supportive relationships where we can share about our struggles. We are emotional beings, so we need to process our grief and emotions—possibly through counseling. He also talked about how part of his healing journey had involved receiving prayer for deliverance from spiritual attacks.

All of this made sense to me. But as J. P. closed, he prayed for those in attendance, and something unusual happened. His prayer began as a loving, though fairly generic, prayer. But at one moment he stopped, as though he was being prompted by God. And he began to pray against any demons in the room, commanding them to leave. As soon as he did, I began to feel a dark presence leave my body and be replaced by a warm flow from the top of my head down to the tips of my toes. I didn't know exactly what was going on, but the best language I could come up with was that I felt like I was being filled with the Holy Spirit. I felt incredibly close to God for the first time in a long time, and I felt God's love. As J. P.'s prayer ended, my experience gently subsided.

I still wasn't quite sure what had just happened, but I thanked God, thanked J. P., and then returned to my lonely grad housing apartment.

When I got back to my apartment, I could tell immediately that something was different, though I wasn't quite sure what. I began to pace through my apartment, trying to piece it together. At one point I realized that I was smiling for the first time in months. I was absolutely astounded. I was actually experiencing joy! Still trying to come to grips with what had just happened, my experience before and after that brief prayer led me to conclude something that was difficult for me to accept—namely, that I had just been delivered from an evil presence. That was the only language that could adequately capture the phenomenology of my experience before and after that event.

That was hard for me to accept, as I had been running on a naive view of spiritual reality. Up to that moment, I had thought that faithful Christians were basically immune from any significant direct spiritual attack. Knowing what I now know of Scripture, theology, and church history, I realize that's a naive view. But I share this so you know that I'm not the sort of person who punted to spiritual attack at the first sign of adversity. Quite the opposite. But two more events transpired over the next several minutes that confirmed the conclusion I had just arrived at.

My phone rang. It was my mom. She said, "You're not going to believe this, but two people had prophetic words for you today." I did not come from a charismatic background, so I'd never received a prophetic word in my life, let alone two in one day! But I was very open, so I encouraged my mom to share. She said, "The first was from Aunt Susan in Colorado. As she was praying for you today, she said she felt like God wanted her to tell you that it's going to be okay. That this isn't going to go on and on."

That was such a relief, as up to that point, I had begun to assume that my life was basically over. That the hell I was going through would continue for the rest of my life. So I shared how that was so encouraging to hear, and I hoped that would be the case.

She went on to say, "The second person is JoLynn DiGrazia." JoLynn is an amazing woman of God who started a ministry in my hometown called Westside Ministries, which ministers to troubled youth. I knew her to be a woman of sterling character and Christian maturity, so I put stock in anything she said. My mom said, "I ran into JoLynn today, and as we were speaking, she said, 'God is giving me a prophetic word for your son. God is allowing him to be sifted right now. But it's not going to go on and on forever. God is allowing it for a greater purpose. And once he has turned, he will strengthen his brothers.'"

I said, "Wow, I don't know exactly what *sifted* means, but that definitely resonates with my experience. I feel like I've been sifted!" At that moment, there was a knock on my door. I said, "Mom, someone's at my door. I'm going to have to call you back."

I opened the door, and standing there was my friend and fellow MA Philosophy student Ed Luk, who lived across the way. He was standing there with an open Bible in his hands and an awkward, sheepish look on his face. I said, "Ed, what's up?" He said, "So I was in the bathroom. And I felt like I heard God say, *Give Michael this Scripture.* But it's a weird one. So I said, *God, are you sure?* And I felt like I heard God say yes. So here I am."

I said, "Well, go for it. What's the Scripture?"

He said, quoting Luke 22:31–32, "Simon, Simon, behold, Satan has demanded permission to sift you like wheat; but I have prayed for you, that your faith may not fail; and you, when once you have turned again, strengthen your brothers" (NASB).

I almost fell over. I said, "Whoa, Ed, you need to come inside, brother!" And then I began to open up to him for the first time about what I had been going through. Through these prophetic words, I became convinced that I had in fact been delivered that night from some terrible form of spiritual oppression. A horrible, dark, and heavy weight had been lifted. After that night, I still had things to process and continue in as part of my healing journey. I continued with the antidepressants I had recently begun to take. I continued to see a Christian counselor. And I continued to process things with God and trusted friends.

But that night was a radical turning point. Joy returned

to my life. Hope returned to my life. Symptoms of depression lessened. The tortured thoughts and feelings of being tormented ceased. It was as though I was still in an ocean amidst a storm, but now there was no longer someone shoving my head under the water, trying to drown me. And it felt like I had just been given a life preserver. My counselor was so stunned at the progress he saw in my life in such a short period of time that he said, "I'm shocked!" He'd never seen anything like it.

This experience made real to me the reality of spiritual warfare described in the Scriptures, as well as the authority that followers of Jesus have been given to confront it. Were it not for J. P. faithfully following the prompting of the Holy Spirit to pray against spiritual attack that night, I'd hate to think what would have happened with me. I will be forever grateful to the Lord for his mercy and deliverance in my life.

In closing, I will add that what Satan meant for evil, God meant for good. And I have seen God use the hell I went through to equip me to bring hope and deliverance to many others, including several people who have struggled with suicidality. So the prophetic words that were spoken have been fulfilled.

Less than thirty minutes after Michael left, I heard another knock on my door, and a student I'll call Jonathan asked if he could chat for a while. To make a long story short, Jonathan had been struggling with a depressive, dark heaviness for months and had not slept well during that time. He then told me—and this is almost the exact wording he used—that when I had prayed the night before, he felt a dark presence leave his body and be replaced by a warm oily feeling that started at his head and "poured" throughout his body down to his feet. He slept well that night for the first time in months. I checked with both men for the rest of the semester and into the summer. Both continued to feel and sleep well, and the darkness never returned.

Case #2 of Demonic Influence

In September 2017, I received a phone call from Cat Guerra, wife of Darren, a faculty colleague of mine. The case involved a high school girl named Kristen (not her real name) who had recently experienced dramatic changes and needed prayer. Kristen and her family were close friends of the Guerras. Here in Cat's own words is what happened:

> In August 2017, it began as nightmares that were so vivid and disturbing that Kristen could not sleep. Then she started convulsing and writhing on the floor, with her eyes rolled back in her head. Kristen was a joyful, energetic, and bright young woman who loved to dance and spend time with others. But that summer something had changed. A friend came and told me that Kristen was having epileptic seizures and asked me to pray. Kristen was a believer who was part of a strong Christian home with parents who are both graduates of Christian universities with deep faith and relationships with God. One is a psychologist; the other is the administrator of a homeschool program. Both of them work in ministry to encourage pastors and church leaders.
>
> When I heard this description of what was happening to Kristen, I was convinced that a demonic presence was involved. So I inquired immediately, both of my church and of a prominent, large church in town, for a pastor or a team to help me with deliverance ministry. This was not successful, so I went to Kristen's house and brought with me a prayer warrior friend to try to pray the demon out and away from Kristen.
>
> Sadly, we all sensed that the dark presence remained.

Soon after, I returned with *The Steps to Freedom in Christ* [a resource by Neil Anderson for deliverance prayer ministry] and spent hours with Kristen in the hope of sensing deliverance.[9] But the presence remained. During this time, another friend of the family came and tried inner healing prayer with Kristen. But the nightmares were worsening. Kristen was now dreaming that she was rising from her sleep in the middle of the night and murdering her entire family.

Because it seemed that the parents and the nearby churches had a typical Western evangelical view of demonology, my husband, Darren, said, "It's unfortunate that most churches aren't equipped to handle these situations; you'll have to go to the charismatics." I reached out to J. P. and Hope Moreland. J. P. replied in part with this message: "Order the book *Defeating Dark Angels* by Charles Kraft. Some demons bring a string of demons with them, and you will need several people to pray against them. Bring her to my church on a Sunday for prayer, and she may well be delivered."

The next evening, I knew that Kristen would be with her mom, Amy, and some other friends, and I prayed my entire way to Amy's house. I prayed that Amy would be open to having Kristen come for prayer. And before I could even begin a conversation with Amy, she turned to me and said, "We will go and do anything you want Kristen to do because I saw it." Shocked, I asked her, "What do you mean?" Amy replied, "I took Kristen to an office that specializes in brain scans. Once she fell asleep, I saw it. The demon was crawling on my daughter's body and licking her and looking at me. It was as if it was taunting me."

The next day, Kristen's family and I met with J. P. at his church. J. P. opened the conversation by stating that a lot of believers have a demon bothering them, but they are often just unaware of it. During the prayer and worship time, Kristen, her family, and I went forward with J. P. and Hope. About eight members of the church surrounded Kristen in a quiet place to the right of the stage. Worship music was playing. It was not dramatic or intensely emotional, but as the prayers and commands were offered and Kristen prayed, the demonic presence left, and Kristen was set free! The joy in her spirit and the peace in her demeanor were restored and evident to all of us. It was clear that Jesus had won the victory over darkness that day, and his once-tormented daughter could now walk in freedom.

Since that day, Kristen's parents said the experience has transformed Kristen and the way they do ministry. Kristen no longer suffers nightmares and continues to live for Christ. She is her normal upbeat and active self and shares her powerful testimony with others. A few days after Kristen's deliverance, an interesting situation occurred. When the book *Defeating Dark Angels* arrived at my home, I stayed up all night until 4:00 a.m. the next morning reading the entire book. I said to Darren, "I don't know why I stayed up all night reading this book." Darren said, "Well, did you see Amy's text?" A text from Amy had come that same morning, stating that Kristen's brother was now having nightmares.

I gathered my two trusted prayer warrior friends, April and Kim, and met at Amy's home once again that evening. Kim prayed that the family would know without a doubt that God's presence was with them and that the enemy was defeated. Now equipped with the knowledge of how to pray, we three gals came to the home and prayed in each room with each family member who was willing. At the end of our closing prayer for the family, Kristen's sister let out a gasp. When asked what it was, she said, "I don't want to say. You'll all think I'm really weird." Her parents and the women encouraged her to share. She stated, "There's an angel now standing in the corner of the room." The enemy was defeated, and God's Spirit had filled their home once again!

Case #3 of Demonic Influence

On July 27 and 28, 2019, I spoke at the Saturday evening service and twice on Sunday morning at SeaCoast Grace Church in Cypress, California (in the Los Angeles area). The pastor is Doyle Surratt, who is a wonderful brother in the Lord. I would estimate there were seven to eight hundred people in attendance at the second Sunday morning service at 10:45 a.m. The sanctuary was divided into six sections—a left, middle, and right section on the lower front level, and the same arrangement farther back in the second tier of seats. Since I was preaching, I sat in the front row about ten feet from the pulpit that was in the center of an elevated stage.

During worship, I suddenly began to sense dark demonic presences over my left shoulder in the top left section (the right section as viewed from the pulpit). I turned around and saw about eighty people sitting in that section. As I turned back in my seat, a series of thoughts came to me. They were short, direct, crystal clear, and authoritative. I was 75 percent sure it was the Lord, saying, *There is a person in that section who does not attend this church but who came today because she is going to commit suicide later this afternoon. She is being degraded by a demon, and when you get up to preach, ask the congregation to join you and command the demon to leave. And tell the person that I love her and have important plans for her life.*

I have preached in about four hundred churches in the fifty-two years I've been a Jesus follower, and never had I done such a thing. But because it seemed very likely that God himself had spoken to me, even though it was risky and a bit embarrassing, I did what I was told to do. When worship was over, I went to the pulpit immediately and began to do what I was told. As of the writing of this book in June 2020, I had just recently spoken to the pastor's son and church staff member, Cody Surratt, about the incident. He reminded me that he was supposed to introduce me, but I got up to the pulpit so fast and began to direct the congregation that he had no time for the introduction! (Sorry, Cody!)

I told the congregation that I sensed a dark demonic presence in the upper left section, and that I believed God had just told me there was a person in that section who was not an attender of the church but who had come that day intending to commit suicide later that afternoon. I went on to share the rest of what the Lord had told me, and I asked the congregation to turn, look up at that section, and hold their hands out with palms directed toward that area. When they did so, I spoke to the demon affecting the person and commanded it to leave in Jesus' name. I invited the Spirit to come and fill the vacated place, said "Amen," and gave my message. The whole thing was recorded.

About two and a half months later, on October 14, 2019, I received this text message from Pastor Cody, which I've saved on my phone:

> Hey, J. P., it's Cody Surratt from SeaCoast Grace. I just wanted to share a story with you. When you were at SCG, you opened up the third service by saying that you felt like someone in the stadium seating was struggling with suicide and you prayed against it. Well, a woman came forward today and shared that she was the woman you were praying for. Long story short, she was, indeed, considering suicide until you said what you did, and she knew you were talking about her. That's the reason she didn't, and she has been coming back ever since.

In a later conversation in June 2020 with Cody, he added a few more details. Besides coming forward at church, the woman had scheduled an appointment with Cody's dad, Doyle, the senior pastor. Doyle reported the content of that appointment to me, using a different name and after receiving the woman's permission to do so. Doyle shared that the woman was in fact demonized, had felt the presence leave her during prayer, was not an attender at the time, and did have plans to commit suicide later that day. And she was now loving the church and seeking to grow spiritually. I thank God I accepted the risk of looking stupid to do what I was confident—but not certain—he had told me to do.

Make no mistake about it. The secular worldview is false. Angels and demons are around us all the time. And there is solid evidence that they are real. In this chapter, we have transitioned from evidence of divine supernatural actions in the world to a broader picture of the reality of the spiritual world in general by focusing on angelic and demonic manifestations. In the next chapter, we will transition one more time to a consideration of near-death experiences and the reality of heaven and hell.

Chapter 9

DEFENDING THE
VERACITY OF NEAR-DEATH
EXPERIENCES

It is beyond reasonable doubt that in 1999, an orthopedic surgeon, Mary Neal, died in a kayaking accident in southern Chile and was taken to heaven by Jesus himself.[1] After her near-death experience (NDE), Mary's life was lastingly transformed, and after reflecting deeply on what had happened to her, she wrote a book on the seven most important lessons she learned. Here they are as she states them:

- Circumstances are seen differently through the lens of heaven.
- Death is not the end.
- God is love, and forgiveness sets us free.
- Heaven is real and grace abounds.
- God wants to be seen and shows His presence in our world through miracles.
- God has a plan for us that is one of hope, purpose, and beauty.
- In God's time, beauty blossoms in all things.[2]

These are not just pious platitudes or Christian slogans. They are life-altering truths we all should set our hearts and minds to believe more strongly as we age in the Lord. The main purpose of this chapter is to present some evidence-based NDEs that I hope will intensify your belief in these lessons and related truths. I commend to you what Mary Neal does in light of the truths she shares. Each day, she writes out and recites the following creed:

- I believe God's promises are true.
- I believe heaven is real.
- I believe nothing can separate me from God's love.
- I believe God has work for me to do.
- I believe God will see me through and carry me when I cannot walk.[3]

My own daily affirmations are similar and have been so real and wonderful to me that I don't have to *try* to believe them. They give me a joy and hope that sustain my daily life. Here is what I write out and say each day:

> I know that God is actually real, that Christianity really is true, that heaven and hell are real and that life does not end at death, and that no matter my age, health, or station in life, God has a hopeful, good plan for my life and a future in heaven forever that is so wonderful that it overrides all the hardship and suffering in my earthly life.

The miracles recounted in this book—including many others I've read or heard about—and especially the NDEs I know about, have had a significant impact on my degree of conviction about this daily affirmation. However, before we look at these cases, I will address the key objections people have to the veracity of NDEs—objections from both naturalists and other Christians who believe that NDEs contradict Scripture.

A BRIEF ASSESSMENT OF THE CASE FOR AND AGAINST THE VERACITY OF NDES

First, let's consider some background information. Contrary to what you might think, NDEs aren't all that rare. For example, it's estimated that about one out of twenty-five Americans have had an NDE, and if you extrapolate this figure, it means around 15 to 16 million Americans now living have experienced one. Statistical studies estimate up to 300 million cases have occurred world-wide.[4] Moreover, scholarly research on NDEs has been ongoing for more than forty years. Most of the prominent, respected NDE researchers have MD or PhD degrees—and many were skeptics before examining the evidence for and against them.[5] I don't know of a single case in which a researcher did not convert to believing in God and the reality of the afterlife after being exposed to the evidence. Numerous books have been published by respectable publishers defending the reality of NDEs, as well as at least one thousand journal articles.[6] Moreover, NDE accounts have been around for centuries, dating back to the ancient Near East, and have been consistently reported throughout human history.[7]

Here is a summary of six lines of evidence for the veracity of NDEs:[8]

1. NDEs are worldwide, numerous, often failing to conform to religious or worldview expectations, and happen to atheists as well as little children. As noted above, thousands upon thousands of NDE cases have been authenticated by scholarly research. They happen frequently, to people from very different cultures and to people who die in different circumstances (for example, in a hospital during cardiac arrest or in a car accident where death was immediate and instantaneous). Yet there are significant and common elements to all of these experiences. People raised in a Buddhist or Hindu culture who expect to be annihilated or lose their individuality—like the proverbial drop of water falling into the ocean—report meeting a personal God, sometimes a Jesus-like figure holding a book of judgment. Many Christians who have been taught erroneous doctrine or unbiblical ideas experience things they never would have dreamed would happen. NDEs cannot be explained as projections of a person's expectations because they happen to very young children (for example, a child eighteen months old) who have no religious ideas as well as to atheists who have no expectations.

2. *NDEs show evidence of enhanced consciousness when there should be no consciousness at all.* A large number of people report that during their NDE, their sense of alertness and awareness of surroundings was so vivid that when compared to ordinary alertness and awareness in daily life, the latter feels like a half-awake dream. Many NDE individuals have no "living" activities or signs—there is no gag reflex, no heartbeat, and no brain activity. Under these conditions, consciousness is impossible, medically speaking. Dr. Eben Alexander has an MD degree from Duke University and served for five years at Harvard Medical School in Boston. He had been an academic neurosurgeon for twenty-five years when he personally had an NDE. Dr. Alexander was attacked by a rare illness on November 10, 2008, and according to Alexander, he immediately went into a weeklong coma in which his brain stopped working altogether. Yet Alexander says he left his body and was vividly and fully conscious of another world when he should not have been conscious at all.[9]

3. *People born blind or deaf and who have never seen or heard anything are able to report accurately specific things they saw and heard that were fully verified by medical personnel.* When these individuals returned to their bodies after their NDE, they were once again blind or deaf. Drs. Kenneth Ring and Sharon Cooper have both been professors at the University of Connecticut (Ring is now retired), and both are trained in research methodology. They performed and subsequently published the results of a

rigorous study of people born blind or who were blinded in some way and who had also had an NDE.[10] Using a carefully crafted questionnaire with only questions whose answers could be objectively, empirically verified, they began by screening forty-six individuals, finally selecting thirty-one who qualified for the study. Fourteen of these individuals had been blind from birth, eleven had lost sight somewhere after the age of five, and six were severely impaired. In just a moment I will present a specific case of this, but suffice it to say that this study showed beyond reasonable doubt that people born blind or currently blind left their bodies during an NDE and saw things that were objectively verified.

4. *In NDEs, there is an odd commonality of the "universal love theme," despite radical cultural differences about what is most important.* John Burke, in his book *Imagine Heaven*, reports that thousands and thousands of NDE individuals report that the "Being of Light" (almost always identified with God) sent them back with the message that the greatest value of all was to love others.[11] As far as I know, there are few if any cases with a different message. The ultimacy of love is the universal message God gives those who have an NDE. In just a moment, I will look at the question of why the gospel is not the universal message (though we should note it is frequently expressed or shared in some way with NDE individuals). For now, consider that it is unusual that this theme is precisely what one would predict regarding the value that is most important if Christianity is true (see John 13:34–35; 1 Corinthians 13). But this is inexplicable if NDEs are not real and do not involve the biblical God. Why? Because various cultures differ significantly about what is the highest good—whether it is respecting ancestors, upholding honor, pursuing success, seeking moral purity, believing in annihilation so suffering and desire will cease, merging with the One—there is a wide variety of opinion on what matters most in life and in death.

5. *We cannot ignore the non-duplicable, long-lasting, radical life changes that result from an NDE.* Something clearly happens to NDE individuals—something that is unlike anything else they have ever experienced. As Jeffrey Long puts it, "When a near-death experience takes place, it is generally completely different from anything people could have imagined ever happening to them."[12] The experience is so unique and magnificent that virtually all NDErs (NDE experiencers) do not want to come back to life on earth, but they do so because of the needs of family or friends or because they have work left to do for God. Many are depressed for months after their return because this world seems so bland and gray compared to what they have seen. NDErs are no longer afraid of dying. They have a greater sense of God's presence and have purpose in life, and their core values are utterly transformed. This impact frequently lasts and is orders of magnitude greater than the impact caused by any other experience.[13]

6. *We have evidential cases with objectively verified confirming corroboration.* This last line of evidence is by far the most important and convincing approach to verifying the veracity of NDEs. People report meeting family members or friends they knew nothing about, such as details about an older brother they did not know had ever existed. Some report meeting people no one knew were dead, including one case where no one believed that an NDEr had just met a deceased relative (who lived hundreds of miles away) in heaven because someone had just talked to that person on the phone earlier that day. The NDEr would not allow the surgeon to do further work until a family member in the waiting room called the relative. They did so and learned the person had died earlier that day. Some people report seeing specific things in the operating room that were impossible for them to see (for example, odd behavior by the doctors, specific clothing worn by the nurses, or the precise recall of medical activities not shown on television). One man died, floated up to the ceiling, looked down

on his body, and noticed a 1984 quarter on top of a cabinet high above his bodily visual field that was later found and verified. Others saw things going on in other parts of the hospital. In such cases, what they claimed to have seen was subsequently verified by nurses, doctors, or others. These cases are simply impossible to explain away or dismiss with a purely naturalistic explanation.

RESPONDING TO TWO NATURALISTIC ARGUMENTS AGAINST NDES

The first common objection to NDEs is that they tend to comport with cultural expectations, are culturally relative, and are mere projections of a person's religious or cultural expectations.[14] We can say several things in response to this objection.

First, many NDErs are little children or atheists who have no cultural expectations to project. And many NDEs actually go against religious or cultural expectations, not conform with them. Furthermore, a common core is observed in NDEs across the world, including such things as an out-of-body experience, heightened awareness and senses, intense and positive emotions (except for NDEs that are hellish), a passing through or over a barrier (a tunnel, for example) to get to the other side, an encounter with a personal Being who manifests a brilliant light and is usually recognized as God, an encounter with angels or deceased friends or relatives, a life review, and an experience of a boundary beyond which there is no coming back.[15]

Where there are cultural or religious differences, these can easily be explained by noting that the core experiences are stable across cultures (the kinds of sights and sensations people actually experience), but the interpretations can vary—though not always. Finally, I would add that this objection does absolutely nothing to explain the evidential NDEs.

The second common objection to NDEs is that they are

merely the result of a dying brain or oxygen deprivation of the brain, and some parts of NDEs can be reproduced by brain stimulation or acceleration during flight by pilots.[16] To this, again, we can give several replies. First, I would note that many NDEs occur when death is instantaneous (for example, someone is immediately killed in a car accident) and are experienced outside of the hospital. Thus, there is no time for oxygen deprivation or brain death to be a factor. And while attempts have been made to duplicate the effects, these reproduced hallucinations are fragmentary, incoherent, and not nearly as vivid as awareness in actual NDEs. Moreover, such hallucinations often lead to mental laziness and an inability to concentrate.

The truth is that many NDEs occur when the brain is completely dead and inactive. Nothing is going on, so the NDE can't be the result of a dying brain or oxygen deprivation. And again, this objection does absolutely nothing to explain evidential NDEs.

RESPONDING TO THREE BIBLICAL OBJECTIONS TO NDES

There are also some common biblical objections, typically raised by Christians, to the reality of NDEs. The first is that many NDE individuals do not report meeting the biblical God or Jesus Christ. Instead, they meet a vague "Being of light" and interpret this meeting in unbiblical ways.

In response, I would simply note that there are many times in the Old Testament when God, angels, and the Angel of the Lord (who many scholars believe was the preincarnate Christ) encounter people and do not reveal their true identity. Rather, they leave it vague as to who is being manifested. For example, the Bible indicates there are times when angels are present but appear as human beings (see Hebrews 13:1–2).

I would also note that the incarnation was the supreme manifestation of God himself, and it provided a golden opportunity for people to understand and acknowledge God. And yet, even though they met God in the flesh in the person of Jesus, many did not recognize Jesus as God.

The Bible teaches that God often hides his identity from us and chooses not to bowl people over, but rather he manifests as much of himself as we can take and can benefit from. Similarly, we do not know God's purposes for each NDE, and we can rest assured that he will reveal as much or as little of himself as is best for an NDE individual as it accords with his purposes.

Another common objection is that in the Bible there are two judgments: (1) the Bema (Judgment) Seat judgment in 1 Corinthians 3:12–15 (see also Romans 14:10; 2 Corinthians 5:10), in which the believer's works will be judged and assessed; and (2) the final Great White Throne judgment (Revelation 20:11–15), at which God will announce a person's final destiny. Yet NDE individuals communicate a "life review" as something positive and not as a judgment, which seems contrary to biblical teaching.

In reply, I would note that in many NDEs, people have hellish experiences of judgment, so not all NDEs are positive.[17] Furthermore, as John Burke points out, the life review is not mentioned in the Bible, so it does not seem to match either of the biblical judgments.[18] It is something that does not contradict Scripture but is, rather, extrabiblical information many NDErs experience that may be done for God's good purposes.

The third objection is that Hebrews 9:27 teaches that "people are destined to die once, and after that to face judgment." NDEs seem to violate this text and as such are cases of an unbiblical second chance to be saved after death.

The Hebrews text is talking about what we would call irreversible, final death from which resuscitation is impossible. Near-death experiences are not this sort of final, irreversible death, so NDEs do not violate the text, nor are they examples of a second chance after final death. In addition, God has the right to override this principle anytime he wants, and Scripture contains examples of him doing so in Elijah's raising of the widow's son (1 Kings 17:17–24), in Jesus' raising of Lazarus (John 11), and in Paul's raising of the man who fell to his death (Acts 20:7–12).

HOPE-INDUCING CREDIBLE NDES

Case #1: An NDE Sparks a Radical Atheist and Cardiologist to Become a Christian

On November 15, 2018, I delivered a lecture at Southeast Christian Church during the national meeting of the Evangelical Theological Society in Denver. At the end of the talk, a gentleman in his fifties hurried up to me and asked if we could talk. The man was Dr. Dan De Girolami, a well-known cardiologist. He asked for my email address because he had something important to send me. A few days later, I received his email in which he told me his story.[19]

By his own admission, since his childhood, Dr. Dan (as his colleagues call him) was a militant, hostile atheist who picked fights with Christians and mocked and cursed God and Christianity. He reveled in his godlessness. According to Dr. Dan, he simply never saw any reason to believe in such nonsense. Further, he was an arrogant, self-made narcissist who had risen to become a top cardiologist. One day while on duty at Saint Joseph Hospital in Chicago, he received an urgent call from two cardiologists at Silver Cross Hospital asking him to come immediately to Silver Cross to attend to a patient. They believed Dr. Dan was this woman's last hope of living.

Upon arrival, Dr. Dan met the cardiologists. They were panicked, their faces white as snow. The patient, a woman named Kay, was already dead. She had been shocked twenty-five times to restart her heart, all to no avail. She had no blood flowing anywhere in her body, and there were no signs of life at all. Kay had been dead for a while, but Dr. Dan decided that no harm would be done if they shocked her a twenty-sixth time. Completely stunning them all, the woman returned to life! More incredible still was her condition. She had absolutely no damage done to her at all, and in a few days, she returned home. She has been a friend and patient of Dr. Dan's up to the present time of this writing.

Two days after Kay's recovery, while Dr. Dan was visiting with his patients, he entered Kay's room without introducing himself. Surprisingly, Kay greeted him with an expression of thanks for saving her life. Dr. Dan was confused, since they had never officially met one another (Kay had already been dead when he arrived and had never gained consciousness while he was present). When he asked her how she knew he had worked on her, she replied that she had left her body, had been with God up near the ceiling, and had watched the entire thing from up there. She proceeded to tell him, as Dr. Dan shared with me, "everything I said while I was in the room!"

It was undeniable to Dr. Dan that she had indeed left her body when she died and had actually seen and heard what was happening in the room. This was not something Dan could square with his existing atheist worldview, and it sparked the beginning of a journey to discover the truth, which led him to Jesus. Eventually, Dr. Dan attended church for the first time at River Valley Christian Fellowship in Bradley, Illinois, and when an invitation to receive salvation was given, he went forward to the altar, fell on his knees, and wept, accepting Christ. Dan has been on fire for Christ ever since, and he regularly engages in evangelism with anyone who will listen.

Case #2: Two Atheists Become Christians after
Having the Same Simultaneous NDE

Hope and I first came across this incredible miracle years ago when reading together Robert Wise's excellent book *Crossing the Threshold of Eternity*.[20] Before including this case in this book, however, I wanted extra verification of its authenticity, so on May 7, 2020, I called Dr. Wise at his home in Oklahoma City, and he confirmed every detail of what follows.

While Wise was residing in Colorado, he lived a short distance from a hospice nurse, Cindi Pursley, and the two were also friends. Cindi told him this story to which she was an eyewitness. Cindi had worked with a hospice organization for seventeen years, and among her responsibilities was making house calls to dying patients. Most of her patients were facing the reality of death well, except for two—one man and one woman—who were both bitter and "fiercely resisted the inevitable." It was a cold winter day, and Cindi had a full caseload that had her scheduled to visit several homes. The two bitter patients were on the schedule for that day's visits; one was the first of the day and the other the last. And Cindi dreaded seeing each of them. The first appointment was with Betty Meier, a woman in her eighties and a cantankerous agnostic. The last appointment was with another agnostic, Al Harris, who was dying, though he was only in his late forties. Neither of them knew each other.

Upon entering Betty's home for her first appointment of the day, Cindi was dreading the time. Betty was always anxious, snarky, and a general pain in the derriere. To Cindi's surprise, however, for the first time Betty was quite happy and in good spirits. Curious, Cindi asked her what had caused the change of spirit. Betty replied that last night while sleeping, she had drifted to "the other side" (which she did not believe existed), and the experience had been so vivid and amazing she knew it was real and not a dream. Betty went on to tell Cindi what she had seen there:

Two little boys had died. Cutest little guys. Of course, they were little fellows and didn't know where in the world they were. I guess you might say that they had come to this holding realm where people arrive immediately after they die. They just didn't know what in the world to do and were afraid . . .

You can understand how two little boys who had just died would be bewildered . . . Their problem was they didn't know how to get across that great divide.[21]

Betty went on to report that eventually the boys discovered a path out of the holding area and, holding hands, had crossed the path into heaven. As they did so, it was as though all heaven broke loose! A wind had begun blowing at their backs, and Betty was so overjoyed to see they had joyfully made it into eternity that all her fears of dying left. Cindi left the house that morning grappling with what she had heard. And she had no idea what was about to happen later that day.

Her last appointment of the day was in the evening with Al Harris. As was the case with Betty, she dreaded seeing Al that day. When Al's daughter let Cindi in, she mentioned she had heard a strange noise the previous night. Al's daughter had installed a listening device in Al's room to better keep track of him, and the noise had come from Al's room. The daughter said it sounded like "my father was blowing on or at something."

As Cindi entered Al's room, she was—once again—stunned to find Al, like Betty, in great spirits and doing quite well. When she asked him how he was doing, Al shared that he was no longer afraid to die, and Cindi asked him why he had changed his mind. Al responded, "Last night I had one of those twilight experiences I've heard about. Never had one before . . . I saw two little boys. Little ones that had lost their way." After Cindi cautiously asked him, "Where?" Al said, "Trying to get into eternity. In that realm where I guess you go right after you die. They weren't sure how to get out of there. Then they found this path and I started blowing as hard as I could to help them go forward. The wind picked up. As I watched them find their way down that route into eternity, my own fears disappeared."[22]

Al went on to tell almost the exact story Cindi had heard earlier that day from Betty. Here were two agnostics, who lived miles apart and had never met or talked with one other, having had the exact same experience at about the same time—and as a result neither one feared death any longer. And they had both abandoned their agnosticism! Dr. Wise sums up this account by saying that while this may sound astonishing to many people, stories like this are not all that unusual for people who regularly work with the dying.

Case #3: Give Me Back My Dentures!

This famous case has been reported frequently, and while it is funny, it also has an important lesson to teach us. The incident was first reported by an eyewitness, a nurse at a coronary care unit. It was subsequently verified by the highly respected Dutch cardiologist Pim van Lommel and was published in one of the leading medical journals in the world (*The Lancet*) and in his book *Consciousness beyond Life*, which was endorsed by the *Washington Post*, the *Sunday Telegraph* (London), and the *Toronto Star*, among others.[23]

During the night shift at Canisius Wilhelmina Hospital in Nijmegen, Netherlands, near the end of 1979, an ambulance brought in a forty-four-year-old man who was purplish-blue, stone-cold with no heartbeat or blood circulation, and clinically dead. He had been found an hour earlier, lying unconscious on the ground in a public park, having suffered a massive heart attack. Resuscitation attempts had failed on the ambulance drive to the hospital, and upon arrival, the senior resuscitation nurse (we'll call him TG), along with two other nurses, immediately took over resuscitation attempts, including heart massage and defibrillation. Every time TG opened one or the other of the patient's closed eyelids and shone a bright light on the pupil, both were light-rigid and unresponsive.

While inspecting the patient's mouth before oral intubation, TG discovered that the man, who was still clinically dead, had dentures, so TG removed the upper set and put them in a drawer in the crash cart. Amazingly, after ninety minutes, the patient's heart rhythm and blood pressure were sufficiently restored to move him to the ICU, though he remained in an unconscious coma the entire time.

Eventually, the patient was stable enough to be returned to the coronary care unit, but he remained in a coma for a little more than a week. TG happened to be on duty a week after the patient was brought in and was distributing medication to various patients. When he walked into the man's room, the patient saw him and said immediately, "Oh, yes, but you, you know where my dentures are." TG was flabbergasted because the man had been completely unconscious and clinically dead when TG was working on him, so the patient had never seen TG. Then the patient said this to TG: "Yes, you took the dentures out of my mouth and put them into that cart; it had all these bottles on it [which was accurate; the bottles contained various medicines], and there was a sliding drawer underneath, and you put my teeth there."

After further questioning, the man told TG that he had seen himself lying in bed and had watched from above as nursing staff and doctors had tried to resuscitate him. He also gave a completely accurate description of the small room he had been in (including a description of items that were not viewable from the comatose patient's location) and of all the medical personnel who were present. The man reported that he had tried to tell the doctors to work harder at his resuscitation, but they could not hear him. Eventually, the man was released from the hospital.

This is an extremely well-documented case supported by high-quality evidence. To me, it seems to show quite clearly that we have (or are) souls and that there is life after death. But there is another lesson here. Dallas Willard used to say that when we die, it may take a long time for us to realize we are gone. The dentures man seems to have not known he had died for several minutes. And there are several similar cases.[24] This means that for believers, while we may go through pain as we near death, death itself is not necessarily—if at all—a negative experience. Indeed, it is so gentle that some don't know it has happened!

Case #4: The Tough Guy Comes Back and Is Pretty Angry

Dr. Chauncey Crandall is a world-renowned cardiologist with postdoctoral training at Yale Medical School. He has been the chief of the cardiovascular transplant program at the Palm Beach Cardiovascular Clinic in Palm Beach Gardens for decades. The following event is reported by Dr. Crandall himself and occurred very early in his career, during the last year of his cardiology fellowship.[25] By his own admission, at that time he believed science and faith were in conflict, so he chose to follow the science. As Crandall put it, "I was always inclined toward science and its rationalism."[26] Consequently, he was what we might call a weak, nominal, or Sunday Christian. All of that was about to change for him though.

One day a man named Gary, a six-foot-five-inch gang member with a body full of tattoos, was scheduled for heart surgery at Hunter Holmes McGuire VA Medical Center in Richmond, Virginia. The surgery was to be performed by Crandall and another senior surgeon, and it involved inserting an arterial PTCA balloon into his diseased heart. During the surgery, however, Gary unexpectedly went into full cardiac arrest. The team prepared to shock him with defibrillator paddles, but the machine was dead. After three attempts to recharge the machine and shock the patient, it became apparent that the machine just wasn't working.

So they began full CPR until another solution was found. During the frantic moments that followed, the number of medical personnel doubled as additional staff rushed in to help. According to Crandall, the scene was chaotic, with some doctors and nurses attending to the patient, while others sought to get the paddles working by plugging them into different electrical outlets around the room. Nothing worked, so as a last resort, some rushed to the radiation department to secure a different set of paddles.

Meanwhile, the EKG leads had come off of Gary's body, and at one point someone tripped over Gary's IV line and Crandall had to crawl under the operating table to reconnect it. When a new defibrillator was brought in, they shocked Gary's heart again, and finally Gary's normal sinus rhythm returned, a necessary but not sufficient condition for normal electrical activity to be restored. Once Gary was in the clear, Crandall left and returned a few days later to check in on his patients, including Gary.

As Crandall walked past Gary's room in the hallway, Crandall suddenly felt himself being hoisted up by the collar onto his tiptoes. He couldn't move. In an angry voice, his patient Gary yelled, "Why did you bring me back?" When Crandall asked Gary what he meant, Gary went on to say that he had been fine right where he was. He had left his body and, looking down, had seen the entire scene in the surgical theater after his cardiac arrest. He reported seeing Crandall crawl under the table to restore his IV line and described in detail what everyone had done to save him, including the failed testing of the paddles and the new machine that had been brought into the room. All the while, said Gary, he had experienced such a perfect peace and serenity that he did not want to come back.

Eventually, Gary released his grip on Crandall. As he reflected on this event, Crandall realized that Gary's description, complete with minute detail, would be simply impossible unless he had witnessed the events from above the operating table. Crandall had no other explanation that was remotely plausible, and the incident marked the beginning of his journey toward a dedicated, thriving Christian life.

Case #5: Seven-Year-Old Katie Makes a Visit Back Home

Melvin Morse, MD, practiced pediatrics in Renton, Washington, for twenty years. He was also an associate professor of pediatrics at the University of Washington in Seattle. He was voted by his peers as one of "America's Best Doctors" in 1997–1998, 2001–2002, and 2005–2006. He has published numerous scientific articles in medical journals over the course of his thirty-year career. As the author of several books, Morse has appeared on many talk shows and television programs to discuss his extensive research on near-death experiences in children, including interviews with Oprah Winfrey and Larry King.

Early in his career, Morse had an experience that spurred a life of research into NDEs and forever changed his life. One day while he was working in the ICU during his internship in a small town in Idaho, a little girl's lifeless body was brought in.[27] An hour earlier, seven-year-old Katie had been found floating facedown in a YMCA pool. An emergency CAT scan showed massive swelling in Katie's brain. She had no gag reflex, and an artificial lung was breathing for her. She was, as Morse put it, a train wreck with a 10 percent chance of living. Fortunately, Morse was able to resuscitate her from her lifeless condition. And three days later, she made a full recovery! As soon as Katie felt well enough, Morse did a follow-up appointment to assess her condition and to ascertain why she had drowned.

Her parents were present at the interview, and as soon as Dr. Morse greeted Katie (who had been lifeless and unable to see Morse), she shocked him by turning to her mother and saying,

"That's the one with the beard. First there was this tall doctor who didn't have a beard, and then he came in." She was correct. Dr. Bill Longhurst, a clean-shaven physician, had been the first into the emergency room, followed by Dr. Morse. Katie went on: "First I was in the big room, and then they moved me to a smaller room where they did X-rays on me." She accurately noted that a tube had been placed down her nose, which is an uncommon practice. The standard way to intubate—the way it is often depicted on television—is oral intubation. And Katie accurately reported to Morse several other details she could not possibly have seen.

Morse asked her about the drowning. Katie replied, "Do you mean when I visited the heavenly Father?" Stunned, Morse told her that was a good place to start, so Katie recounted that she had met Jesus and the Father while underwater. A shy girl, Katie became embarrassed, so Morse scheduled another follow-up appointment for a week later. Morse acknowledges that what he heard in that second appointment "changed my life."

Katie recounted that while she was underwater, a tunnel opened up and a tall golden-haired person named Elizabeth came through the tunnel to greet her. Katie went with Elizabeth through the tunnel, and once on the other side, she saw her late grandfather and several other people. At one point, Katie was allowed to return to her home, with Elizabeth as her escort. While moving through her house, she saw her brother pushing a GI Joe jeep around his room and one of her sisters combing her Barbie doll's hair and singing a specific, popular rock song. She drifted into the kitchen and noticed her mother cooking roast chicken and rice and saw her father sitting on the living room couch, staring off into the distance.

Later when Katie told all this to her parents, she stunned them by presenting vivid details about the clothes her family members were wearing and their positions in the house.

According to Morse, the parents reported that everything Katie claimed to see was completely accurate. Finally, the angel Elizabeth took Katie to heaven to meet Jesus, who asked her if she wanted to go back and be with her mother. Katie said yes, and then she awoke.

Katie was very shy and only seven years old, but for an hour, she confidently recounted her story to Morse. And he found her completely believable. She was not yet old enough to have a set of religious concepts required to fabricate such a story. Moreover, her family was a fairly uninvolved, middle-of-the-road Mormon family who did not believe in angelic guides, tunnels, or guardian angels. Morris did extensive research and concluded that nothing Katie reported was "taught" to her before her drowning. In fact, quite the contrary. This was a fresh report from actual memory that was subsequently corroborated by the family.

Case #6: A Person Born Blind Sees for the First Time during Her NDE

The case of Vicki Umipeg was reported, along with other similar cases examined professionally, in a meticulous research study performed by two professors at the University of Connecticut, Drs. Kenneth Ring and Sharon Cooper.[28] Vicki, a married, forty-three-year-old woman living in Washington State, was born prematurely after only twenty-two weeks. As was common in the mid-twentieth century, along with fifty thousand other premature babies, Vicki was placed in an airlock incubator with a dangerous level of oxygen such that her optic nerve was damaged, leaving her completely blind for life. On February 2, 1973, at the age of twenty-two, Vicki died in a car accident while in a Volkswagen bus driven by an inebriated person. At that time, she had a vivid NDE.

Vicki reports that immediately after the crash, she felt herself leave her body and had a brief view of the crumpled bus. After arriving at Harborview Hospital's emergency room (she does not remember the ambulance ride), she again left her body and found herself on the ceiling watching a male doctor and a woman working on her body. Vicki could overhear their conversation, in which they expressed concern about possible damage to her eardrum. She also recognized her own body, though she had never seen herself before:

> I knew it was me . . . I was pretty thin then. I was quite tall and thin at that point. And I recognized at first that it was a body, but I didn't even know that it was mine initially. Then I perceived that I was up on the ceiling, and I thought, 'Well, this must be me. Am I dead? . . .' I just briefly saw this body, and . . . I knew that it was mine because I wasn't in mine. Then I was just away from it. It was that quick.[29]

She then saw herself going through the ceiling of the hospital until she was above the hospital roof, during which time she saw a panoramic view of the surroundings. Next she was sucked through a tube and moving toward a light. Once she came out of the tube, Vicki found herself lying on grass, surrounded by trees, flowers, and a number of people. According to Vicki, everything there seemed to be made out of light, and the light radiated love from everywhere. She then became aware of five specific persons she had known on earth who welcomed her to that place: Debby and Diane (Vicki's blind schoolmates who had died years before), two of her childhood caretakers (Mr. and Mrs. Zilk, both of whom had previously died), and her grandmother, who had died two years earlier.

Then Vicki noticed a figure next to her with a radiance greater than anything or anyone else, and she understood somehow that this was Jesus. Jesus acknowledged that everything there was beautiful, and it all fit together, and that one day, she would come back. But for now she had to return to do further work, especially to learn more about forgiving and loving. She grudgingly agreed, but before she was sent back, Jesus said, "But first, watch this," and he showed her a complete panoramic review of her life. Jesus commented on several things that she needed to learn before she returned to her body. When she finally did return, she experienced "a sickening thud" and found herself feeling heavy and full of pain. Her visual sight was once again gone.

Many of the things Vicki saw were capable of verification, proven accurate, and yet completely inexplicable from a naturalistic perspective.

Case #7: The Incredible, Completely Documented Case of Pam Reynolds

The case of Pam Reynolds (aka Pam Reynolds Lowery, 1956–2010), an American songwriter from Atlanta who experienced an NDE in August 1991 at the age of thirty-five, is one of the most powerful evidential cases I have ever heard. It has been called one of the most impressive and medically well-documented NDEs that exists in the literature.

After Pam experienced a number of symptoms, among them regular dizziness, her doctor referred her to a neurologist, who performed a CAT scan on her, revealing a large and very dangerous aneurysm near her brain stem. It was a ticking time bomb in her brain, and doctors predicted she would have no chance of surviving the surgery needed to remove it. As a last-ditch effort, Pam was referred to Dr. Robert Spetzler, a neurosurgeon at the Barrow Neurological Institute in Phoenix, Arizona. Spetzler had invented a dangerous and rarely performed surgical procedure for cases like Pam's, and he agreed to do the surgery. The following account is based on recorded or written reports by members of the surgical team, including neurosurgeons Spetzler and Karl Greene, along with Pam Reynolds's own account.[30]

Spetzler had pioneered a surgical procedure known as hypothermic cardiac arrest. Briefly, the operation required Pam's body temperature to be lowered to 60 degrees, her heartbeat and breathing stopped, her brain waves flattened, and all of the blood drained out of her head. In other words, Pam would die. At 7:15 a.m. on the morning of the surgery, Pam was brought into the operating room, numerous IVs were inserted, and penthathol was administered. She was tied down on the operating table; her eyes were lubricated to prevent dryness and taped shut; an oral endotracheal tube was inserted; and she received a deep-sleep anesthesia. She was completely unconscious. For the next hour and twenty-five minutes, her body was subjected in a number of ways to various medical devices, including EEG electrodes taped to Pam's head to monitor cerebral cortical brain activity. The brain's auditory nerve center would be tested repeatedly using 100-decibel clicks emitted from tiny speakers inserted into her ears. More than twenty doctors and nurses had scrubbed in for the operation. A diagram of the operating theater exists.[31]

Shortly after 8:40 a.m., Spetzler began the surgery by using a Midas Rex drill (it looked like a dentist's drill) to carve out a large portion of Pam's skull. When Pam recovered, she reported hearing the sound of the drill ("it was a natural D"), leaving her body, and seeing and hearing the entire operating room while looking down. Her awareness, and especially her vision, was more focused and clearer than during normal life. She noticed that the way they had shaved her head seemed peculiar since they left some hair unre-moved. She described accurately the Midas Rex drill: "The saw . . . looked like an electric toothbrush, it had a dent in it . . . and the saw had interchangeable blades [that] were in what looked like a socket wrench case." She was expecting the operation to use a saw of some sort, yet she accurately reported, contrary to her expectation, that the instrument looked like a dentist's drill. She also saw and accurately described a number of other tools she did not recognize.

While Spetzler was opening Pam's skull, a female cardiac surgeon located the left femoral artery and vein, but they were too small to be useful. Pam reported, "Someone said something about my veins and arteries being very small. I believe it was a female voice and that it was Dr. Murray, but I'm not sure." Pam then heard a male doctor recommend that they try the other side. Eventually, they successfully used a femoral artery (a large artery in the thigh), and Pam reported the details of what happened. At 10:50 a.m., Pam's blood was drained from her body through a large bypass machine, cooled, and returned to her body. At 11:00 a.m., her body temperature had decreased by 25 degrees. Five minutes later, her heart stopped all activities, and twenty minutes after that, all brain activity ceased. Pam Reynolds was completely dead.

The operating table was tilted up, the bypass machine was turned off, and the blood was drained from Pam's body. At this point, Pam recalls that she "heard" her grandmother calling to her, so Pam followed her into a dark shaft with a light at the other end that grew lighter as she drew closer to it. Everything she saw seemed to be made out of light. Pam met her great-great-aunt Maggie and her uncle Gene, along with others she knew who had died. It suddenly dawned on Pam, a self-described Christian, that she was standing in the very light and presence of God! Then Pam reached a point beyond which she was not permitted to go.

With Pam's blood drained out, Spetzler removed the aneurysm, the bypass machine was turned on, and warmed blood began to reinter Pam's body. After a while, her brain activity slowly came back and her body began waking up. As Pam began her return, she reported that her grandmother would not bring her back, so her uncle took her back through the tunnel. Everything was fine until she saw her body. It looked horrible and dead, and Pam was scared. Nevertheless, she "dove" back into her body and said that it hurt.

As she was returning, rock music was being played in the operating room, and Pam noticed. "When I came back, they were playing 'Hotel California' and the line was 'You can check out anytime you like, but you can never leave.'" At 2:10 p.m., Pam was taken to the recovery room in stable condition.

Think carefully about this case. Pam Reynolds was completely dead with no brain activity, no heat activity, and all the blood drained from her body. She was put into a deep sleep and her eyes were taped shut before the operation began. The theater was populated by many people, and medical instruments were set up to record her body activities. Yet she reported accurately a number of events, people, and instruments that were in the room (hearing the female doctor complain about her arteries and veins being too small, hearing "Hotel California," the exact nature of the drill and the toolbox, the location of some of the doctors, the different things that happened to her), and all of these things were verified and confirmed by doctors on the medical team. And best of all, Pam went to heaven and met some of her family and God himself. It is hard to see how an honest seeker of truth would not be persuaded by this evidence that God, the soul, and heaven are real.

TWO FINAL REFLECTIONS

In June 2003, having been born with a genetic predisposition to anxiety and raised in a very anxious home, and after finishing one of the most stressful years of my life, I had a seven-month nervous breakdown that I have recounted elsewhere.[32] After recovering, I started a journey to remove my anxiety as much as possible. At the time, Hope and I were reading together five nights a week, and we both admitted we had a little anxiety about dying. So we started working on our anxiety and fear of death. We would strengthen ourselves by recalling texts like John 11:25–26 and Philippians 1:21–26 and the evidence for Jesus' resurrection, and we added reading about NDEs to our strategy.

Over the next several years, we read about forty NDE books together, which not only reinforced our confidence that heaven is real but also provided clear visual images for dreaming about and joyfully anticipating heaven. In August 2015, I began a two-and-a-half-year period of eight surgeries and various rounds of chemo and radiation, and I had three different life-threatening cancers. But I had no fear of death. I used to think that the removal of the sting of death and the apostle Paul's desire to be with Christ after death rather than remain here on earth were unachievable. But Hope and I have actually reached that point, and at seventy-two years of age, not only do we truly have no fear of death, but we also are excited about our future! Again, I want you to know that we are no different from you. By reading credible, Christ-honoring NDE accounts, you can begin to lose your fear of death too.

Trudy Harris was a hospice nurse for many years and also served as the president of the Hospice Foundation for Caring. Trudy aided and was present when multitudes of people passed into the next life. When asked to reflect on her career, Trudy marveled at how time after time, God orchestrated just the right events, tailored to each individual person, to bring comfort and alleviate fear for the dying. At the very end of our earthly lives, God brings comfort, peace, and grace. One example is the case of a woman named Mary Anne. Trudy comments:

God loves each of His children so deeply and wants them to know Him. His desire for them is to find peace and to come home to Him when He calls. It is wonderful to watch the lengths to which He will go to make that happen. He gives us ample time and uses the everyday gifts we have had all our lives to help us find Him. Mary Anne was gifted with great curiosity and determination, which she had used in her successful business life. God enabled her to use those very same gifts in searching for and finding Him. What an awesome and loving God we have at our disposal all the days of our lives.[33]

Interestingly, on May 30, 2020, the very day I began writing this chapter on NDE cases, I received an email from a dear friend on the East Coast about some close friends of theirs, Manny and Connie Barton, whose daughter, Analicia, has a twelve-year old son, Randy, who is dying from heart failure and complications with pneumonia. Here's a text my friends received from them:

Randy is struggling and is refusing to take his medications because they've been coming back up. He has been eating but no meds will stay down. Today is Analicia's birthday. She is remarkably filled with love and peace, even though nights are most often very rough for Randy and she's tired.

Randy told Analicia last night before bed, "I was just talking to Jesus. I told him I really, really want to just go to heaven now so I can eat good food and walk again and hug him all day long. He was right here, Mom . . . I was hugging him! But I don't want to leave you, Mom."

And right before he fell asleep . . . "Mom, Jesus is in my bed with me. I can feel him next to me, touching my leg. He's taking care of me."

Where, O death, is your sting?

Chapter 10

WHERE DO WE GO
FROM HERE?

Years ago, a student I will call Rod Pennington (he has asked to remain anonymous) met me during office hours to share an edifying story. Rod and his wife, Sue, lived in the Hollywood area and attended a church there. Sue had been sexually abused by her father, and during her late teen years and early twenties, she had one abusive boyfriend after another. Eventually, she became a Christian, began to heal, and married Rod, whom she had met at church. Rod was bringing Sue to meet me the next week, and he wanted to share their story before that meeting so I could be prepared to ask Sue any questions I might have for her.

According to Rod, an older man in their church named Simon Falk had for many years established a mentor relationship with several women, many of them in the entertainment industry. He focused on women who had abusive backgrounds and was a very godly, loving man who served as an ideal father figure—now a grandfather figure—for these women and helped facilitate their healing. His reputation had grown, and while numerous women wanted to be discipled by Simon, he would only take six or seven at a time. Simon would meet with each woman biweekly at a safe place and work with them for about six months.

Happily, Simon had agreed to mentor Sue, and they had been meeting for a few months with wonderful spiritual and psychological results. At any given time, Simon's mentees did not meet each other and their identities were kept anonymous. However, during one appointment with Sue, Simon disclosed, under the condition of confidentiality, that he had been meeting with a woman named Tammy Strauss for six weeks, that she was struggling terribly, and that he needed to recruit safe people who would commit to praying daily for Tammy. Simon granted permission for Sue to include Rod in the prayer effort.

Tammy was no ordinary person. To be blunt, arguably, she was the leading sex goddess in the Western world, the fantasy of millions upon millions of men. If I were to tell you her real name, you would immediately know who she is. Tammy was exotically gorgeous in every way and knew how to project her sensuality effectively. She was the featured star in a highly successful, weekly prime-time television program watched by several million viewers in the United States, Canada, and Europe. Before the television series, she had been in some pornographic movies; was a regular, treasured presence at the Playboy Mansion; and was one of Hugh Hefner's "girls."

Rod and Sue were deeply troubled for Tammy and prayed earnestly for her conversion and subsequent growth in the Lord. They went so far as to pray daily that, somehow, God would let one of them meet Tammy and witness to her. Unfortunately, according to Rod, accomplishing that would take a miracle, since her personal information was impossible to get and she was always surrounded by bodyguards. Still, Rod and Sue continued to pray for the impossible.

Rod's job required him to fly bimonthly to Toronto, Canada, to work for two days and then return home. About two months after Rod and Sue had started praying for Tammy, Rod was sitting in the Toronto airport, waiting to board a direct flight back to Los Angeles. While reading the newspaper, Rod happened to glance around, and suddenly he thought he saw Tammy in the distance, apparently waiting to board the same flight. In reality, he thought he was seeing things, and not wanting to keep staring, he got out of his seat and walked across the gate area to get a closer look. Sure enough, it was Tammy.

Rod walked back to his seat with his heart pounding. *Lord, he prayed, give me the courage to talk to her.* Unfortunately, Rod was too afraid, and he didn't know how he would manage it, since there were no empty seats near Tammy and he didn't want to make a scene. And once they boarded the plane, he knew his chance to talk would be over. He was seated in coach and Tammy would be sitting in first class. He remained frozen in his seat.

When the time came to board, Rod noticed that Tammy had not moved, and he suspected she would wait until the plane was fully boarded before she got on. So Rod took his seat about halfway back in coach, praying against all hope that God would do something. In complete honesty, Rod told me that the entire plane was full except for one empty seat—right next to him. And then at the last minute, he saw Tammy get on. But instead of sitting in first class, she took the empty seat right next to him!

Rod froze up and was tongue-tied, but he comforted himself with the knowledge that he had several hours to loosen up and talk to Tammy. About an hour into the flight, he introduced himself to her, and they struck up a conversation. Tammy had never been to Toronto before, but she had been there for a few days of filming when she received word that she had to return to Los Angeles immediately due to a tragedy that had happened to her close friend. Tammy had booked the next flight she could find, and since no first-class seats were available, she had taken the only seat she could get—the one next to Rod!

When Tammy asked Rod if he had a family, he knew this was his chance. He shared about Sue's abusive father and how men had regularly used her for their own gratification. He went on to share how Sue had come to Jesus and they had been married, and now she was being mentored by a wonderful man named

Simon Falk. Tammy burst into tears because she was also being mentored by Falk and felt it was clearly a divine appointment she was having with Rod.

They talked about Jesus for the rest of the trip, and Tammy received Jesus on that flight! Tammy also wanted to meet Sue, and Rod reported to me that the two women met several times. Tammy was also still regularly seeing Simon for guidance. The following week, Rod brought Sue to see me, and she shared that this whole experience had been such an answer to prayer—a truly miraculous answer to prayer.

Let me ask you to do something right now. Set aside your doubts and skepticism. From what you've read in these pages, it should now be clear and beyond reasonable doubt that numerous miracles are happening all over the world each day. Sadly, however, in our secular culture, the word is just not getting out.

It doesn't take a rocket scientist to know that we live in a culture that is rapidly slouching toward a secular Gomorrah. Christianity is increasingly scorned and ridiculed. Many look to science as the only rational means of gaining truth about reality. Religion is viewed as outdated, superstitious, and sustained by stupid people—on par with believing in the flying spaghetti monster. The morality of the Bible is seen as repugnant, oppressive, and dangerous. Our universities are populated by a large percentage of the professoriate who disdain Christianity and believe their calling is to turn young believers into leftist skeptics. We are losing our children, our courage, and the confidence needed to sustain vital, attractive, countercultural Jesus followers, families, and churches.

Since the second decade of the twentieth century, believers have attempted to erect a firewall of protection against this onslaught by retreating from the public square, withdrawing from cultural engagement, and severing faith and reason in the employment of a blind, privatized faith as a way of insulating

Christian truth claims from rational attacks. The price we have paid for this nonresponse is incalculable. We have lost our courage, confidence, and spiritual power. We are moving unwaveringly closer toward the outcomes we see in secular Western Europe. Our religious rights are eroding right in front of our eyes, and the way we practice our Christianity is uninformed, spiritually thin, and anemic.

This must stop. But what can we do? After more than a half century in vocational ministry, I believe I have an answer to this question. Intentionally and with perseverance, we must do three things the church has always done when she has been at her best.

1. We must recapture the value of learning why we believe what we believe. Simplistic calls to "faith" are no longer adequate.
2. We must recapture the habits at the center of a richer approach to spiritual formation.
3. We must regain our confidence in and practice of experiencing the supernatural, miraculous power of God's Spirit and kingdom.

In this book, I've attempted to provide help with the first and third points in particular, with a special focus on the latter. If you wish to be a part of the solution to the problem of weak and anemic Christianity, you must do whatever it takes to internalize, actually believe, and live daily in the awareness of the things I've borne credible witness to in this book. My goal has been to build our confidence that we can *know* the reality of the biblical God, to increase our *expectation* and *hope* that God can and often does miraculously intervene to bring help and comfort, to show that the spirit world of angels and demons is real and must be wisely factored into the way we approach our daily lives, to demonstrate that it makes rational sense to step out and engage in the employment of kingdom power, and to strengthen our courage to witness and act on behalf of the gospel of Jesus.

These different aspects of the book's purpose center on building strong, confident, mature disciples who increasingly manifest a supernatural lifestyle to a watching world. I've tried to offer and defend fresh new insights and understanding about the different topics within the book's purview and to provide credible, confirmed, inspiring, and motivating cases of five kinds of miraculous events that are happening to ordinary believers like you and me.

Unfortunately, given the secular influence we absorb daily, it's easy to slide back into a deistic, even naturalistic way of seeing the world and living in it. It takes dedication, effort, persistence, and a team effort to resist this tendency. Failure at this point will lead to an increasingly marginalized church and to a boring and powerless Christian life. Ultimately, the way we are living today can lead to an unattractive presentation of Jesus to a world that desperately needs him.

Peppered throughout the preceding chapters are my suggestions for where to go next to enter more deeply into a supernatural Christian life and the practices that constitute it. But I want to close by boiling things down to two related aspects of our strategy going forward: *exposure* and *enactment*.

EXPOSURE

The first is what I call exposure—putting ourselves in a position to see, hear, read, learn about, and experience the supernatural power of God. Be aggressive in exposing yourself to supernatural miracles happening all around you. Make a habit of reading credible books that tell biographical stories of supernatural events and miracles. Start with the books in the bibliography at the back of this book. Form the habit of reading the Bible as though it recounts divine interventions that actually happened and are happening today. Read as though these things can take place in your life and your church. Bring up the topic when meeting with a Christian friend, at the dinner table, or in a small group or Sunday school class. Create room in your church services for teaching about these things.

Ask questions (Have you had a specific answer to prayer lately? Have you heard God's voice, encountered a demon or angel, known someone who had an NDE?), and make people feel safe to share without embarrassment or rejection. Visit credible churches that are more steeped in signs and wonders than your church is. Look, listen, and learn. Don't be critical. Your purpose is to absorb anything worth receiving. Hope and I have been doing this for fifteen years, and the benefits have been transformative. We have to continue to find ways to remind ourselves that the visible world really isn't the only reality. To believe this is not our problem; to live daily within its reality is. Constant exposure to manifestations from the other side remind us that the world is a thin place after all.

ENACTMENT

Exposure is needed, but it alone is not enough. We also must take risks and exercise faith, doing the supernatural works God wants to do through us. Taking a page from real estate agents, the key to a supernatural lifestyle is practice, practice, practice. John Wimber used to say that faith was spelled r-i-s-k. With certain qualifications, I believe this is a trustworthy saying. Start asking for specific things to happen, and record answers to prayer in a journal. What do you have to lose? If nothing happens, try to learn from it, and keep on going, perhaps with another request. Share your answers to prayer with others to build their faith, and ask them what they have seen. Start reading about the healing of the sick by the laying on of hands, and start praying for people this way. Promise to bless people. See what happens, and keep learning and practicing.

Since we have compelling reasons to believe that God is real, that Christianity is true, and that God still speaks to us in various ways, pray each morning for the Lord to speak to you if he wishes. At night, ask him to speak to you as you sleep and your guard is down. If you are 60 percent sure it was God who spoke, either seek additional confirmation (especially if something important hangs in the balance) or step out and take a risk. If you are fifty-fifty, why not err on the side of taking it as a real communication from God? Of course, we want to be wise, but why not place the burden of proof on a skeptical stance? Why not make our default position to take a supposed communication from the Lord as authentic? Pray for angelic protection, and make deliverance prayers part of an overall strategy of helping others with mental illness. Be aggressive in getting rid of any fear of death you may have. Do whatever it takes.

Here's the bottom line: learn, practice, and seek. And never forget what the great apostle Paul taught us: "For the kingdom of God is not a matter of talk but of power" (1 Corinthians 4:20).

SELECT ANNOTATED BIBLIOGRAPHY

T he following bibliography is meant to help us continue to grow in a supernatural, miraculous life and ministry. There are several categories of books from which to choose, and I have limited my listings to the ones that have helped me the most.

If you were to ask me what you should read next about such and such, this bibliography provides my answer. I have placed three stars (***) in front of a book I consider a must-read. I also list each book as basic (B), intermediate (I), or advanced (A) as a guide to the book's level of difficulty. I hope you meet some new "friends" on this list.

One more thing. If I were forced to select the *first* books to read for encouragement regarding miracles and the supernatural, I would select these in alphabetical order: John Burke, *Imagine Heaven*; Tom Doyle, *Dreams and Visions: Is Jesus Awakening the Muslim World?*; James Garlow and Keith Wall, *Miracles Are for Real*; and Judith MacNutt, *Angels Are for Real*.

ARGUMENTS FOR GOD'S EXISTENCE

***Boa, Kenneth D., and Robert M. Bowman. *Twenty Compelling Evidences That God Exists: Discover Why Believing in God Makes So Much Sense.* Rev. ed. Colorado Springs: Cook, 2005. (B)

This book contains an accessible presentation in brief form of a large number of solid arguments for God's existence. Each argument is presented in a usable form.

Craig, William Lane. *On Guard: Defending Your Faith with Reason and Precision.* Colorado Springs: Cook, 2010. (I)

An excellent, brief overview of the case for God and Christianity by its ablest defender.

Moreland, J. P. *The God Question.* 2nd ed. Downers Grove, IL: InterVarsity, 2021. (I) ·

Contains two chapters on God's existence, defends the reliability of the New Testament, and provides fresh insights for becoming a growing Jesus follower.

***Moreland, J. P., and Tim Muehlhoff. *The God Conversation: Using Stories and Illustrations to Explain Your Faith.* Downers Grove, IL: InterVarsity, 2007. (B)

A basic book that focuses on learning the arguments for God and using illustrations to communicate them to others. A simple read.

ARGUMENTS FOR THE HISTORICAL RELIABILITY OF THE NEW TESTAMENT DOCUMENTS

***McDowell, Josh, and Sean McDowell. *Evidence That Demands a Verdict: Life-Changing Truth for a Skeptical World.* Rev. ed. Nashville: Nelson, 2017. (I)

This is an updated edition of a Christian classic that has changed lives all over the world. A great reference tool.

Strobel, Lee. *The Case for Christ: A Journalist's Personal Investigation of the Evidence for Jesus.* Grand Rapids: Zondervan, 1988. (B)

The gold standard in defending the historicity of Christianity.

Wallace, J. Warner. *Cold-Case Christianity: A Homicide Detective Investigates the Claims of the Gospels.* Colorado Springs: Cook, 2013. (B)

In this absolutely fascinating, easy-to-read book, Wallace, a homicide detective who has appeared on shows such as Dateline, FOX News, and Court TV, applies his detective craft to the claims of the Gospels and concludes there is overwhelming evidence of their historical reliability.

Williams, Peter J. *Can We Trust the Gospels?* Wheaton, IL: Crossway, 2018. (B)

A brief, excellent resource for learning why it is most reasonable to accept the historical reliability of the Gospels.

ARGUMENTS FOR THE HISTORICITY OF THE RESURRECTION OF JESUS

Craig, William Lane. *The Son Rises: The Historical Evidence for the Resurrection of Jesus.* Eugene, OR: Wipf & Stock, 2000. (B)

A good, basic overview of the evidence.

***Habermas, Gary R., and Michael R. Licona, *The Case for the Resurrection of Jesus.* Grand Rapids: Kregel, 2004. (I)

A thorough case for the resurrection that leaves no stone unturned.

McDowell, Josh, and Sean McDowell. *More Than a Carpenter.* Rev. ed. Carol Stream, IL: Tyndale, 2009. (B)

A wonderfully readable book defending the resurrection.

GENERAL ARGUMENTS FOR MIRACLES

Keener, Craig. *Miracles: The Credibility of the New Testament Accounts.* 2 vols. Grand Rapids: Baker, 2011. (A)

A massive tome that many call the best books (it's a two-volume set) defending miracles on the market today.

***Strobel, Lee. *The Case for Miracles: A Journalist Investigates Evidence for the Supernatural.* Grand Rapids: Zondervan, 2018. (B)

This is the first book I'd read to learn the case for and against miracles.

GENERAL COMPENDIA OF MIRACLE STORIES, ANSWERS TO PRAYER, ANGELIC ENCOUNTERS, AND NDES

These books are tremendously inspiring and will strengthen your faith. They contain credible accounts of people who have experienced God's miraculous interventions.

Canfield, Jack, Mark Victor Hansen, and LeAnn Thieman. *Chicken Soup for the Soul: A Book of Miracles.* Cos Cob, CT: Chicken Soup for the Soul Publishing, 2010. (B)

A very readable book containing brief accounts of numerous miracle stories that are inspiring and faith-building.

Canfield, Jack, Mark Victor Hansen, and Amy Newmark. *Chicken Soup for the Soul: Miracles Happen.* Cos Cob, CT: Chicken Soup for the Soul Publishing, 2014. (B)

This is a further exploration of miraculous events by two of the same authors.

***Crandall, Chauncey. *Touching Heaven: A Cardiologist's Encounters with Death and Living Proof of an Afterlife.* New York: Faith Words, 2015. (B)

This book will change your life. It is a must-read.

***Fazzina, Daniel. *Divine Intervention: Fifty True Stories of God's Miracles Today.* Lake Mary, FL: Charisma House, 2014. (B)

This exciting and very credible book contains fifty miraculous accounts by the people who experienced them. Contact information is provided for each contributor and an appendix contains medical documentation of a number of cases where relevant.

***Garlow, James, and Keith Wall. *Miracles Are for Real: What Happens When Heaven Touches Earth.* Bloomington, MN: Bethany House, 2011. (B)

The best book to get for credible, moving, brief accounts of contemporary miracles. A great read.

————. *Real Life, Real Miracles: True Stories That Will Help You Believe.* Bloomington, MN: Bethany House, 2012. (B)

This book is also excellent and faith building.

Books about the Present Reality of the So-Called Miraculous Spiritual Gifts

Grudem, Wayne, ed. *Are Miraculous Gifts for Today? Four Views.* Grand Rapids: Zondervan, 1996. (I)

A solid biblical study presenting advocates of four different views about miraculous gifts. Objective and accessible.

***Storms, Sam. *The Beginner's Guide to Spiritual Gifts.* Ventura, CA: Regal, 2002. (B)

A must-read for solid teaching about miraculous spiritual gifts.

How to Practice Kingdom Power in the Local Church

***Scott, Alan. *Scattered Servants: Unleashing the Church to Bring Life to the City.* Colorado Springs: Cook, 2018. (B)

In this book that is chock-full of authentic accounts of miracles, Pastor Scott places the focus on using the Spirit's power for outreach and ministry.

***Storms, Sam. *Practicing the Power: Welcoming the Gifts of the Holy Spirit in Your Life.* Grand Rapids: Zondervan, 2017. (B)

The best book available about the wise, biblical way to make room for the practice of the Spirit's power in the local church.

How to Practice and Receive Answers to Specific Petitionary Prayers

***Hazen, Craig. *Fearless Prayer: Why We Don't Ask and Why We Should.* Eugene, OR: Harvest House, 2018. (B)

This power-packed little book is one you won't be able to put down. It contains excellent perspective on petitionary prayer.

THE PRACTICE OF HEALING PRAYER

***MacNutt, Francis. *Healing*. Rev. ed. Notre Dame, IN: Ave Maria, 1999. (B)

This is the best book on learning to heal the sick.

Wimber, John. *Power Healing*. San Francisco: HarperSanFrancisco, 1987. (B)

This is the story of how John Wimber learned to practice healing prayer with a special focus on its use in evangelism.

GENERAL BOOKS ON HEARING GOD

***Jersak, Brad. *Can You Hear Me? Tuning In to the God Who Speaks*. Rev. ed. Abbotsford, BC: Fresh Wind, 2012. (B)

A very practical guide with plenty of exciting cases for learning to hear God.

***Virkler, Mark and Patti. *Dialogue with God: Opening the Door to Two-Way Prayer*. Alachua, FL: Bridge-Logos, 1986. (B)

Another exceptional guide for discerning God's voice.

***Willard, Dallas. *Hearing God: Developing a Conversational Relationship with God*. 3rd ed. Downers Grove, IL: InterVarsity, 1999. (B)

This classic Dallas Willard book provides deep, instructive teaching about cultivating the ability to hear God's voice.

BOOKS ON PROPHECY, WORDS OF KNOWLEDGE, AND WORDS OF WISDOM

***Deere, Jack. *The Beginner's Guide to the Gift of Prophecy*. Ann Arbor, MI: Servant, 2001. (B)

The first book to read on this topic.

***Storms, Sam. *Understanding Spiritual Gifts: A Comprehensive Guide.* Grand Rapids: Zondervan, 2020. (B or I)

The most comprehensive biblical study available. Outstanding biblical treatment of spiritual gifts; full of real-life examples.

***Sullivant, Michael. *Prophetic Etiquette: Your Complete Handbook on Giving and Receiving Prophecy.* Lake Mary, FL: Creation House, 2000. (B)

Written by an authentic, well-regarded practitioner, this book is at the top for learning how and how not to practice the prophetic.

BOOKS ABOUT CONTEMPORARY DREAMS AND VISIONS IN THE MUSLIM WORLD

***Doyle, Tom. *Dreams and Visions: Is Jesus Awakening the Muslim World?* Nashville: Nelson, 2012. (B)

If you don't believe that Jesus himself is appearing to Muslims in the Middle East, you will after you read this.

Malick, Faisal. *Ten Amazing Muslims Touched by God.* Shippensburg, PA: Ambient, 2012. (B)

This book contains accounts of miraculous conversions of Muslims. It would be the book to give to a Muslim.

BOOKS ABOUT ANGELS

***MacNutt, Judith. *Angels Are for Real: Inspiring, True Stories and Biblical Answers.* Bloomington, MN: Chosen, 2012. (B)

An informative and inspiring account of angelic manifestations.

***————. *Encountering Angels: True Stories of How They Touch Our Lives Every Day.* Bloomington, MN: Chosen, 2016. (B)

Another great book on angels. It will strengthen your faith in the supernatural.

BOOKS ON THE DEMONIC

***Arnold, Clinton E. *Three Crucial Questions about Spiritual Warfare.* Grand Rapids: Baker, 1997. (I)

Written by a world-class New Testament scholar, this is the first book to read about biblical teaching regarding the demonic.

Dickason, C. Fred. *Demon Possession and the Christian: A New Perspective.* Wheaton, IL: Crossway, 1989. (I)

A thorough treatment of what the Bible says about a Christian's relationship to the demonic.

***Kraft, Charles H. *Defeating Dark Angels: Breaking Demonic Oppression in the Believer's Life.* 3rd ed. Grand Rapids: Chosen, 2016. (B)

The best practical guide for dealing with the demonic. My first choice in this area.

***Storms, Sam. *Understanding Spiritual Warfare: A Comprehensive Guide.* Grand Rapids: Zondervan, 2021. (I or A)

This is the most thorough treatment of the subject available today.

BOOKS MAKING THE CASE FOR THE REALITY OF NDES

These books contain wonderful stories of NDEs, but their strength is that they give the evidence for why we should trust these accounts and respond to all the objections skeptics raise against NDEs. Very persuasive books.

Atwater, P. M. H., and David H. Morgan. *The Complete Idiot's Guide to Near-Death Experiences.* Indianapolis, IN: Alpha, 2000. (B)

I don't agree with everything in this book, but it is fair and contains a careful presentation of a number of credible accounts.

***Burke, John. *Imagine Heaven: Near-Death Experiences, God's Promises, and the Exhilarating Future That Awaits You.* Grand Rapids: Baker, 2015. (B)

Burke's book is the very best of its kind. The first book to read on this subject.

***Long, Jeffrey. *Evidence of the Afterlife: The Science of Near-Death Experiences*. San Francisco: HarperOne, 2010. (B)

This book contains a nice presentation of responses to all the major objections raised against NDEs.

Miller, J. Steve. *Near-Death Experiences as Evidence for the Existence of God and Heaven: A Brief Introduction in Plain Language*. Acworth, GA: Wisdom Creek, 2012. (B)

Miller writes well, thinks clearly, and possesses a pastoral heart. This is a great read, especially for evidence of NDEs.

***Rivas, Titus, Anny Dirven, and Rudolf H. Smit. *The Self Does Not Die: Verified Paranormal Phenomena from Near-Death Experiences*. Durham, NC: International Association of Near-Death Studies, 2016. (I)

While not a Christian perspective, the book is very friendly to a religious worldview, including distinctively Christian accounts that are recorded. This may be the best researched book available.

COMPENDIA OF NDES

These books contain a different NDE story in each chapter, with the result that many brief and inspiring stories fill these books.

Bell, James Stewart, comp. *Angels, Miracles and Heavenly Encounters: Real-Life Stories of Supernatural Events*. Bloomington, MN: Bethany House, 2012. (B)

A solid book with a number of authentic stories about heavenly encounters.

Garlow, James L., and Keith Wall. *Encountering Heaven and the Afterlife: True Stories from People Who Have Glimpsed the World Beyond*. Bloomington, MN: Bethany House, 2010. (B)

Garlow and Wall are extremely credible, excellent writers who have gathered a number of exciting cases.

***_____. *Heaven and the Afterlife*. Bloomington, MN: Bethany House, 2009. (B)

Ditto.

***Morse, Melvin. *Closer to the Light: Learning from the Near-Death Experiences of Children*. New York: Ivy, 1990. (I)

This is a very special, heartwarming book.

Sabom, Michael. *Light and Death: One Doctor's Fascinating Account of Near-Death Experiences*. Grand Rapids: Zondervan, 1998. (B)

Sabom is a solid Christian and writes a very persuasive book with wonderful stories.

Individual Biographies of NDE Stories

These books tell the story of an individual's life, including their NDE and how it changed their life.

Alexander, Eben. *Proof of Heaven: A Neurosurgeon's Journey into the Afterlife*. New York: Simon & Schuster, 2012. (B)

This was a bestseller that provided very strong evidence of the afterlife. Unfortunately, some of the interpretations Alexander gives to his experience are contrary to biblical teaching. Still, it is a good read.

***Anderson, Reggie. *Appointments with Heaven: The True Story of a Country Doctor's Healing Encounters with the Afterlife*. Carol Stream, IL: Tyndale Momentum, 2013. (B)

This may be the most moving book Hope and I have read in this area. Incredible!

Besteman, Marvin. *My Journey to Heaven: What I Saw and How It Changed My Life*. Grand Rapids: Baker, 2012. (B)

A persuasive, insightful book about the author's visit to heaven.

Burpo, Todd. *Heaven Is for Real: A Little Boy's Astounding Story of His Trip to Heaven and Back.* Nashville: Nelson, 2010. (B)

The basis for a movie, this touching book is hard to deny in its claims.

McVea, Crystal, and Alex Tresniowski. *Waking Up in Heaven: A True Story of Brokenness, Heaven, and Life Again.* New York: Simon & Schuster, 2013. (B)

A sad story about Crystal's horrible life and how her NDE changed all that.

***Neal, Mary C. *Seven Lessons from Heaven: How Dying Taught Me to Live a Joy-Filled Life.* New York: Convergent, 2017. (B)

It's hard to overstate how excellent this book is. Extremely credible and full of practical life lessons.

————. *To Heaven and Back: A Doctor's Extraordinary Account of Her Death, Heaven, Angels, and Life Again.* Colorado Springs: WaterBrook, 2011. (B)

A New York Times bestseller, Dr. Neal's account has a deep feel of authenticity.

Storm, Howard. *My Descent into Death: A Second Chance at Life.* New York: Doubleday, 2005. (B)

Storm was an arrogant, narcissistic atheistic professor who died and experienced demons taking him to hell. The book recounts what followed.

A Daily Devotional on Heaven Containing Scripture and Daily NDE Accounts

Burke, John, and Kathy Burke. *Imagine Heaven Devotional: 100 Reflections to Bring Heaven to Your Life Today.* Grand Rapids: Baker, 2018. (B)

This book contains one hundred devotional reflections, each about two pages in length, that ponder a Scripture text and give a short NDE account, followed by daily application.

ACKNOWLEDGMENTS

Several people have helped me in developing this book. First, I thank those who sent me their stories and let me query them about their veracity: Tim Bayless, Ed Bort, Peter Crawford, Dan De Girolami, Tom Doyle, Cat Guerra, Joe and Kay Harding, Ruth and Bill Henderson, Klaus Issler, Craig Keener, Chris Linamen, Jason Martin, Sean McDowell, Tim Newell, Lance Pittluck, Alan Scott, Hermoz Shariat, Ben Shin, Mayme Shroyer, Ken Slezak, Mark Step, Michael Sullivant, Doyle and Cody Surratt, Michael Swanson, Jane Willard, Carol Wimber, and Robert L. Wise. Second, my agent, Mark Sweeney, was so helpful to me in developing my main focus and purpose. Finally, I am so grateful to my wife, Hope, for reading the entire manuscript and giving me excellent suggestions for improvement.

NOTES

Introduction

1. See Joel C. Rosenberg, *Inside the Revolution: How the Followers of Jihad, Jefferson, and Jesus Are Battling to Dominate the Middle East and Transform the World* (Carol Stream, IL: Tyndale, 2009), 393–94.

2. See Daniel J. Siegel, MD, *Mindsight: The New Science of Personal Transformation* (New York: Bantam, 2010), 167; for more on this, see chapter 9 in his book (pp. 166–89).

3. Quoted in Jim Wilder, *Renovated: God, Dallas Willard, and the Church That Transforms* (Colorado Springs: NavPress, 2020), 6.

4. Dallas Willard, "Spiritual and Emotional Maturity," in Wilder, *Renovated*, 21.

5. Kevin DeYoung and Greg Gilbert, *What Is the Mission of the Church? Making Sense of Social Justice, Shalom, and the Great Commission* (Wheaton, IL: Crossway, 2011); see especially 110–13, 118–19, 139.

Chapter 1: Why So Many Westerners Are Embarrassed by Miracles Stories

1. Michael Green, *Evangelism in the Early Church*, rev. ed. (1970; repr., Grand Rapids: Eerdmans, 2003), 26.

2. Tertullian, *Apology* 37, in *Tertullian, Minucius Felix*, trans. T. R. Glover and Gerald H. Rendall, Loeb Classical Library 250 (Cambridge, MA: Harvard University Press, 1931), 173.

3. Tertullian, *To Scapula* 4, in *The Fathers of the Church*, vol. 10, *Tertullian: Apologetical Works and Minucius Felix: Octavius*, trans. Rudolph Arbesmann (Washington, DC: Catholic University of America Press, 1950), 173.

4. Charles Kraft, *Christianity with Power: Your Worldview and Your Experience of the Supernatural* (Ann Arbor, MI: Servant, 1989), 27, italics in original.
5. Kraft, *Christianity with Power*, 41.
6. Dallas Willard, *The Divine Conspiracy: Rediscovering Our Hidden Life in God* (San Francisco: HarperSanFrancisco, 1998), 92, italics in original; see also 75, 79, 134, 184–85.
7. The phrase comes from Robert Bork's book *Slouching towards Gomorrah: Modern Liberalism and American Decline* (New York: HarperCollins, 1996); the concept of "slouching towards" something comes from W. B. Yeats's 1919 poem "The Second Coming," in which he writes of the "rough beast" that "slouches towards Bethlehem to be born."

Chapter 2: Miracles: What They Are and How to Recognize Them

1. We tell this story in J. P. Moreland and Klaus Issler, *In Search of a Confident Faith: Overcoming Barriers to Trusting in God* (Downers Grove, IL: InterVarsity, 2008), 142–43.
2. For a brief and helpful discussion of the definition and characteristics of a miracle, see Yujin Nagasawa, *Miracles: A Very Short Introduction* (Oxford: Oxford University Press, 2017), 17–20.
3. See William Dembski, *Intelligent Design: The Bridge between Science and Theology* (Downers Grove, IL: IVP Academic, 1999), 127–49. I have adopted Dembski's discussion for our present purposes.
4. For more on this point, see Dembski, *Intelligent Design*, 127–46.
5. A version of this section can also be found in J. P. Moreland, *The God Question*, rev. ed. (Downers Grove, IL: IVP Academic, 2021).
6. See Lee Strobel's interview of Shermer in Lee Strobel, *The Case for Miracles: A Journalist Investigates Evidence for the Supernatural* (Grand Rapids: Zondervan, 2018), chapters 1–3.
7. This is a phrase popularized by Carl Sagan, who used the statement on his television program *Cosmos*.
8. Thomas Nagel, *The Last Word* (New York: Oxford University Press, 1997), 130–31.

9. Craig Keener, *Miracles: The Credibility of the New Testament Accounts*, 2 vols. (Grand Rapids: Baker, 2011).

10. See John Earman, *Hume's Abject Failure: The Argument against Miracles* (Oxford: Oxford University Press, 2000), 20–70.

11. William Lane Craig, *Reasonable Faith: Christian Truth and Apologetics*, 3rd ed. (Wheaton, IL: Crossway, 2008), 270.

Chapter 3: Cleaning Up Some Unproductive Misunderstandings about Prayer

1. Helen Roseveare, *Living Faith: Willing to Be Stirred as a Pot of Paint* (Minneapolis: Bethany House, 1980), 44–45, http://living-testimony.blogspot.com/2006/10/hot-bottle-water-true-story-by-helen.html.

2. In this section, I am deeply indebted to Loyola University professor Michael J. Murray (see his "God Responds to Prayer," in *Contemporary Debates in Philosophy of Religion*, ed. Michael L. Peterson and Raymond J. VanArragon [Malden, MA: Blackwell, 2003], 242–54, http://philosophyfaculty.ucsd.edu/faculty/ewatkins/Murray-PetitionaryPrayer.pdf). See also Eleonore Stump, "Hoffman on Petitionary Prayer," *Faith and Philosophy* 2 (January 1985): 30–37; Peter Forrest, "Answers to Prayer and Conditional Situations," *Faith and Philosophy* 15 (January 1998): 41–51.

3. See Murray, "God Responds to Prayer."

4. Murray, "God Responds to Prayer," 247–48.

Chapter 4: Miraculous Answers to Prayer

1. See Christian Smith, *American Evangelicalism: Embattled and Thriving* (Chicago: University of Chicago Press, 1998), 155–60.

2. See J. Warner Wallace, *Cold-Case Christianity: A Homicide Detective Investigates the Claims of the Gospels* (Colorado Springs: Cook, 2013).

3. See Wallace, *Cold-Case Christianity*, 69–78 (see p. 73 for list of criteria). I have selected six out of the fourteen criteria Wallace provides because they are the most relevant ones for our present purposes. I have also modified some principles to make them clearer when applied to answers to prayer.

4. See William Dembski, *Intelligent Design: The Bridge between*

Science and Theology (Downers Grove, IL: IVP Academic, 1999), 139–48.

Chapter 5: Understanding the Nature and Importance of Miraculous Healing

1. Now is not the time to present a defense of the historical reliability of the New Testament documents. Fortunately, that defense has been adequately provided elsewhere. See the bibliography at the back of this book for key books in this area.
2. Quoted in Eusebius, *Ecclesiastical History* 4.3.2.
3. Irenaeus, *Against Heresies* 2.31.2.
4. Irenaeus, *Against Heresies* 2.32.4.
5. Origen, *Against Celsus* 3.24.
6. See J. C. Blumhardt, "The Early Years: A Church Triumphant," in *Healing through the Centuries: Models for Understanding*, ed. Ronald A. N. Kydd (Peabody, MA: Hendrickson, 1998), 20–33.
7. Augustine, *The City of God* (Washington, DC: Catholic University of America Press, 1954), 22.8. Chapter 8 of book 22 is filled with several examples of documented miraculous healings. It makes for a very inspiring read.
8. Ramsay MacMullen, *Christianizing the Roman Empire: A.D. 100–400* (New Haven, CT: Yale University Press, 1984).
9. For a more in-depth treatment of what happened, see Francis MacNutt, *The Nearly Perfect Crime: How the Church Almost Killed the Ministry of Healing* (Grand Rapids: Chosen, 2005), chapters 10–18.
10. See John Calvin, *The Institutes of the Christian Religion*, 4.19.18; see also 4.19.6.
11. Francis MacNutt, *The Healing Reawakening: Reclaiming Our Lost Inheritance* (Grand Rapids: Baker, 2006), 69.
12. See John Wimber, *Power Evangelism*, rev. ed. (1985; repr., Bloomington, MN: Chosen, 2009).
13. Quoted in Judith MacNutt, *Encountering Angels* (Bloomington, MN: Chosen, 2017), 60.
14. See Philip Jenkins, *The Next Christendom: The Coming of Global Christianity* (New York: Oxford University Press, 2002), 1–3.
15. Jenkins, *Next Christendom*, italics added.
16. Jenkins, *Next Christendom*, 77; cf. 124–27.

17. See George Eldon Ladd, *The Gospel of the Kingdom: Popular Expositions on the Kingdom of God* (Grand Rapids: Eerdmans, 1959), 18–23.

18. For these next two lines of evidence, I have borrowed heavily from my book *Kingdom Triangle: Recover the Christian Mind, Renovate the Soul, Restore the Spirit's Power* (Grand Rapids: Zondervan, 2007), 174–75, 177–79. Used by permission.

19. Thomas C. Oden, *Life in the Spirit*, vol. 3 of *Systematic Theology* (San Francisco: HarperSanFrancisco, 1992), 47.

20. Gerald F. Hawthorne, *The Presence and the Power: The Significance of the Holy Spirit in the Life and Ministry of Jesus* (Waco, TX: Word, 1991), 234.

21. See Wayne Grudem, ed., *Are Miraculous Gifts for Today? Four Views* (Grand Rapids: Zondervan, 1996).

22. See Grudem, *Are Miraculous Gifts for Today?* 341–49.

23. Dallas Willard, *Hearing God: Developing a Conversational Relationship with God* (Downers Grove, IL: InterVarsity, 1999), 35.

24. Willard, *Hearing God*, 36, italics in original.

25. Jack Deere, *Why I Am Still Surprised by the Power of the Spirit: Discovering How God Speaks and Heals Today* (Grand Rapids: Zondervan, 2020), appendix 4.

26. Clarissa Romez, David Zaritzky, and Joshua W. Brown, "Case Report of Gastroparesis Healing: 16 Years of a Chronic Syndrome Resolved after Proximal Intercessory Prayer," *Complementary Therapies in Medicine* 43 (April 2019): 289–94, www.sciencedirect.com/science/article/pii/S0965229918313116.

27. Clarissa Romez et al., "Case Report of Instantaneous Resolution of Juvenile Macular Degeneration Blindness after Proximal Intercessory Prayer," *Explore* 17, no. 1 (January–February 2021): 79–83, www.sciencedirect.com/science/article/pii/S1550830720300926.

28. See Sam Storms, *Practicing the Power: Welcoming the Gifts of the Holy Spirit in Your Life* (Grand Rapids: Zondervan, 2017), 75–81; John Wimber and Kevin Springer, *Power Healing* (New York: HarperCollins, 1991), chapters 9–12. I have modified these approaches to comport with my own experience.

29. Jack Deere, *Surprised by the Power of the Spirit: Discovering How God Speaks and Heals Today* (Grand Rapids: Zondervan, 1993), 153–54.

30. While the comments and insights are mine, I have learned a lot about this topic from two key sources: Deere, *Surprised by the Power of the Spirit*, 145–59; Francis MacNutt, *Healing*, rev. ed. (1974; repr., Notre Dame, IN: Ave Maria, 1999), 193–204.

31. See J. P. Moreland, *Finding Quiet: My Story of Overcoming Anxiety and the Practices That Brought Peace* (Grand Rapids: Zondervan, 2019), 120–28; see also Joel McDurmon, *What Would Jesus Drink? A Spirit-Filled Study* (White Hall, WV: Tolle Lege, 2011); Kenneth L. Gentry Jr., *God Gave Wine: What the Bible Says about Alcohol* (Fountain Inn, SC: Victorious Hope, 1999).

Chapter 6: Encouraging Credible Testimony of Cases of Miraculous Healing

1. Reginald Cherry, MD, *Healing Prayer: God's Divine Intervention in Medicine, Faith, and Prayer* (Nashville: Nelson, 1999), 134–35.

2. "Millions All Over China Convert to Christianity," *Washington Times*, August 2, 2005, www.washingtontimes.com/news/2005/aug/2/20050802-115449-8165r.

3. See J. P. Moreland, *Kingdom Triangle: Recover the Christian Mind, Renovate the Soul, Restore the Spirit's Power* (Grand Rapids: Zondervan, 2007), 168–70.

4. Cited in James Rutz, *MegaShift: Igniting Spiritual Power* (Colorado Springs: Empowerment, 2005), 21; Rutz identifies a letter from Paul Eshleman as the source of the story (p. 46).

5. Jim Green, JESUS Film Project Update (January 14, 2011), 1–2, italics in original.

6. Based on the story in Tom Doyle, *Dreams and Visions: Is Jesus Awakening the Muslim World?* (Nashville: Nelson, 2012), 72–83; quotes throughout this account come from Doyle's book.

7. "Padina's Story," YouTube, November 7, 2012, www.youtube.com/watch?v=rVCj26fdJpQ.

8. "Sheep among Wolves Volume II," YouTube, August 23, 2019, www.youtube.com/watch?v=9SAPOLKF59U; see also www.sheepamongwolvesfilm.com.

9. Scott J. Kolbaba, MD, *Physicians' Untold Stories: Miraculous Experiences Doctors Are Hesitant to Share with Their Patients,*

or Anyone! (North Charleston, SC: CreateSpace, 2016). Barb's story is told by one of her attending physicians, Thomas Marshall, MD, who had cared for her for more than ten years at the time of writing (see pp. 115–22).

10. See Lee Strobel, *The Case for Miracles: A Journalist Investigates Evidence for the Supernatural* (Grand Rapids: Zondervan, 2018), 101–5.

11. My account is based on the stories told in Strobel, *Case for Miracles*, and Kolbaba, *Physicians' Untold Stories*.

12. Quoted in Strobel, *Case for Miracles*, 101.

13. Quoted in Kolbaba, *Physicians' Untold Stories*, 121–22; see http://searchingdeeper.com/SearchingForMiracles.html.

14. Quoted in Strobel, *Case for Miracles*, 105.

Chapter 7: Hearing the Supernatural Voice of God

1. "Lily Tomlin: Quotes," IMDb, https://m.imdb.com/name/nm0005499/quotes.

2. While a bit dated, see Dallas Willard, *Hearing God: Developing a Conversational Relationship with God* (1984; repr., Downers Grove, IL: InterVarsity, 1999), 15–29.

3. It is true that in the next few verses, God finally did give specific guidance to David through Nathan. But this is irrelevant to my point. The simple fact that Nathan would express the idea to David that he was free to do whatever he had in mind and the Lord would go with him shows that this was not at all a foreign notion to either Nathan or David. And that's all I am saying here (see also 1 Kings 8:17).

4. It is beyond the scope of this chapter to explicate how we can grow in hearing God's voice with discernment. For help in this area, see Dallas Willard, *Hearing God*; Brad Jersak, *Can You Hear Me? Tuning In to the God Who Speaks* (Abbotsford, BC: Fresh Wind, 2003); Mark and Patti Virkler, *Dialogue with God: Opening the Door to Two-Way Prayer* (Alachua, FL: Bridge-Logos, 1986).

5. C. S. Lewis, *The Abolition of Man* (1947; repr., San Francisco: HarperOne, 2001), 26.

6. Jack Deere, *The Beginner's Guide to the Gift of Prophecy*, rev. ed. (2001; repr., Ventura, CA: Regal, 2008), 53.

7. Gordon Fee, *God's Empowering Presence: The Holy Spirit in the Letters of Paul* (Peabody, MA: Hendrickson, 1994), 216.

8. Sam Storms, *Practicing the Power: Welcoming the Gifts of the Holy Spirit in Your Life* (Grand Rapids: Zondervan, 2017), 92.

9. In a personal email on August 15, 2017. The professor wishes to remain anonymous.

10. John Wimber, *Power Evangelism*, rev. ed. (1985; repr., Bloomington, MN: Chosen, 2009), 74–76.

11. Wimber, *Power Evangelism*, 75.

12. For more on this, see Deere, *Beginner's Guide*, 81–102.

13. Michael Sullivant, *Thinking Biblically about the Life Model* (West Hollywood, CA: Life Model Works, 2017).

14. See Judith MacNutt, *Angels Are for Real: Inspiring True Stories and Biblical Answers* (Bloomington, MN: Chosen, 2012); *Encountering Angels* (Bloomington, MN: Chosen, 2016).

15. MacNutt, *Angels Are for Real*, 127–29.

16. I first shared this story in J. P. Moreland and Klaus Issler, *In Search of a Confident Faith: Overcoming Barriers to Trusting in God* (Downers Grove, IL: InterVarsity, 2008), 145–47.

17. Lonnie Frisbee, *Not by Might, nor by Power: The Great Commission* (Santa Maria, CA: Freedom Publications, 2016), 27–34.

Chapter 8: *The Nature, Reality, and Purposes of Angels and Demons*

1. A version of the following three sections can also be found in J. P. Moreland, *The God Question*, rev. ed. (Downers Grove, IL: IVP Academic, 2021).

2. John Calvin, *The Institutes of the Christian Religion* 1.14.6.

3. Judith MacNutt, *Encountering Angels: True Stories of How They Touch Our Lives Every Day* (Bloomington, MN: Chosen, 2016), 122.

4. For a credible book on authentic angelic encounters, see MacNutt, *Encountering Angels*.

5. James L. Garlow and Keith Wall, *Encountering Heaven and the Afterlife: True Stories from People Who Have Glimpsed the World Beyond* (Bloomington, MN: Bethany House, 2010), 258–59.

6. For fuller, authoritative treatments of this issue, see Clinton E. Arnold, *Three Crucial Questions about Spiritual Warfare*

(Grand Rapids: Baker, 1997), 73–141; C. Fred Dickason, *Demon Possession and the Christian: A New Perspective* (Wheaton, IL: Crossway, 1987), 73–127.

7. See Charles Kraft, *Defeating Dark Angels: Breaking Demonic Oppression in the Believer's Life* (Ann Arbor, MI: Servant, 1992), 119–38, especially 131–35; Arnold, *Three Crucial Questions*, 101.

8. See Sheila Flynn, "Demonic Possession Is Real, Says Psychiatry Professor Who's Spent 25 Years Viewing Exorcisms," *Daily Mail*, June 19, 2018, www.dailymail.co.uk/news/article-5857677/Psychiatrist-prof essor-says-demonic-possession-real-witnessing-exorcisms-25-years .html; see Richard Gallagher, MD, *Demonic Foes: My Twenty-Five Years as a Psychiatrist Investigating Possessions, Diabolic Attacks, and the Paranormal* (San Francisco: HarperOne, 2020).

9. See Neil T. Anderson, *The Steps to Freedom in Christ*, rev. ed. (Ventura, CA: Gospel Light, 2001); see also "Steps to Freedom in Christ," Freedom in Christ Ministries, www.ficm.org/steps -to-freedom-in-christ.

Chapter 9: Defending the Veracity of Near-Death Experiences

1. See Mary C. Neal, MD, *To Heaven and Back: A Doctor's Extraordinary Account of Her Death, Heaven, Angels, and Life Again* (Colorado Springs: WaterBrook, 2011). For her powerful thirteen-minute TED Talk about her experience, see "Death Brings Context to Life | Dr. Mary Neal," www.youtube.com /watch?v=C-M9zR17egA.

2. Mary C. Neal, MD, *Seven Lessons from Heaven: How Dying Taught Me to Live a Joy-Filled Life* (New York: Convergent, 2017), 192–93; see also Robert L. Wise, *Crossing the Threshold of Eternity* (Ventura, CA: Regal, 2007), 157–73.

3. Neal, *Seven Lessons from Heaven*, 177.

4. See Janice Miner Holden, Bruce Greyson, and Debbie James, eds., *The Handbook of Near-Death Experiences: Thirty Years of Investigation* (Santa Barbara, CA: Praeger, 2009), especially chapters 1, 2, and 7.

5. For a list of prominent NDE researchers, along with their credentials, see P. M. H. Atwater, *The Big Book of Near-Death Experiences: The Ultimate Guide to What Happens When We Die* (Charlottesville, VA: Hampton Roads, 2007), 175–93.

6. See Holden, Greyson, and James, *Handbook of Near-Death Experiences*, chapter 1.
7. For documentation of this information, see Holden, Greyson, and James, *Handbook of Near-Death Experiences*, 1–16; J. Steve Miller, *Near-Death Experiences as Evidence for the Existence of God and Heaven* (Acworth, GA: Wisdom Creek, 2012), 19–23; Gary R. Habermas, "Evidential Near-Death Experiences," in *The Blackwell Companion to Substance Dualism*, ed. Jonathan Loose, Angus Menuge, and J. P. Moreland (Oxford: Wiley Blackwell, 2018), 227–46.
8. Radiation oncologist and onetime skeptic of NDEs Jeffrey Long has studied thousands of NDE cases, all subjected to rigorous research questionnaires containing more than one hundred questions, and on that basis he provided nine lines of evidence for the veracity of NDEs (see Jeffrey Long, MD, *Evidence of the Afterlife: The Science of Near-Death Experiences* [San Francisco: HarperOne, 2010]). Long's website—Near-Death Experience Research Foundation—contains close to five thousand NDE reports (see www.nderf.org).
9. See Eben Alexander, *Proof of Heaven: A Neurosurgeon's Journey into the Afterlife* (New York: Simon & Schuster, 2012).
10. See Kenneth Ring and Sharon Cooper, *Mindsight: Near-Death and Out-of-Body Experiences in the Blind*, 2nd ed. (Palo Alto, CA: William James Center for Consciousness Studies, 1999).
11. See John Burke, *Imagine Heaven: Near-Death Experiences, God's Promises, and the Exhilarating Future That Awaits You* (Grand Rapids: Baker, 2015).
12. Long, *Evidence of the Afterlife*, 173.
13. See Long, *Evidence of the Afterlife*, 176–95; Pim van Lommel, MD, *Consciousness beyond Life: The Science of the Near-Death Experience* (San Francisco: HarperOne, 2010), 45–79.
14. For more on these arguments, see Long, *Evidence of the Afterlife*, Miller, *Near-Death Experiences*, 31–48; Habermas, "Evidential Near-Death Experiences," 239–42; Holden, Greyson, and James, *Handbook of Near-Death Experiences*, 213–34; Atwater, *Big Book of Near-Death Experiences*, 195–224.
15. See Long, *Evidence of the Afterlife*, 6–7; Atwater, *Big Book of Near-Death Experiences*, 10–17; van Lommel, *Consciousness beyond*

Life, 7–43; Burke, *Imagine Heaven*, 44–52; Holden, Greyson, and James, *Handbook of Near-Death Experiences*, 135–58.

16. Besides the sources listed in the previous endnote, see Neal, *Seven Lessons from Heaven*, 54–74.

17. See Burke, *Imagine Heaven*, 215–36; see also Howard Storm, *My Descent into Death: A Second Chance at Life* (New York: Doubleday, 2005).

18. Burke, *Imagine Heaven*, 237–51.

19. "From Atheist to Christian, the Full Testimony of Dr. Dan Degirolami," YouTube, September 3, 2018, www.youtube.com /watch?v=xY5mSlOxlqs.

20. Robert L. Wise, *Crossing the Threshold of Eternity: What the Dying Can Teach the Living* (Ventura, CA: Regal, 2007), 15–23.

21. Wise, *Crossing the Threshold*, 17.

22. Wise, *Crossing the Threshold*, 18–19.

23. See Pim van Lommel, MD, et al., "Near-Death Experience in Survivors of Cardiac Arrest: A Prospective Study in the Netherlands," *Lancet* 358, no. 9298 (December 2001): 2039–45; van Lommel, *Consciousness beyond Life*, 20–21. Titus Rivas, Anny Dirven, and Rudolf H. Smit, *The Self Does Not Die: Verified Paranormal Phenomena from Near-Death Experiences* (Durham, NC: International Association for Near-Death Studies, 2016), 62–68; "An Interview with TG on the 'Man with the Dentures,'" *Terugkeer* 19, no. 3 (Autumn 2008), http://net werknde.nl/wp-content/uploads/trnursetg.pdf; Jime Sayaka, "Interview with Afterlife Researcher and Philosopher Titus Rivas," July 7, 2014, www.titusrivas.nl/public/articles/read/867.

24. In my opinion, the best one is told by psychiatrist George G. Ritchie, *Return from Tomorrow*, rev. ed. (1978; repr., Grand Rapids: Chosen, 2007). More than 500,000 copies of this book have been sold.

25. Dr. Chauncey Crandall, *Touching Heaven: A Cardiologist's Encounter with Death and Living Proof of an Afterlife* (New York: Faith Words, 2015), 9–11.

26. Crandall, *Touching Heaven*, 9.

27. See Melvin Morse, MD, *Closer to the Light: Learning from the Near-Death Experiences of Children* (New York: Random House, 1990), 1–8.

28. See Ring and Cooper, *Mindsight*, 22–28.
29. Ring and Cooper, *Mindsight*, 25.
30. See van Lommel, *Consciousness beyond Life*, 169–76; Rivas, *Self Does Not Die*, 95–104, 311–15; Michael Sabom, MD, *Light and Death: One Doctor's Fascinating Account of Near-Death Experiences* (Grand Rapids: Zondervan, 1998), 37–47; Kevin Williams, "People Have Near-Death Experiences While Brain Dead," www.near-death.com/science/evidence/people-have-ndes-while-brain-dead.html.
31. See Sabom, *Light and Death*, 40; Williams, "People Have Near-Death Experiences."
32. See J. P. Moreland, *Finding Quiet: My Story of Overcoming Anxiety and the Practices That Brought Peace* (Grand Rapids: Zondervan, 2019).
33. Trudy Harris, RN, *Glimpses of Heaven: True Stories of Hope and Peace at the End of Life's Journey* (Grand Rapids: Revell, 2008), 30.

Finding Quiet

My Story of Overcoming Anxiety and the Practices That Brought Peace

J. P. Moreland

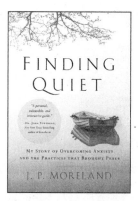

Bracing and honest, *Finding Quiet* will validate the experiences of believers with mental illness, remind them that they are not alone, and provide reassurance that they can not only survive but thrive again.

In May 2003, prominent philosopher, author, and professor J. P. Moreland awoke in the middle of the night to a severe panic attack. Though often anxious by temperament and upbringing, Moreland had never experienced such an incident before. Thus began an extended battle with debilitating anxiety and depression.

More than a decade later, Moreland continues to manage mental illness. Yet along the way, he has moved from shame and despair to vulnerability and hope. In *Finding Quiet*, Moreland comes alongside fellow sufferers with encouragement and practical, hard-won advice. According to the Substance Abuse and Mental Health Services Administration, nearly 20 percent of Americans suffer from mental illness, and people in the pews are not immune. Moreland explores the spiritual and physical aspects of mental illness, pointing readers toward sound sources of information, treatment, and recovery.

Available in stores and online!